AN EXPOSITION

OF

THE THIRTY-NINE ARTICLES.

A COMMENTARY

ON

THE THIRTY-NINE ARTICLES

FORMING

AN INTRODUCTION TO THE THEOLOGY OF THE CHURCH OF ENGLAND

BY

T. P. BOULTBEE, LL.D.

PRINCIPAL OF THE LONDON COLLEGE OF DIVINITY, ST. JOHN'S HALL, HIGHBURY
LATE FELLOW OF ST. JOHN'S COLLEGE, CAMBRIDGE

FIFTH EDITION

Wipf & Stock
PUBLISHERS
Eugene, Oregon

Wipf and Stock Publishers
199 W 8th Ave, Suite 3
Eugene, OR 97401

A Commentary on the Thirty-Nine Articles
Forming an Introduction to the Theology of the Church of England
By Boultbee, T. P.
ISBN: 1-59752-356-9
Publication date 9/7/2005
Previously published by Longmans, Green, and Co., 1880

PREFACE.

———◆———

THIS WORK has at least been produced by a natural
process. It originated, and has gradually assumed
shape, out of a necessity which has long pressed upon
the Author. Having been engaged for some years in
teaching theology, he has sought in vain for a manual
containing the definitions and terms of that science,
and distinctly enunciating the received doctrines of the
Church of England.

The plan of this work is precisely that which is indicated by its title. It is meant to be an introduction to
the Theology of the Church of England. We are so
accustomed to magnify our own divisions, and our opponents so habitually mock them, that some may be
inclined to doubt whether there is such a theology.
The Author would be far from saying that our differences on the doctrine of justification and the nature and
efficacy of the sacraments are trivial. But, setting
aside those extremes which do not really belong to our
Church, though they struggle to find foot-hold within
her limits, it is believed that our differences are, to say
the least, very manageable, so long as they are discussed on the platform of Holy Scripture. No one

accustomed to teach the subjects which, with consider
able uniformity, are required by our bishops of the
candidates for Holy Orders, can hesitate to acknowledge the solid basis of recognised English Theology.
To this it is the object of this work to introduce the
Student. It is desired to embarrass him as little as
possible with extra subjects or extraneous matter. The
time at his disposal is all too little. He is required to
read and know many books, sometimes too many. He
often fails to trace any unity of teaching or of system
throughout his prescribed course. One object of this
work is to be a guide to that unity, and to show how
each portion of his prescribed reading falls into its
place in this great doctrinal code of his Church. For
example, the Student as a matter of course reads
Pearson's great work on the Creed. There he finds
Scripture applied with unexampled copiousness in the
text, and abundant patristic learning in the notes. It
is most undesirable to confuse his mind with a different
arrangement when he comes to the Articles. Accordingly in the first five Articles Pearson's treatment of
the subjects is epitomised, with the addition of such
illustrative and explanatory matter as appeared necessary

Paley's unrivalled clearness still maintains for him
an acknowledged position in the defence of our faith.
The student will certainly read at least the first part of
his Evidences. It is, therefore, very unwise to disturb
the arrangement of the historical proof of the Canon of
the New Testament which he has given. And, after
all, excepting some matters of detail, that proof re-

mains where Paley left it. Therefore this is taken as the basis of the proof of that portion of the Sixth Article.

In doctrinal subjects, for obvious reasons, Hooker occupies a foremost place. He has therefore been freely quoted, and his true place in theology is attempted to be defined. These examples will serve to illustrate the nature of the work. Everywhere references are given, sufficient to guide the more thoughtful and studious minds to greater research, and to verify the statements in the text.

Further, remembering that the Articles were written by men who had been trained in the Roman system, it is essential for their proper understanding (to say nothing of our own necessities) that the Roman theology should be fully exhibited. This has always been done from unquestionable authorities, and generally from the Council of Trent itself.

It is taken for granted that ecclesiastical history has been carefully read, and that its main outlines and principal details are borne in mind. Early heresies, the papal developments, the schoolmen, the chief characters and controversies of the Reformation, gather around us at every step as we make our way through the Articles. It must be assumed that there is a sufficient knowledge of these before a close study of the Articles is commenced. It has not been deemed necessary to add more than cursory details to the needful historical allusions.

The English text of the Articles is that adopted in Hardwick's 'History of the Articles of Religion,' a work distinguished by much careful research. In all matters connected with the history of the text the Author is much indebted to it. The Latin text is taken from Sparrow's collection. The chief preceding works on the Articles have been consulted, but, it is believed, have had but little influence in forming the opinions, or moulding the arrangements, here adopted. With very rare exceptions it has been thought the wiser as well as the more respectful course, not to allude to living writers. It is better to prepare the Student for controversy hereafter, if it must needs be, than to entangle him in it prematurely.

It has been the desire of the Author to retire as far as possible into the background in the composition of this work. He is conscious that his own individual opinions can have little weight. He desires the Student to feel that confidence which is natural when he knows that the exposition of a given doctrine is that of divines of our Church, some of whom have been for centuries its pride and its ornament. He who knows that he is at one with Hooker on Justification; that he follows Pearson in dealing with the mysteries of the Holy Trinity; and has Barrow's masterly hand in traversing the thorny path of the Papal Supremacy, must feel those convictions strengthened, which it is hoped he has already based on the Word of God. In the more original portions the Author has anxiously endeavoured to furnish the Student with such information and explanations as shall at once be fair and sufficient to put him in a position to understand the men and the questions he will have to encounter in practical life.

The Author has no desire to conceal or reserve his own convictions, but these are of consequence to but few beside. Whereas the true grounds and reasons and bearings of the great religious questions being once clearly grasped, the Student's own convictions will be maturely formed, and will usually be stedfast. In this case there is no more reason to fear what the general result will be, than there was in the days of our fathers.

It is hoped that the method here pursued will be distinguished from a mere catena of authorities on the one hand, and from a mere *cram-book* on the other. The object certainly has been to stimulate research and enquiry, instead of resting in the mere manual. But this must depend on the earnestness of the student.

The rarity of patristic quotations may strike some as a serious defect. Those who think so will find brief extracts of this kind in Welchman's little work, so long used at Oxford; and more copious citations in the well-known Exposition of the present Bishop of Ely. But the Author must further add that he thinks rather lightly of the benefit of such quotations to the ordinary Student. Their use is rather for reference than for 'getting up.' Few indeed are those who can retain them in their memory, and even their time may be generally more usefully spent in other practical matters which are insufficiently mastered.

But besides this, the Author must confess that he agrees with the present Bishop of Ossory in the Preface to his 'Sermons upon the Nature and Effects of Faith' when he says, 'the early divines from whom I draw so largely were certainly at home in the Fathers; and they were led to conduct the great contest, so as to furnish any one who desires to make an array of ancient authorities, with an ample store of citations, and with great facility for enlarging it. But Romish controversial writers produced counter-authorities from the same sources; and though I am far from believing that upon this, any more than upon the other points which divide the Churches, there is room for reasonable doubt about the opinions, or at least the principles, of the ancient Fathers, yet to fix with precision the meaning of writers who, confessedly (at least before the Pelagian controversy), wrote somewhat loosely upon this doctrine, would require much reading and thought.' This fully illustrates the Author's conviction as to the practical utility of partial patristic extracts to the tyro in theology. For example, in the course of this work the valuable chapter of Waterland 'On the Eucharist' is referred to, in which he treats of the Eucharist as a sacrifice. What would the unassisted Student make of the numerous passages in early writers in which the Eucharist is called *a true sacrifice*, if he were not led to understand the real meaning of their phraseology? There must be something fundamentally unsound in the system itself, apart from mental unfairness, which has led to such opposite results. Jewel, for instance, in his Apology, produces a selection of Protestant quotations on the Eucharist from Fathers of the first four centuries; some modern writers amongst ourselves exhibit extracts from the same Fathers which look, to say the least, very like transubstantiation.

It is impossible, without a thoughtful study of their theological phraseology and general system, to understand rightly the true position of those ancient writers. Even our own Hooker may be, and has often been, misunderstood on some important points from want of this. Much more must this be the case when mediæval or modern theological glossaries are used to interpret the meaning of the earliest Christian writers. The Author has no misgivings as to the general result of that meaning. Our great Reformation divines were not mere men of indices and cyclopædias. They wrought our their systems by painful and laborious study of the Scriptures and the early authors. The mind and intent of primitive writers were familiar to them, and their appeal to antiquity was unwavering and decisive. Modern criticism has produced very little change in the general position as they left it. An excrescence, an inaccuracy, a spurious document, may have been lopped off here or there ; but, substantially, the patristic bearing of the main controversies remains where our Reformers believed it to lie.

On the grounds, then, of the limited nature of this work, as well as of doubt as to their practical utility at this stage of advance, and their somewhat dubious value in themselves, patristic authorities have been scarcely at all referred to.

Some may desiderate a more important matter, a more distinct and copious demonstration of each Article from Holy Scripture. The Author by no means undervalues judicious selections of this kind from Holy Writ. At the same time, if the divine is ultimately to be

' mighty in the Scriptures,' it is thought that the
Student should be guided rather to the *manner*, than
to the *details*, of thus applying the Bible. Such at
least is the course followed in the College over which
the Author presides. The Scriptural examination and
instruction in the Articles is oral, and precedes their
more theological interpretation.

More, perhaps, need not be added in explanation of
the objects and principles of this work. To write
at greater length would have been in some respects
an easier task. To unite compression of style with
sufficient fulness of matter and reference, in dealing
with subjects which invite discussion and amplification
at every turn, requires a self-restraint not always easy
to practise. But that compression is absolutely necessary when the object is not to make a display of
learning, but to provide the theological student with a
safe guide through his early difficulties. That some
such treatise is greatly needed is very generally confessed. Should this attempt in any measure supply
that necessity, it is not doubted that the criticism it
may meet with will make considerable improvements
possible on a future occasion.

CONTENTS.

PART IV.

THE CHURCH: ITS SACRAMENTS AND MINISTERS.

PART V.

REGULATIONS AFFECTING THE CHURCH OF ENGLAND IN PARTICULAR.

PART VI.

CIVIL RIGHTS AND DUTIES.

HISTORICAL INTRODUCTION.

THE code of doctrine known as the Thirty-nine Articles of the Church of England has experienced several modifications. It has also its roots in yet earlier documents. Of these it appears necessary to give some account.

The earliest doctrinal formulary of a Reformed Church is that known as 'the Confession of Augsburgh.' It was the work of Melanchthon, revised by Luther and other divines, and was presented to the Diet at Augsburgh in 1530. To a great extent this suggested the several Confessions of Faith published by different Reformed National Churches in that century. But in the case of the English Church it had a more direct influence. Our Articles have borrowed from it some considerable portion of their theological statements. It may be found at length, together with other similar documents, in the 'Sylloge Confessionum,' published at Oxford.

We may notice here the Wurtemberg Confession, which belongs to the same school, and was consulted in the formation of our Articles. It was intended for presentation to the Council of Trent in 1552, by the ambassadors of Wurtemberg, but the Council refused to hear them.

The first independent attempt of English divines to deal with doctrine, after the rejection of the papal supremacy, was the publication of the Ten Articles in 1536. These were set forth by royal authority, and the approval of the clergy in

a

Convocation.[1] In most essential points they contain Roman doctrine, modifying, however, some things, and substituting the royal for the papal supremacy. They are of great historical value in tracing the growth of the Reformation, but have no authority whatever.

It is well known how Henry's course oscillated in the latter years of his reign, under the action of the conflicting influences of foreign and domestic policy.

At certain times the German alliance appeared to attract him. Cranmer's influence was thrown into this scale, and there was more than one negotiation with the German Protestant princes with a view to some agreement on matters of faith. These negotiations assumed the most practical form in 1538, when a Lutheran embassy arrived in England, consisting of three members. They held repeated interviews with Cranmer and certain other commissioners appointed by the king. They appear to have taken the Augsburgh Confession as the basis of their deliberations. They finally broke off their discussions on the following points, on which Henry would not yield: the administration of the Lord's Supper in both kinds; private propitiatory masses; and clerical celibacy. After the interruption of these negotiations the reactionary influence of Gardiner prevailed; and the ' Act of Six Articles ' made any such plan of union with the German Protestants impossible for the present. There still remains among Archbishop Cranmer's papers a manuscript, containing Articles of Religion, evidently founded on the Confession of Augsburgh. This is believed to contain the result of the conferences between the German and English commissioners. It not only possesses historical interest, but it is probable that, in drawing up the Forty-two Articles in Edward's reign, Cranmer had recourse to this document. If so, the Augsburgh Confession has influenced our doctrinal code not directly, but *indirectly*,

[1] See ' Formularies of Faith during the Reign of Henry VIII.'

through this revised formula. Hardwick[1] gives as a reason for this opinion, that in matter common to the Augsburgh Confession and our Articles, the divergencies from the former are frequently contained in the document in question. It will be found in ' Cranmer's Remains.'[2]

The death of Henry in 1547 introduces us to another stage of the Reformation. Cranmer still adhered to his long-cherished plan of a scheme of doctrine which should embrace the whole of the Reformed Church. But from various causes his efforts failed. Perhaps, among other reasons, the fact that the Archbishop abandoned the idea of the corporal presence, whether under the transubstantiation or consubstantiation theory, proved a serious impediment to union with Lutheran divines in such a formulary. There appears to have been a collection of Articles of Religion drawn up by Cranmer as early as 1549. What this may have been is unknown, but it may probably have served as the basis of the Forty-two Articles. In 1551 the Archbishop was directed by the Privy Council to ' frame a book of Articles of Religion, for the preserving and maintaining peace and unity of doctrine in this Church, that being finished they might be set forth by public authority.'[3] This was done, and the Articles were sent for inspection to some other bishops, and to other eminent persons. The Articles, forty-two in number, were finally issued under the authority of a royal mandate in 1553. This document is accordingly referred to by Hardwick as the Articles of 1553. But as they were discussed and completed in the previous year, they are more generally known as the Articles of 1552, and are, therefore, so styled in this work.

It has been much disputed whether this formulary was ever sanctioned by Convocation, or whether it was imposed by royal

---

[1] History of Arts. c. iv. [2] Parker Soc. p. 472.
[3] Strype's Cranmer, ii. 27.

authority only. It would seem to be a matter of no great consequence, since this code has been superseded some centuries ago. But, on the score of precedent bearing on ecclesiastical legislation, this question has been deemed by some to possess importance.

There is no record of any action of Convocation on this subject, and there are some other difficulties in the way. But Hardwick is of opinion that Convocation did approve the Articles. He rests on the fact that all extant copies purport in their title to have been ratified ' in the last synod of London.' Statements to the same effect are found in other contemporary documents.

The very year which saw the authoritative publication of the Forty-two Articles, witnessed also their abrogation on the accession of Mary.

The first parliament of Elizabeth, 1559, restored the English Liturgy. The Articles of Religion, however, remained in abeyance for some time. In 1563 Convocation took action upon them, and ultimately sanctioned a revised copy, containing Thirty-eight Articles. But for lack of royal authority subscription could not be enforced. In 1571 Elizabeth [1] finally sanctioned another revision, which was subscribed by Convocation in that year. The Articles so ratified and sanctioned, thirty-nine in number, have remained to our time without any alteration.

The Latin and English versions of the Articles have equal authority. We have, therefore, the advantage of a reference from one version to the other in the case of any ambiguity occurring.

The reader who desires further information on this subject will find it fully treated in Hardwick's 'History of the Articles of Religion.'

---

[1] See the Ratification usually appended to the Thirty-nine Articles in the Prayer-book.

THE PRINCIPAL

DIVISIONS AND ARRANGEMENT OF THE ARTICLES.

THE arrangement of the Articles deserves notice. They may be divided into six parts corresponding to the principal divisions of their subjects.

Part I. (Arts. I.–V.) treats of the nature of the Deity in this order. The essential attributes of God, and His mode of existence in three Persons. The Deity, incarnation, sufferings, and death of Christ for sin. The descent of Christ into hell; His resurrection, and ascension, and the future judgment. The Deity and Personality of the Holy Ghost.

Part II. (Arts. VI.–VIII.) treats of the rule of faith thus. The sole authority of Holy Scripture in matters of faith is asserted. The relation of the Old Testament to the New, and the degree of obligation of the Mosaic law, are set forth. The three Creeds are accepted, but are denied any authority independent of Holy Scripture.

Part III. (Arts. IX.–XVIII.) The basis of doctrinal authority having been laid down, the main doctrines of man's salvation are next defined in this order. The lost condition of man by nature is described, and it is denied that he is able to turn to God without preventing grace, or to do what is pleasing to God without co-operating grace. It is then declared that man can only be accounted righteous before God for the merits of Christ, and that faith only is the grace regarded by God in thus justifying the sinner; for which purpose God is pleased to isolate it from other graces present with it simultaneously. Thenceforward the good works of the justified sinner surely follow, and are pleasing to God in Christ, although themselves imperfect. But works, although in themselves good, done before justification, are not regarded in Christ, and therefore of necessity retain the sinful taint of the nature from which they come.

Further, however pleasing in God's sight the gracious works of His children in Christ may be, none can render to God by the utmost self-sacrifice more than He has invited us to give. No human being, save the Son of God in His human nature, has escaped the universal corruption. The baptised, on falling into sin, have the way to God still open to them through repentance; nor can a sinless state be attained on this side the grave.

Next, the original ground of calling, justifying, and sanctifying sinners, is traced in the gracious purpose and predestinating love of God. This ought to call forth in them warm spiritual affections, but the opposite doctrine of reprobation is regarded as one calculated to harden the sinner.

Finally, salvation can be obtained through Christ only. There is no other way to God. ·

Part IV. (Arts. XIX.–XXXIV.) We now come to the Church which holds these doctrines. It is defined as consisting of an assembly of faithful men, possessing the pure word of God and the sacraments complete in all essentials. But the most famous individual churches have not been exempt from serious error. The Church may appoint rites, and can judge in controversy, subject to the supreme authority of Scripture. But even General Councils, being composed of fallible men, have no collective infallibility, and are subject to the authority of Scripture. In particular, purgatory, indulgences, saint and image worship, are errors which have prevailed, contrary to the Word of God.

The ministers of the Church ought to be lawfully appointed, and the services performed in the vulgar tongue.

The nature and number of the sacraments of Christ are next set forth; the five Romish sacraments are repudiated; and the exhibition, as distinguished from the use, of the sacraments is rejected. Evil ministers cannot annul that grace which Christ bestows on the faithful in the use of His ordinances. Yet such ministers should receive due ecclesiastical discipline.

The efficacy of Baptism follows, and the privilege of infants to receive it. The nature of the communion of Christ's body and blood in the Lord's Supper is described; and all participation of Christ by those who have not living faith is denied. To partake of the Cup as well as the Bread is the right of the laity. Christ cannot be offered again in the Eucharist, for His sacrifice is complete and sufficient. The clergy have full liberty to marry. Excommunicated persons ought to be avoided. Rites and ceremonies may vary according to the convenience of national Churches. But private persons ought not to disobey them.

Part V. (Arts. XXXV.–XXXVII.) A few special regulations affecting the Church of England in particular come next in order. The two Books of Homilies are approved for general use in churches. The ordinal is sanctioned for setting apart the ministers of the English Church. The royal supremacy is decreed, and the papal authority in England repudiated.

Part VI. (Arts. XXXVII.-XXXIX.) A few civil rights and duties, at that time called in question by some sectaries, are defined. Capital punishments and military service are lawful. Community of goods is not the law of Christianity. Judicial oaths may be taken.

It is hoped that this rapid recital of the substance of the Articles may be deemed fairly accurate.   It will at least show their coherence and consecutive arrangement, which is the purpose for which it has been drawn out.   That this renowned code possesses scientific order as well as accuracy is too often lost sight of.

PART I.

THE HOLY TRINITY.

ARTICLE I.

Of Faith in the Holy Trinity.

There is but one living and true God, everlasting, without body, parts, or passions, of infinite power, wisdom, and goodness, the Maker and Preserver of all things, both visible and invisible. And in unity of this Godhead there be three Persons, of one substance, power, and eternity, the Father the Son, and the Holy Ghost.

De fide in sacro-sanctam Trinitatem.

Unus est vivus et verus Deus, æternus, incorporeus, impartibilis, impassibilis, immensæ potentiæ, sapientiæ ac bonitatis, creator et conservator omnium, tum visibilium, tum invisibilium. Et in unitate hujus divinæ naturæ tres sunt personæ, ejusdem essentiæ, potentiæ, ac æternitatis, Pater, Filius, et Spiritus Sanctus.

NOTES ON THE TEXT OF ARTICLE I.

Comparing the Latin with the English text, we may notice the following expressions :—

Without body : Latin, *incorporeus.* *Without parts :* Latin *impartibilis,* i.e. insusceptible of division into parts. *Without passions :* Latin, *impassibilis,* i.e. incapable of suffering. *Infinite :* Latin, *immensæ,* immeasurable.

This Article remains as it was in the original formula of 1552.

It has been chiefly derived from Art. I. of the Augsburg Confession, as may be seen from the following quotation from that document:—

' There is one divine essence, which is called, and is, God, everlasting, without body, without parts, of infinite power, wisdom, and goodness, the Creator and Preserver of all things, visible and invisible, and yet there are three Persons, of one substance and power, and coeternal: the Father, the Son, and

the Holy Ghost.' The original Latin corresponds in the
same exact manner with that of our present Article. As the
definitions of so great a divine as Melancthon must be valuable,
it may be well to add from the same Article of the Augsburg
Confession the definition of the word *Person*: 'The name
Person is used in the same sense in which ecclesiastical writers
have used it in this matter, to signify not a part or quality of
something else, but that which has a proper existence of its
own '—(*quod proprie subsistit*).

OBSERVATIONS ON ARTICLE I.

It is assumed that the reader is sufficiently aware of the
principal varieties of belief as to the nature of the Deity which
have prevailed in different times and countries. It is beyond
the limits of this work to give even a sketch of the history of
the misbelief of man on this fundamental subject; and a mere
catalogue of names is a worthless thing for practical purposes.
It may, however, be desirable to name the principal classes
under which the varieties of human notions of the Deity are
arranged. The dire name of *Atheism* needs no definition :
'The fool hath said in his heart, There is no God.'

Deism is a general expression for the notions of those who
believe in One God, the Creator, and in some moral relation
to Him, but who reject revelation.

Theism is an ill-defined term, often used as equivalent to
deism, but sometimes as including something more, and as
the opposite to atheistic ideas.

Polytheism holds that 'there be Gods many,' personal ex-
istences, sharing among themselves in various degrees the
divine power.

Pantheism holds that 'the universe is itself God, or of the
divine essence.' All organised matter, all sentient being, it
views as appertaining to the Deity, coming from Him, returning
to Him, and always in Him. There is, therefore, no personal
God distinct from the creature he has made. This was the
inner belief of many of the ancient philosophers. It is also
that of the Buddhists, and lies at the root of Brahminism. It

has also been revived in various forms in some schools of modern European philosophy. In further illustration of these portentous aberrations of the human intellect, a passage full of indignant eloquence is subjoined from a charge of the late Bishop of Peterborough (Dr. Jeune).

' *Material Atheism.*—In the last and at the beginning of the present century, it was a material and mechanical athe-.sm which attracted the vulgar of scientific men. It was the atheism which denies all existence but the existence of matter —of matter eternal, and containing a divinity called Force in every atom ; the atheism which regards thought as a mere secretion of the brain, and vice and virtue simply as products, " like sugar or vitriol " ; the atheism which sees order, but not design, in the universe—laws, not Providence, in the course of things.

' *Pantheism.*—To this blank and revolting materialism suc-ceeded pantheism, as revived in Germany—the system which confounds the Infinite and the finite, and which makes God the sum of all things. God, it teaches, is brutal in brute matter, mighty in the forces of nature, feeling in the animal, thinking and conscious only in man. This system is, in its first aspect, more noble than material atheism, but in truth it is not less fatal to all that is noble and good. It, indeed, makes man—nay, the beast that perisheth ; nay, the very dung on the earth—divine; but it also makes God human, animal, ma-terial. It degrades what is high by exalting what is low. Better to deny God, after all, than to debase Him. Pantheism is, if possible, a worse atheism.

' *Positivism.*—Of both these systems, positivism—the system which at this moment claims exclusive possession of truth; positivism, for such is its barbarous name, to which all thought, we are told by a leading review, in Germany and England, as well as in France, its birthplace, is now converging—speaks with no less contempt, though with less hatred, than it speaks of Christianity. " Day-dreams," it says, " are all the assertions, all the negations alike, of philosophers : impotent attempts to compass impossibility." Of God, if there be a God ; of the soul, if there be a soul ; of revelation, if revelation there be, man can know, man need know, nothing. Away, then, it cries, with mere hypothesis! To the positive, to the material, to the teaching of the senses, to observation of facts, philosophy must limit itself. This system is mean, though supercilious. Perhaps, however, positivism rises in comparison with atheism, which itself is less base than pantheism; for it is better to ignore than to deny, as it is better to deny than to degrade God.

'*Suicide of Philosophy.*—Human reason, then, left to itself, leaves us, as to God, a threefold choice: we may deny God, we may degrade God, we may ignore God. A noble result! A godless philosophy ends in suicide! So it will ever be. To quote from the noble close of the Dunciad—

> ' Philosophy, which leaned on Heaven before,
> Sinks to her second cause, and is no more.

'*Destruction of Morality.*—As is the theology, so is the morality of all these systems. One specimen of their ethical teaching will suffice for all. Hear Spinosa, the greatest of pantheists:—" Every act of man, as every fact of nature, is produced by fated laws. Free-will is a chimera, flattering to our pride and founded on our ignorance. Not only has every man the right to seek his pleasure, he cannot do otherwise. He who lives only according to the laws of his appetites is as much in the right as he who regulates his life according to the laws of reason, in the same manner as the ignorant man and the madman has a right to everything that his appetite compels him to take. A compact has only a value proportioned to its utility; when the utility disappears, the compact disappears too. There is folly, then, in pretending to bind a man for ever to his word, unless at least that the man so contrive that the breach of the contract shall entail for him more danger than profit."

'*Practical Results of false Philosophy.*—Utter heartless selfishness, restrained by cowardice, is then to be our sole rule of life! Our final destiny is to perish like the brute; or, like bubbles, to be absorbed, when we burst into the ocean of being on which we now float!

'These systems may for a time prevail; but their prevalence cannot be permanent or universal.'

Amongst Christians, there are, strictly speaking, only two divisions on this subject, *Trinitarians* and *Unitarians*. The former include the vast majority of the Christian world. The *Unitarians* include persons holding a great variety of opinions, verging downwards from Arianism and Socinianism, with more or less belief in Holy Scripture as a revelation from God, to mere deism.

I. *The Unity of God.*

It is the object of this work to bring into one focus, as far as possible, the somewhat scattered reading of the theological student. Looking also to the scanty time allowed the aspirant to the ministry of the English Church for acquiring the rudiments of theological science, it is most desirable to give him, as far as possible at this stage of his progress, *one* treatise only on each main doctrine. And this *one* treatise ought in each case to be that which has gained the general approval of the Church, and is recognised as a text-book for holy orders. In this point of view, it seems essential to take the guidance of Bishop Pearson under this and the four following articles. The student in divinity will either have read, or is purposing to read, the great work of that prelate on the Creed. But for the sake of completeness, and at the same time not to take the student over superfluous ground, there is subjoined a sketch of such portions of 'Pearson on the Creed' as bear on the present Article.

1. '*There is but one living and true God*,' the passage with which our Article begins, will receive illustration from 'Pearson on the Creed' (Art. I. § 2, 'I believe in God'), the substance of which may be thus given :—

The true notion of God is that of a Being, self-existent, independent of any other, on whom all things else depend, and governing all things.

We are assured of His existence, not by a connate idea (for God has never held us responsible on this score), nor as a

self-evident truth or axiom; but by the necessity of assigning
an origin to things having existence, and from the perfect
adaptation of means to ends in creation, or the relation of final
causes to the efficient cause. Pearson would give weight also
to the testimony of conscience, and the universal consent of
mankind to the existence of God.

That God is *One* is deduced first from the primary notion
of God, which has been defined as implying *independence*, and
there cannot be two independent beings coexistent and acting
together. It further follows from the unity of design and of
government in creation. Thus God is *One*, and not only
actually One, but the *only possible* Supreme. He has an
intrinsic and essential singularity.

2. ' *Everlasting*.'—That God is everlasting will follow from
the notion of His self-existence and independence, for He has
His existence from none. And it is asserted in numerous passages of Scripture, which need not be here specified.

3. ' *Without body, parts, or passions*.'—This doctrine is in
several places asserted by Pearson (see the Articles 'Which was
conceived' and 'Suffered'), but is not separately handled. It
follows from the fundamental notion of the self-existence and
independence of God. A body is subject to the laws of space
and of limitation, it is divisible and local, it can suffer from
other bodies; the whole notion is subversive of the true idea
of God. There will be no difficulty in quoting sufficient passages of Scripture under this head.

4. ' *Of infinite power, wisdom, and goodness*.'—Pearson deals
with the almightiness of God in Art. I. § 4, and Art. VI. § 3,
and treats it as involving these main particulars: the absolute
power of free-will, the absolute right of possession of all
things, the absolute right of using and disposing of all things;
further, that God is the source of all power in any creature,
that there can be no resistance to His will, and no limit to
His power, save that which involves a contradiction, physical,
rational, or moral. The infinite wisdom and goodness would
follow in like manner from a survey of the divine perfections;
and all these attributes will be readily confirmed by Holy
Scripture.

· 5. ' *The Maker and Preserver of all things, visible and invisible.*'—These attributes of the Godhead are arranged by Pearson under Art. I. § 5, 'Maker of heaven and earth;' where he shows that *heaven and earth* must be understood as including all things visible and invisible. (Col. i. 16, &c.) Hence follows the definition ' Everything is either made or not made. Whatsoever is not made is God. Whatsoever is made is not God.'

This creation is further to be conceived of as the bringing all things out of that which had no previous existence, in opposition to ancient fallacies about the eternity of matter. Several passages of Scripture imply this. But it follows from the primary notion of God ; for to suppose anything existing independent of God, and coeval with Him, detracts from His independence and self-sufficiency.

In regard of motive, we are to believe that nothing but the goodness of God moved Him to create. No necessity lay upon Him, and His own will was a sufficient cause for the production of all that He willed to exist.

In respect of time, all created things were called into existence at definite times known unto God.

That God is *the Preserver* of all things follows also from the necessary idea of the dependence of all things upon Him.

II. *The Trinity in Unity.*

We have already noticed the definition of the term *person* given in the Augsburg Confession. It may be desirable, before entering on the details of the present section, to pursue that subject somewhat further. Waterland, in his ' Second Defence of Some Queries ' (qu. xv.), thus defines the term : ' A single person is an intelligent agent, having the distinctive characters of I, thou, he ; and not divided nor distinguished into more intelligent agents capable of the same characters.' The rationality or intelligence is meant to distinguish a person from an individual of the brute creation, to which he allows personality only in a modified analogous sense. The absence of division is intended to exclude a collective intelligent agent, as an army or a senate.

In this sense the Trinity is not a person. A man, an angel, the Father, the Son, the Holy Ghost, the separated soul, the God-man, are each of them single persons. 'All other persons, save the three divine Persons, are divided and separate from each other in nature, substance, and existence. They do not mutually include and imply each other. . . . But the divine Persons being undivided, and not having any separate existence independent of each other, they cannot be looked upon as substances, but as one substance distinguished into several *supposita*, or intelligent agents.'

There are compound persons also. Man's soul and body together make a compound person, and yet only one person.

A man does not say we, but I. The God-man is a compound Person, consisting of soul, body, and the Logos. But the result is one Person. 'The same Christ made the world, increased in wisdom, was pierced by a spear.' He is spoken of in Scripture as 'one I, one He, one Thou, whether with respect to what He is as the Logos, or as having a soul or a body.'

In our discussion of the great doctrines now before us, it will be necessary to anticipate in some measure Articles II. and V.; for we shall have to take these three separate propositions. The Father is God. The Son is God. And the Holy Ghost is God.

The first of these needs no proof. There is no question about it. We pass, therefore, to the second. It must be noted that this is a matter of pure revelation. It is believed as a direct deduction from certain passages; and, if possible, it follows still more certainly from the whole spirit of the New Testament, that the Son is God, and a distinct Person in Himself.

This subject is handled by Pearson (Art. II. §§ 3 & 4, ' His only Son our Lord '). Having spoken of Jesus Christ as the Son of God, Pearson proceeds with the following argument:—

1. Jesus Christ had a real existence before His incarnation, as will appear from the following passages: ' What and if ye shall see the Son of Man ascend up where He was before ? '

(John vi. 62); 'He that cometh after me is preferred before me, for He was before me' (John i. 15); 'Before Abraham was, I am' (John viii. 58); 'By the Spirit He went, and preached to the spirits in prison. . . . in the days of Noah' (1 Pet. iii. 18–20); 'By whom also He made the worlds' (Heb. i. 11); &c.

2. The pre-existent nature of the Son was not created, but essentially divine, as appears from the following arguments.

a. It follows of necessity from the fact of *creation* being ascribed to Him; for this is absolutely a divine attribute.

b. It follows also from the familiar passage Phil. ii. 6, 7, which, being argued out, shows that the Son was in the form of a servant as soon as He was made man, but that before this He was in the form of God. The word *form* ($\mu o \rho \phi \grave{\eta}$), being used in both clauses, applies as really to the divine as to the human nature.

c. Jehovah describes Himself thus, 'I am the First, I also am the Last' (Isa. xlviii. 12). The same is said of the Son (Rev. i. 11).

d. That which in Isaiah vi. is spoken of Jehovah is in John xii. 41 referred to Christ.

e. In several passages Christ is called God, especially Col. ii. 9.

f. In several other places (e.g. Jer. xxiii. 6; Mal. iii. 1; Isa. xl. 3) the name Jehovah is used, and the same is referred in the New Testament to Christ.

Hence we conclude that the Son of God has an essentially divine nature.

3. Next, He has this divine nature not of Himself, but as communicated from the Father.

a. Because of the absolute unity of the divine essence, which will not permit the existence of two divine Persons independently existing.

b. The divine nature being indivisible, the whole and not a part of the Deity must be thus communicated. 'I and the Father are one.' This is the $\delta \mu o o \acute{v} \sigma \iota o \nu$ of the Nicene fathers.

4. This communication of the divine essence is of such a

nature that it is called in Scripture the generation of the Son (Heb. i. 5).

In the case of human generation, man begets a son in his own likeness, but with a separate individuality from his own. God, *as the Father*, has a more perfect relation to God *the Son*, in that He communicates the whole nature and properties of the Deity, not by dividing Himself, but by a full communication of Himself.

Hence it is concluded that the Son is God. But that He is not the same Person as God the Father, inasmuch as they stand in a peculiar relation in respect of origin, and because in many passages they are plainly distinguished from each other in will and operation (e.g. John v. 30, 37 ; xvi. 26, &c.).

The third main proposition before us is this : *The Holy Ghost is God.*

We refer again to Pearson (Art. VIII. ' I believe in the Holy Ghost'). The mode of dealing with this subject may be thus exhibited :—

1. The Holy Ghost is a *Person*, and not a mere quality or influence, because—

a. He is contrasted with evil spirits, who are *persons.* See the cases of Saul and Micaiah.

b. He can be grieved, He makes intercession, searches all things, distributes spiritual gifts, spake to Peter and to prophets at Antioch. As the Paraclete, He is sent, teaches, testifies, comes, reproves, guides, speaks. All these are Personal acts.

2. The Holy Ghost is not only a Person, but uncreated and divine.

a. See 1 Cor. ii. 11.

b. The sin against the Holy Ghost is irremissible. Since all sin against God is not so, sin against a created being cannot be unpardonable.

c. (John i. 3). All created things were made by the Son. But the Spirit of God was in the beginning (Job xxvi. 13), and therefore is not a creature.

d. (Luke i. 35). Jesus is called the Son of God as being conceived by the Holy Ghost, who must, therefore, be God.

e. Further proofs are alleged from the following passages :—

2 Cor. iii. 15–17. Acts v. 3, 4. The lie to the Holy Ghost is a lie to God. 1 Cor. vi. 19. The inhabitation by the Spirit makes man a temple of God. Acts xxviii. 25. The Holy Ghost is identified with Jehovah.

f. The divine attributes—Omniscience, Omnipotence, Omnipresence—are attributed to the Holy Ghost.

3. But though a Person and divine, the Holy Ghost is not to be confused with the Father or the Son. For—

a. He proceeds from the Father (John xv. 26); therefore He is not the Father.

b. He receives of that which is the Son's, and glorifies the Son. He is sent on condition of the Son's departure (John xiv. 26, and xvi. 7, 14); therefore He is not the Son.

c. He is distinguished from both Father and Son (Matt. iii. 16; Eph. ii. 18, &c.).

The above is a brief sketch of the argument of Pearson in support of the doctrine before us, that *in the unity of the Godhead there be three Persons, of one substance, power, and eternity : the Father, the Son, and the Holy Ghost.*

The Trinitarian controversy in the Church of England belonged chiefly to the commencement of the eighteenth century. In 1685 the celebrated work of Bishop Bull appeared, the *Defensio Fidei Niceni.* It is a learned investigation of the opinions of the fathers of the first three centuries on the doctrine of the Trinity. It remains the standard work on that part of the subject. Bishop Bull died in 1709, and the controversy took another form, mainly in consequence of the publications of Dr. Samuel Clarke, which were considered to be a revival of Arian opinions. This led to the valuable treatises of Waterland on the Trinity ; they appeared in succession for some years, and remain as a copious storehouse of theology on the various points of the doctrine of the Holy Trinity.

A short treatise, entitled ' The Catholic Doctrine of a Trinity proved from Scripture,' by Jones of Nayland, of which there is an edition published by Rivington, will be found a brief and able compendium, which may be useful.

ARTICLE II.

Of the Word, or Son of God, which was made very Man.

The Son, which is the Word of the Father, begotten from everlasting of the Father, the very and eternal God, of one substance with the Father, took Man's nature in the womb of the blessed Virgin, of her substance; so that two whole and perfect natures, that is to say, the Godhead and Manhood, were joined together in one Person, never to be divided, whereof is one Christ, very God, and very Man; who truly suffered, was crucified, dead and buried, to reconcile His Father to us, and to be a sacrifice, not only for original guilt, but also for all actual sins of men.

De Verbo, sive Filio Dei, qui verus homo factus est.

Filius, qui est verbum Patris, ab æterno a Patre genitus, verus et æternus Deus, ac Patri consubstantialis, in utero beatæ virginis, ex illius substantia naturam humanam assumpsit : ita ut duæ naturæ, divina et humana, integre atque perfecte in unitate personæ fuerint inseparabiliter conjunctæ, ex quibus est unus Christus, verus Deus et verus homo, qui vere passus est, crucifixus, mortuus et sepultus, ut Patrem nobis reconciliaret, essetque hostia, non tantum pro culpa originis, verum etiam pro omnibus actualibus hominum peccatis.

Notes on the Text of Article II.

The Latin text invites no special comment. The substance of this Article is identical with that of Edward, excepting that the clause, ' begotten from everlasting of the Father, the very and eternal God, of one substance with the Father,' was added in Elizabeth's time from the Wurtemberg Confession, and one or two slight verbal changes were made.

The Article itself is derived from the Third of the Augsburg Confession, which runs thus:—

'The Word, that is, the Son of God, took man's nature in the womb of the Blessed Virgin Mary, so that two natures, the divine and human, were joined together in one person, never to be divided (whereof is), one Christ, very God and very Man, born of the Virgin Mary, (who) truly suffered, was crucified, dead, and buried, to reconcile His Father to us, and to be a sacrifice, not only for original guilt, but also for all actual sins of men.'

It is manifest that no code of Christian doctrine could be complete without an explicit confession of faith on this fundamental Article. But the circumstances of the age of the Reformation also made it needful; for, omitting for the present any reference to the more ancient heresies, it is certain that in the confusion created by the great movements of the Reformation every conceivable misbelief about the nature and person of the Lord Jesus Christ found some utterance. For this we may refer to the notice of the Anabaptists, under Art. VII. We may further illustrate it by some lamentable occurrences in the reign of Edward VI. These will show how strong was the hold on men's minds of the persecuting principles of the middle ages. It was perceived to be an intolerable wrong that the Gospel should be resisted. But it was held to be the inviolable duty of the civil ruler to punish blasphemy with death, according to the precepts of the Mosaic law and the example of Jewish sovereigns. The taunts of Romanists quickened zeal in this matter. The Reformers were anxious to clear themselves of any complicity with those who in any way denied the Saviour. Thus we read of sundry heretics being brought before Cranmer, Latimer, and others, sitting as the King's Commissioners, and being compelled to recant.[1] A more terrible example is the death of Joan Bocher, who was burnt by warrant of the Council of Regency. Latimer[2] gives an account of her, evidently without the slightest misgiving on his own part or that of his hearers that the slightest wrong had been committed in dealing with her. 'I told you,' says he, 'the last time, of one Joan of Kent,

---

[1] Strypes' 'Cranmer,' book ii. ch. viii.   [2] 'Remains,' p. 114.

which was in this foolish opinion, that she should say our Saviour was not very Man, and had not received flesh of His mother Mary, and yet she could show no reason why she should believe so. Her opinion was this. The Son of God, said she, penetrated through her, as through a glass, taking no substance of her. But our Creed teacheth us contrariwise.' Two others likewise suffered for a similar reason. And in like manner, it is notorious that Servetus was put to death at Geneva, how far with the co-operation of Calvin is disputed. If the Romanists, like ourselves, had been led to repudiate and detest this mode of casting out false doctrine, such instances as these (however few, comparatively speaking) would prevent our reproaching them on this score. Our just ground of indignant rebuke is this, that all the authorita-tive utterances of their Church, down to the encyclical of the present Pope, maintain the right of persecution for the sake of religion, and complain of their present state as one of discouragement and oppression, because the civil power no longer enforces the ecclesiastical domination.

Observations on Article II.

For reasons already stated, we shall again recur to ' Pearson on the Creed ' for the exposition of this Article, and, as far as possible, confine ourselves to his treatment of the several doctrines it contains. We may conveniently break up the Article into these principal sections :—

    I. The Deity and Sonship of the Second Person of the Trinity.
    II. The Incarnation.
    III. The Nature of the Person of the Incarnate Son.
    IV. The sufferings of Christ.
    V. The purpose of those sufferings.

I. *The Deity and Sonship of the Second Person of the Trinity.*

It has already been needful, in commenting on the first Article, to prove that the Son is very God, and of one substance with the Father. It was also shown that the mode of communicating the divine essence from the Father is such as to make the Second Person of the Trinity properly the Son of God. 'For,' says Pearson, 'the most proper generation which we know is nothing else but a vital production of another in the same nature, with a full representation of him from whom he is produced. . . . But God the Father hath communicated to the Word the same divine essence by which He is God; and consequently He is of the same nature with Him, and thereby the same image and similitude of Him, and therefore His proper Son.'

The Arians of old, though they allowed the ineffable dignity of the Son of God, yet allowed not this communication of the divine essence which makes the Son properly ὁμοούσιος, of the *same* substance, with the Father. They maintained that He is ἀνόμοιος, *unlike* in substance; while the semi-Arians were willing to go a step further, and to acknowledge that He is ὁμοιούσιος, *similar* in substance to the Father. The Arians also asserted the formula ἦν ποτε ὅτε οὐκ ἦν, *there was a time when He was not.* We maintain, therefore, the true and proper communication of the divine nature to the Son, and we now further assert that *He was begotten from everlasting of the Father.* Upon this we again quote Pearson (Art II. § 3): ' In human generation the son is begotten in the same nature with the father, which is performed by derivation or decision of part of the substance of the parent. But this decision includeth imperfection, because it supposeth a substance divisible, and consequently corporeal. Whereas the essence of God is incorporeal, spiritual, and indivisible; and therefore His nature is really communicated, not by derivation or decision, but by a total and plenary communication. In natural conceptions the father necessarily precedeth the son, and begetteth one younger than himself. It is sufficient if the parent can produce another to live after him, and continue the existence of his nature when his person is dissolved. But this presupposeth the imperfection of mortality wholly to be removed, when we speak of Him who inhabiteth eternity; the essence which God always had without beginning, without beginning he did communicate, being always Father, as always God. Animals, when they come to the perfection of nature, then become prolifical; in God, eternal perfection showeth His eternal fecundity. And that which is most remarkable, in human generations the son is of the same nature with the father, and yet is not the same man, because, though he hath an essence of the same kind, yet he hath not the same essence: the power of generation depending on the first prolifical benediction, 'Increase and multiply,' it must be made by way of multiplication, and thus every son becomes another man. But the divine essence being, by reason of its simplicity, not subject to division, and, in respect of its infinity, incapable of multiplication, is communicated so as not to be multiplied; insomuch that He which proceedeth by that communication hath not only the same nature, but is also the same God.'

Nothing need be added to this clear and masterly theological statement of the proper divinity and eternal generation of the Son of God.

II. *The Incarnation.*

This portion of the doctrine before us corresponds to the third Article of the Apostles' Creed: 'Conceived by the Holy Ghost, born of the Virgin Mary.' In the second section of that Article Pearson considers the action of the Holy Ghost in the conception, and lays down these positions :—

1. The action of the Spirit *excludes* all human agency, even that of the Virgin herself, as the *cause* of the conception. This appears from passages in the gospels, describing what took place previously to the birth.

2. What this action of the Spirit *includes* cannot further be defined from the words of Scripture than to say, whatever ' was necessary to cause the Virgin to perform the actions of a mother ' must be attributed to the Holy Spirit. But this did not involve any communication of the substance of the Holy Ghost, which is uncreated. The flesh of Christ was not formed of any substance but that of the Virgin.

Further, under the third section of the same Article, it is

shown, from the testimony of Scripture, that, in accordance with prophecy, Mary was a virgin at the time of the birth of our Lord, and that her maternity involves of necessity these three things:

1. The reality of the conception of the real substance of our Saviour in her womb and of her substance.

2. The reality of the growth from her substance in her womb of that which was so conceived.

3. That what was so conceived and grew was brought forth by her with a true and proper nativity.

III. *The Nature of the Person of the Incarnate Son.*

The consideration of this in Pearson falls chiefly under Art. III. § 1, 'Who was conceived.' In this part of Pearson's treatise we find statements to the following effect: He who was conceived and born partook of the same human nature which is in all men. He is often called man. A parallel is drawn between Him and Adam. He is the seed of Eve, of Abraham, of David. Being thus truly man, His manhood consisted of body and soul. The body was real, for Scripture speaks of its growth, nutrition, and sufferings. The soul was a rational human soul, for He increased in *wisdom*, as well as in *stature*, which is impossible for the Godhead. Moreover, He experienced the various human affections and sorrows whose seat is in the soul. And He commended this human spirit to His Father at the moment of death.

This opposes the heresy of the Apollinarians, who held that though Jesus had a human body and animal soul, yet in Him the divine Logos was a substitute for the spiritual part of man (the νοῦς or ψυχὴ λογικὴ [1]).

Next, it is maintained that in this incarnation there is no conversion of one nature into the other, nor any confusion between them. There is no confusion or mixture of the two natures, for otherwise a third something would result, which would be neither God nor man. The affections and infirmities of our nature could not belong to such a being. More-

---

[1] Neander, 'Hist.' vol. iv. p. 119.

over, the Godhead being indivisible in *substance*, a confusion
of substance must intermix the Father also.

Further, the divine cannot be converted into the human
nature, for the uncreated Godhead cannot be created or made.

Nor can the human nature be converted into the divine, as
the Eutychians and other monophysites taught.

Finally, it is concluded that, though different actions and
qualities are attributed in Holy Scripture to Christ, some of
which belong to the divine and some to the human nature,
yet they must all be attributed to *one and the same Person*.
Otherwise there would be two Christs, two Mediators, contrary
to the spirit, as well as the language, of all Scripture.

Hence we confess in this present Article of our Church
(against the Nestorians of old), that the two natures *were
joined together in one Person*.

One more topic falls under this head. The Article further
asserts that the two natures in Christ are ' never to be divided.'
In the first place, Pearson[1] argues that they were not divided
when the Lord Jesus died, because God ' doth never subtract
His grace from any without their abuse of it, and a sinful de-
merit in themselves; we cannot imagine the grace of union
should be taken from Christ, who never offended, and that
in the highest act of obedience and the greatest satisfaction
to the will of God.' And further,[2] while it is granted, from
1 Cor. xv. 24, 28, that the mediatorial kingdom shall cease
when its work shall be finally completed, ' yet we must not
think that Christ shall cease to be a king or lose any of the
power and honour which before He had. . . The kingdoms
of this world are become the kingdoms of the Lord and of His
Christ, and He shall reign for ever and ever ' (Rev. xi. 15);
not only to the modificated eternity of His mediatorship, so
long as there shall be need of regal power to subdue the enemies of God's elect, *but also to the complete eternity of the
duration of His humanity, which for the future is coeternal
with His divinity*.'

<hr>

[1] ' Creed,' Art. IV. § 4.   [2] Ibid. Art. VI. § 2.

IV. *The Sufferings of Christ.*

These we find summed up by our Article in these words of
the Creed, ' *Who truly suffered,* was crucified, dead, and buried.'
A slight abstract of some portions of the fourth Article of
' Pearson on the Creed' will bring out the principal theological
points belonging to this section. The Person who suffered
is distinctly *one*, the Son of God. But *the nature in which* He
suffered is as distinctly the human and not the divine. For
the two natures are united ' not by confusion of substance,
but by unity of person.' The nature of the Deity is in itself
' *impassibilis* ' (Art. I.), incapable of suffering. It follows,
therefore, that the union of the divine nature with the human
nature in Christ does not modify the divine nature so as to
make it capable of suffering.

The intimate conjunction of the two natures in Christ
has led divines to the use of language which ascribes to
that *one Person* the attributes which properly belong to *one
only* of the *two united natures.* Such a transfer of language is
called in theological language '*communicatio idiomatum.*' Thus
it is said that the Son of God suffered. Yet He suffered in
that He was man, not in that He was God. Or, *vice versâ,* we
say that Christ is omnipresent. Yet he is so as God, not as
man. Still, properly speaking, the *one Person*, the Son of
God, is omnipresent. But if we permit this mode of speech
to confuse our thoughts, we shall fall into some shape of
monophysite error. Some such error pervades all systems of
consubstantiation and transubstantiation. For they not only
claim that *the Person*, the Son of God, is present, but that His
human nature has acquired (in some sense) the omnipresence
of the divine nature.

The sufferings of the human nature of Christ consist in the
bodily sufferings before the crucifixion which are spoken of
in so many parts of the gospels ; and in the anguish of soul,
including emotions of fear, sorrow, and other pains, endured
during His whole life, and more especially in Gethsemane ;
and, finally, in the acerbity and ignominy of the cross itself.

With regard to the *death* of Christ, the chief theological

points are its certainty and the description of that wherein it consisted.

That Jesus did '*truly* die' is asserted from the testimony of His worst enemies, of nature itself, and of the water and blood which flowed from His wounded side.

Death in Him consisted in the same fact as in other men— the separation of the soul from the body. This appears from the expressions of the Evangelists who describe His death. For this there was an adequate cause in the anguish, bodily and spiritual, which He endured.

It must further be understood that His death was *voluntary* (John x. 18), in the sense that of His own will He submitted Himself to that which would cause death. It was *involuntary* in the sense that, without divine interposition, the human frame subjected to such anguish must suffer dissolution; and also that He did not anticipate the natural moment of death. Otherwise the actual death itself would not have been the deed of His enemies, but His own.

The fact of the *burial* of our Lord, omitting the circumstances relating to it recorded in Scripture, may here be chiefly noticed as sealing the truth of His death.

V. *The Purpose of the Sufferings of Christ.*

' To reconcile His Father to us, and to be a sacrifice, not only for original guilt, but also for actual sins of men.'

It will be noticed that the doctrine here set forth is the more abstract one of the *general* nature and purport of Christ's sufferings; not the particular and individual one of the application of the merit of those sufferings to a sinful soul. This latter will find its place further on, under the Articles on sin, justification, &c.

And it is also this more general view of the subject that Pearson chiefly treats [1] when commenting on the clause 'The forgiveness of sins.' Pearson there deduces from the consideration of many passages of Scripture that the forgiveness of sins promised to us ' containeth in it a reconciliation of an

[1] ' Creed,' Art. X.

offended God, and a satisfaction to a just God: it containeth a reconciliation, as without which God cannot be conceived to remit ; it comprehendeth a satisfaction, as without which God was resolved not to be reconciled.' These are the two particulars of the present section of our Article.

On the first of these two points, ' The reconciliation of His Father to us,' Pearson proceeds thus : ' Christ by His death hath reconciled God unto us, who was offended by our sins ; and that He hath done so we are assured, because He, which before was angry with us, on the consideration of Christ's death becomes propitious to us, and did ordain Christ's death to be a propitiation for us. For we " are justified freely by His grace through the redemption that is in Christ Jesus, whom God hath set forth to be a propitiation, through faith in His blood" (Rom. iii. 24, 25). "We have an Advocate with the Father, and He is the propitiation for our sins " (1 John ii. 1). For God " loved us, and sent His Son to be the propitiation for our sins " (1 John iv. 10). It is evident, therefore, that Christ did render God propitious unto us by His blood (that is, His sufferings unto death), who before was offended with us for our sins. And this propitiation amounted to a reconciliation, that is, a kindness after wrath. We must conceive that God was angry with mankind before He determined to give our Saviour ; we cannot imagine that God, who is essentially just, should not abominate iniquity. The first affection we can conceive in Him upon the lapse of man is wrath and indignation. God, therefore, was most certainly offended before He gave a Redeemer ; and though it be most true that He " so loved the world that He gave His only begotten Son " (John iii. 16), yet there is no incongruity in this, that a father should be offended with that son which he loveth, and at that time offended with him when he loveth him. Notwithstanding, therefore, that God loved men whom He created, yet He was offended with them when they sinned, and gave His Son to suffer for them, that through that Son's obedience He might be reconciled to them. This reconciliation is clearly delivered in the Scriptures as wrought by Christ ; for " all things are of God, who hath reconciled us to

Himself by Jesus Christ" (2 Cor. v. 18), and that by virtue of His death, for "when we were enemies we were reconciled unto God by the death of His Son" (Rom. v. 10).'

This doctrine needs close attention in the present day, when much is made of what Pearson calls 'the Socinian exception, that in the Scriptures we are said to be reconciled unto God, but God is never said to be reconciled unto us.' He shows from the language of Scripture, in many instances (e.g. 1 Cor. vii. 11), that to be reconciled to a person implies that person becoming favourable to the other. We turn to the second part of the present section—the death of Christ viewed as a sacrifice for all sin.

The definition of sin, based on 1 John iii. 4, given by Pearson, is this: 'Whatsoever is done by man, or is in man, having any contrariety to the law of God, is sin.' And after including in this definition all acts of omission or commission contrary to God's law, and 'every evil habit contracted in the soul,' he says that 'any corruption or inclination in the soul to do that which God forbiddeth, and to omit that which God commandeth, howsoever such corruption and inclination came into the soul, whether by an act of his own will, *or by an act of the will of another*, is a sin, as being something dissonant and repugnant to the law of God.'

Sin thus regarded manifestly comprehends under one term the double expression of our present Article, 'original guilt' and 'actual sins of men.' For sin, in this comprehensive sense, Christ's death was a sacrifice. In proof of this, Pearson alleges many passages of Scripture, such as these, which may be easily multiplied: 'Once in the end of the world hath He appeared to put away sin by the sacrifice of Himself' (Heb. ix. 26); 'He was delivered for our offences' (Rom. iv. 25); 'He died for our sins, according to the Scriptures' (1 Cor. xv. 3). Pearson further shows how the life of Christ was laid down as a price: 'Ye are bought with a price' (1 Cor. vi. 20); 'We are not redeemed with corruptible things . . . but with the precious blood of Christ' (1 Pet. i. 18, 19). 'Now, as it was the blood of Christ, so it was a price given by way of compensation: and as that blood was precious, so it was a full and perfect satisfaction. For as the gravity of the offence and iniquity of the sin is augmented and increaseth, according to the dignity of the person offended and injured by it, so the value, price, and dignity of that which is given by way of compensation is raised according to the dignity of the person making the satisfaction. God is of infinite majesty, against whom we have sinned; and Christ is of the same divinity, who gave His life a ransom for sinners; for God "hath purchased *His Church* with His own blood" (Acts xx. 28). Although, therefore, God be said to remit our sins by which we were captivated, yet He is never said to remit the price without which we had never been redeemed; neither can He be said to have remitted it, because He did require it and receive it.'

Before we dismiss this important Article, which deals with the very foundation of the Christian hope, a few words of caution may be needful. That side of the atonement which looks towards God, rather than towards man, is confessedly mysterious. In other words, any doctrinal statement is so which seeks to answer the question, ' Why God required and accepts the atonement on man's behalf,' rather than the practical question, ' How man may obtain the benefit of that atonement.'

On that mysterious side, the analogy of revelation will not permit us to expect more information than may satisfy us that God's attributes are really united in the mode of salvation He has provided. The origin of evil, its permitted existence, the extent to which it has permeated the whole of human nature, and, as Scripture intimates, spiritual regions of unknown amplitude besides, are appalling, and to us unintelligible subjects. They render it absolutely impossible for us to attempt to account for the present immense scope and sway of evil in the universe of God. We may further consider, that to prevent its grosser and more ruinous manifestations in human society is the very utmost which the effort of man has attained, and scarcely attained; and that the absolute conquest of evil in a single human heart has never yet been accomplished. Hence we may well hesitate in presuming to judge of the

means by which it has pleased God to deal with this gigantic
enemy, initially for the present, and completely, as He has
intimated to us, in the future. The dealing of God with sin,
whether through His attribute of Love or of Justice, is therefore beyond human criticism. The past and the future are
alike beyond our ken. The subjection or destruction of
evil, in the establishment of the great kingdom of God that
is to be, will be accomplished, but we cannot judge of the
necessary means. Meanwhile we are able to say that Christianity, of which the atonement is the animating principle, has,
in point of fact, proved itself the most powerful agent yet
known in overcoming sin.

But if all this is undeniable, it is manifest that great
caution is needed in stating the doctrine of the atonement. It
is in theology, as a science, as it is in other sciences. In as-
tronomy the results of multitudinous observations give certain
facts, which must be all accounted for and included in any
theory of the science which claims acceptance. In theology
each passage of Scripture is a fact; and the undoubtedly ascertained qualities of man's nature are other facts. Any doctrinal theory, in order to be true, must unite in itself, and take
account of, all these facts. If it fails to unite them (within
those limits which are possible to man), it is not a true doctrine.
If the results of our induction, carefully conducted, lead to two
apparently conflicting doctrines, it does not follow of necessity
that either is false. For example, the free-will of man, to
such an extent at least as to make him responsible, is an
unquestionable fact of Scripture and experience. The foreknowledge of God, and His universal sovereignty, are necessary deductions of reason and clear assertions of Scripture.
Perfectly to reconcile these with man's free-will may be
impossible. This need not distress us when we have carefully
followed our facts to the verge of the infinite or the unknown.
There we must leave them, and we need have little difficulty
in feeling assured that the missing facts which would reconcile
the apparent contradictions in our deductions lie within, and
probably not many steps within, the dark margin at which we
pause.

Turning again to the doctrine of the atonement, the greatest care is needed in so stating it that the justice of the Father shall not seem in stern opposition to the love of the Son. The popular opposition to the doctrine of the present Article is mainly fostered either by the incaution of the orthodox divine in so apparently stating it, or else by the misapprehension or disingenuousness of the opponent so invidiously expressing it. We need not particularise names. With varying degrees of refinement or of coarseness, the great doctrine of the atonement is travestied. It is profanely represented as a tyrannical wrath seeking satisfaction with a blind fury, and mitigated at length by exhausting itself even on an innocent victim. If divines of some considerable reputation can be found to make such misrepresentations as this, it behoves us to be very careful in our statements. And the point of all others to be wary upon is that which Pearson (p. 23) presses, that God infinitely loved the Son whom He gave, and man for whom He gave the Son. His justice was offended, and yet He did not cease to love. Let us gather together briefly the facts from which we are to make our induction. If any fact of experience be manifest, this is. There are marks of divine wrath and punishment visible everywhere throughout the whole history of man.[1] There are also visible in the world everywhere signs of divine love and care for God's creatures. So also in Scripture there are unquestionable declarations of divine wrath against all unrighteousness of man. There are also most gracious declarations of divine love and care for man. These are our facts, equally unquestionable in nature and in revelation. Any theory which fails to embrace both the wrath and the love must be false. Any theory which either ignores one of these, or so deals with both as to rend them apart, is untrue to the unity and perfection of God, and must be false. The great doctrine of the atonement, truly stated, embraces and harmonises both, so far as we are

---

[1] See Butler, part i. chaps. ii. iii.

competent to follow it. It is not that coarse idea of God's justice, rent away from his love, seeking a victim, and finding it in Christ. God is *One*. He is not made up of conflicting and contending attributes. But His perfection can only be described to us under different names, varying with the action of the divine Will. Towards sin it has the nature of Justice, and can only be described by that name. And yet this is only another phase of that infinite perfection which, looked at another way, is Love, verily such in name and in nature. Thus the atonement may be truly described as God's justice receiving satisfaction, according to the full measure of the demands of an infinite wrong. It may also be as truly and more fully described as the last inconceivable effort of Infinite Love. Sin had produced an apparently irretrievable breach between God and man. There was not put forth a destructive vengeful effort of Infinite Power. At least not yet. But instead, Infinite Love, with Infinite Self-Sacrifice, gave *itself*. He who thinks that he is competent to gage and define all the results in the spiritual world of such a transaction as this, is confident indeed. We are content to believe that it will take eternity to unfold them.

We may observe, finally, that Pearson's mode of stating this doctrine has something of an antique hardness. The present Archbishop of York, therefore, warns us[1] that in this mode of treatment ' there is the danger lest the atonement degenerate into a transaction between a righteous Father on the one side, and a loving Saviour on the other, because in the human transaction from which the analogy is drawn two distinct parties are concerned ; whereas in the plan of salvation one Will operates, and in the Father and the Son alike Justice and Love are reconciled.' The student who desires to meet some modern phases of this doctrine may read with instruction the essay of the archbishop above referred to. And it is scarcely necessary to remind him, that in Butler's ' Analogy ' [2] he will find the *à priori* objections against the appointment of a

---

[1] ' Aids to Faith,' VIII. ii. 10.   [2] Part ii. ch. **v.**

Mediator and the satisfaction wrought by Christ effectually parried, and the right place which human reason may occupy in relation to the divine action accurately defined.   The Thirty-first Article returns to the subject of Christ's death as the sacrifice for sin, and the subject will there receive some further notice.

ARTICLE III.

Of the going down of Christ into Hell.	*De descensu Christi ad Inferos.*
As Christ died for us, and was buried : so also it is to be believed that he went down into Hell.	Quemadmodum Christus pro nobis mortuus est et sepultus, ita est etiam credendus ad Inferos descendisse.

Notes on the Text of Article III.

The present Article consists of the first clause only of the original Article of 1552. In that formula these words followed : ' For the body lay in the sepulchre until the resurrection ; but His Ghost, departing from Him (*ab illo emissus*), was with the ghosts that were in prison or in hell (*in carcere sive in inferno*), and did preach to the same, as the place of St. Peter doth testify.' It must be confessed that we are happily freed from the obligation of maintaining such a comment on that passage.

It appears that controversy had been very busy with this Article. Hence the necessity was felt for stating it in more general terms. Foreign controversies in the time of Edward VI. are spoken of in a letter of Micronius to Bullinger, 1550.[1] ' The Churches of Bremen and the rest are strengthening themselves ; but . . . they are disputing about the descent of Christ into hell, and about the allowance or prohibition of things indifferent. Marvellous is the subtlety of antichrist in weakening the Churches of Christ ! ' The diocese of Exeter also was harassed with controversy on this subject, as appears from a paper presented to Convocation in 1562 by the bishop

---

[1] ' Original Letters,' p. 561 : Parker Society.

of that diocese : [1] 'There have been in my diocese great invectives between the preachers, one against the other, and also partakers with them; some holding that the going down of Christ His soul to hell was nothing else but the virtue and strength of Christ His death, to be made manifest and known to them that were dead before. Others say . . . Thus your wisdoms may perceive what tragedies and dissensions may arise from consenting to or dissenting from this Article.' That this was not limited to the West, or soon appeased, is gathered also from a letter of Secretary Cecil to Archbishop Parker, 1567 : [2]

'It may please your grace to receive my humble thanks for your care taken in the discreet advice given to me concerning the appeasing of the unprofitable rash controversy newly raised upon the Article of the Descent of Christ into Hell.'

Observations on Article III.

If the space or object of this work allowed the discussion, it is manifest from what has been so far said that there is abundant scope for investigation into some of the darker passages of Scripture, and for statements of conflicting opinions. But we may well dismiss the greater part of these with the verdict above quoted from the great Cecil, 'unprofitable and rash.' We shall be content, as before, to give an account of Bishop Pearson's discussion of this Article of the Creed.

Three passages, says Pearson, are usually quoted as the basis of this doctrine. First, Eph. iv. 9. There are such conflicting interpretations of the expression in that text, ' the lower parts of the earth ' (τὰ κατώτερα μέρη τῆς γῆς), that it cannot be relied upon as a proof.

2. 1 Pet. iii. 19, has been interpreted of a local descent of the soul of Christ to preach to the souls in hell. Pearson rejects this, as encompassed with difficulties. He takes the meaning to be that Christ by His Spirit spoke to the disobedient in Noah's days, as in all other times of the world.

---

[1] Strypes' 'Annals,' ch. xxxi.   [2] Strypes' 'Parker,' book iii. ch. xviii.

3. It remains that Acts ii. 26, 27, be accepted as the basis of this Article. For if His soul was not left in hell (Hades), and was not there before His death, it must have descended there after His death. The question, therefore, resolves itself into the interpretation of this passage. We shall have to ask what that hell (Hades) was, and how He descended thither.

Pearson then proceeds to give some account of the principal varieties of opinion which have been advanced on this subject, and which may be thus condensed :—

1. Durandus (an early schoolman) held that it was not a local descent, but one of efficacy and influence.

2. Calvin, Beza, and others maintained that Christ actually suffered the torments of the damned to save men from them. This is denied on the sufficient ground that remorse, despair, alienation from God, were far from Him.

3. Some have taken it as an expression simply equivalent to *buried*.

4. Others have varied the last by making it signify a *continuance* in the *state* of the dead.

5. The usual opinion is, that this Article means that the body having been buried, the soul (as distinguished from the body) was carried into those parts where the souls of men before departed were. In this opinion nearly all the fathers agree. They therefore used this Article of the Creed against the Apollinarians, urging that as the Deity did not descend into hell, Christ must have had a human soul capable of such a descent.

As to the purpose of Christ's descent, the fathers widely differed. But the leading varieties of their opinions may be displayed thus :—

1. He descended to the faithful dead, and removed them to a better place.

2. He descended to them, but did not so remove them.

3. He descended to hell in its proper sense, and preached the gospel to the souls detained there. It was generally thought heretical to believe (as some did) that He delivered them all. But it was widely held that He delivered some.

Finally, in the middle ages the first of these three prevailed, and was stated as an article of faith by the schoolmen with most marvellous elaboration of locality and other particulars. The solid earth was described as the bars of the infernal dungeon; volcanoes, its vent, and their roarings the cries of the damned.

Keeping aloof from profitless speculation about that which has been (not without Divine purpose) concealed from us, we may thus state the end of the descent. Christ bore the condition of a dead man, as He had done that of a living one. His body was laid in the grave. His soul was conveyed to the same receptacles as the souls of other men. He has thus assured His people of His power and presence in death as well as in life.

Finally, we may thus represent the usual simple mode of presenting this subject. We may combine the words of our Lord to the dying thief with the quotation of St. Peter from the Psalms. If the thief was to be with Him that day in Paradise, and yet He descended into Hades, that part of Hades to which He descended must be the place where the souls of the just await the resurrection.

THE ROMAN DOCTRINE ON THE DESCENT INTO HELL.

That audacity of assertion which is so marked a character of Roman theology, and which is one of the chief weapons with which it maintains its ground, is well exemplified in its treatment of this doctrine. The Catechism of the Council of Trent (P. I. c. 6) contains the authorised doctrine on this subject.

Q. 2 defines *Hell* as 'those hidden abodes in which are detained the souls that have not obtained heavenly bliss.'

Q. 3 states that this region contains three different receptacles : 1st. ' the most loathsome and dark prison, in which the souls of the damned, together with the unclean spirits, are tortured in eternal and inextinguishable fire; ' 2nd. ' the fire of purgatory, in which the souls of the just are purified by punishment for a stated time ; ' 3rd. the 'receptacle (commonly called *Limbus patrum*) in which were received the souls

D

of the saints who died before the coming of Christ our Lord;
and where, without any sense of pain, sustained by the
blessed hope of redemption, they enjoyed a tranquil abode.
The souls, then, of those pious men who, in the bosom of Abraham, were expecting the Saviour, Christ the Lord liberated,
descending into hell.'

Q. 5, scarcely in consistency with the preceding, asserts
that Christ 'liberated from the *miserable wearisomeness* of
that captivity the holy and the just.'

Q. 6 further dilates upon the same subject, ' Christ descended into hell in order that, having seized the spoils of the
devil, He might conduct into heaven those holy fathers, and
the other just souls liberated from prison. . . . His august
presence at once brought a glorious lustre upon the captives,
and filled their souls with boundless joy and gladness.   Unto
them He also imparted that supreme happiness which consists
in the vision of God.'

ARTICLE IV.

Of the Resurrection of Christ.	*De resurrectione Christi.*
Christ did truly arise again from death, and took again his body, with flesh, bones, and all things appertaining to the perfection of Man's nature, wherewith he ascended into Heaven, and there sitteth, until he return to judge all men at the last day.	Christus vere a mortuis resurrexit, suumque corpus cum carne, ossibus, omnibusque ad integritatem humanæ naturæ pertinentibus, recepit: cum quibus in cœlum ascendit, ibique residet, quoad extremo die ad judicandos homines reversurus sit.

NOTES ON THE TEXT OF ARTICLE IV.

The Latin text presents no points of sufficient consequence to be noted. No special sources are suggested for this Article. It is possible that some doctrinal follies of Anabaptists may have been in the view of its writers; but the obvious necessity of enunciating a complete faith in Christ would, in any case, have required the statement now before us.

OBSERVATIONS ON ARTICLE IV.

This Article is so manifestly a recapitulation of a portion of the Creed, that nothing need be added to a sketch of the treatment by Bishop Pearson of this portion of the Christian faith.[1] He first shows from prophecy that the Messiah was to rise again, and enumerates varied testimonies from Scripture to the *fact* of Christ's resurrection. Then follows the definition of a resurrection, thus stated—' A substantial change by which that which was before, and was corrupted, is repro-

---

[1] 'Creed,' Art. V. § 2.

duced the same thing again.' For a resurrection must be distinguished from a creation, or a mere alteration of state. A resurrection can only be predicated of a rational being who can retain personal identity. The reunion of the same soul to the same body, in all that is requisite to secure that personal identity, is a perfect and proper resurrection. It must be noted that Pearson in the above definition does not forget that Christ's body 'saw no corruption' (Acts ii. 31). For he further defines 'the separation of the rational soul from its body to be the corruption of a man.'

In the sense above stated Christ did properly rise. He had a *real* body; for He said, 'Handle me and see.' He had the *same* body; for He offered His wounds to be examined. The *animal* soul was present; for He ate before the disciples. The *sensitive* part was there: He conversed, He saw, He heard. The *rational* soul was present: He reasoned with them out of the Scriptures. It was the *same* soul; for the Deity was united to human nature in one man only. And the conjunction of the Godhead with the risen body of Jesus is manifest from His display of divine power after the resurrection. It thus appears that Christ did truly rise again from the dead, with all things appertaining to the perfection of man's nature, and with His own body.

The ascension, which follows next in the Article, will in like manner refer us to Pearson.[1] Having shown from type and prophecy that the Messiah was to ascend, he asserts that Christ ascended into heaven neither metaphorically nor figuratively by virtue of the hypostatic union, but actually by a local transfer of the human nature (body and soul), which was upon earth, into heaven. In testimony of this it was necessary that the ascension should be *visible*, because the ascended body disappeared. Accordingly we have the testimony of the apostles (Acts i. 9, 10), and of angels (Acts i. 10, 11). Further it is asserted that He ascended into that which in the most eminent sense is called *heaven*, as appears from many passages (e.g. Heb. iv. 14; Eph. iv. 10).

[1] 'Creed,' Art. VI. § 1.

The session 'at the right hand of God' is the next doctrine contained in this Article. This is treated by Pearson in the following manner : [1]

The *fact* that Christ was thus enthroned at the right hand of God is asserted frequently in Scripture (e.g. Mark xvi. 19 ; Eph. i. 20). This was covenanted to none but the Messiah (Heb. i. 13). The session itself is shown not to refer necessarily to a corporeal posture; but chiefly to imply rest, dominion, majesty, and judicial power. It, therefore, imports the entry of the Messiah into His full dominion. The place, *the right hand of God*, is not named in our Article, but is necessarily implied. It is interpreted as conveying no corporeal position, since God is a Spirit ; but as signifying power, honour, and the place of highest felicity.

That this session shall continue until the judgment day is asserted by the word *until*. This appears from many passages of Scripture (e.g. 1 Cor. xv. 25, 28 ; Acts iii. 21 ; 1 Thess. iv. 16).

Lastly, the return to judgment is the subject of the Seventh Article of Pearson 'On the Creed.' The principal points of doctrine there elaborated are these:—That Christ shall return is declared frequently in the New Testament (e.g. Acts i. 11), as it is also stated that His purpose then shall be judgment.

The propriety of the judgment being committed to Him appears from these considerations:—It is a part of His exaltation, the reward of His sufferings and obedience (John v. 22, 23). The Judge will thus be *visible*. He will know human infirmities by His own experience.

The judicial action itself is sparingly described. But it involves the eternal disposal of the souls and bodies of all persons. As to the *manner*, we can only say that it is represented to us under judicial terms. A judgment-seat is spoken of (2 Cor. v. 10). A personal appearance of all before the tribunal (Rev. xx. 12); the manifestation of all thoughts and actions (1 Cor. iv. 5); a definitive sentence (Matt. xxv. 34, 41); execution of the sentence (Matt. xxv. 46), are among the judicial particulars set forth in Scripture.

[1] 'Creed,' Art. V. § 2.

That this judgment shall take place *at the last day*, the very closing hour of this dispensation, is manifest from every consideration of its nature and purpose ; and further is clearly declared—2 Pet. iii. 7—which predicts the destruction of the existing frame of heaven and earth. at the time of the judgment.

ARTICLE V.

Of the Holy Ghost.	*De Spiritu Sancto.*
The Holy Ghost, proceeding from the Father and the Son, is of one substance, majesty, and glory, with the Father and the Son, very and eternal God.	Spiritus Sanctus, a Patre et Filio procedens, ejusdem est cum Patre et Filio essentiæ, majestatis, et gloriæ, verus ac æternus Deus.

Notes on the Text of Article V.

The Latin text is closely coincident with the English. No verbal comment is required on either.

This Article is not found amongst those of 1552; it was added in the time of Elizabeth. It is said by Hardwick to have been borrowed from the Wurtemberg Confession, presented to the Council of Trent in 1552.

The observation made under other Articles may be repeated. It is obviously essential to such a code of doctrine as this that the truth about the nature of the Holy Ghost should be declared. But it is also certain (omitting mention of the ancient Macedonians) that in the age of the Reformation there were some Anabaptists, also the elder Socinus and others,[1] who denied the personality of the Holy Ghost.

Observations on Article V.

This Article defines the nature and Person of the Holy Spirit; it does not speak of His office in dealing with the Church or individuals. It may be divided into two principal sections—the procession of the Holy Ghost, and His divine

[1] Mosheim, 'Cent. XVI.' iii. part ii. ch. iv. § 3.

nature. We were compelled to anticipate the latter of these in commenting on the First Article. The procession of the Holy Ghost now remains for consideration.

The history of this doctrine may be briefly recapitulated. The original form of the Nicene, or rather the Constantino-politan, Creed declared that the Holy Ghost proceeded from the Father (ἐκ τοῦ Πατρὸς ἐκπορευόμενον). At the close of the sixth century the words *and from the Son* were added by the Provincial Council of Toledo, in Spain. Thence the clause appears to have gradually found its way into Gaul, in portions of which kindred Gothic races were settled. Nearly two hundred years afterwards, this dogma of the procession of the Holy Ghost from the Son, as well as from the Father, found a strenuous supporter in Charlemagne. He called a council of his own bishops at Frankfort, in which this doctrine was affirmed, and the Pope was afterwards addressed on the subject of the defect of the Creed on this important matter. The Pope declined to make any change in the Creed. Nor, so far as can be clearly ascertained, was the alteration ever made officially and authoritatively. Gradually and stealthily the change spread. About the year 1014 it had established itself in Rome, and was adopted in the Pontifical services.

The opposition called forth in the Eastern Church is well known. The presumption of the Western portion of the Church in venturing to alter the Creed confirmed by all the great General Councils, added to the assumptions of the Pope, made the great schism between the East and the West which has never been closed. It has, perhaps, been a divine mercy that, in the midst of so general a corruption of Christian doctrine, the Papal tyranny should have thus received a check; and that a perpetual protest should have been made against it by a Church scarcely purer than itself in point of doctrine.

Nothing could well be more unsatisfactory than the mode in which this additional clause found its way into the Creed. Nevertheless we see that it is distinctly affirmed by the Church of England; and the fact of its truth, or otherwise, is quite distinct from any particular time or mode of its promulgation.

We turn, therefore, as before to Pearson's treatment of this doctrine.[1] The procession of the Holy Ghost from the Father is confessed by both parties, and is commonly taken to be expressly declared in John xv. 26 (ὁ παρὰ τοῦ Πατρὸς ἐκπορεύεται). This is also said to be evident on this ground. 'Since the Father and the Spirit are the same God, and being the same in the unity of the nature of God, are yet distinct in their personality, one of them must have the same nature from the other ; and because the Father hath it from none, it followeth that the Spirit hath it from Him.'

The procession of the Holy Ghost from the Son is said to be 'virtually contained' in the Scripture. 'Because those very expressions, which are spoken of the Holy Spirit in relation to the Father, for that reason because He proceedeth from the Father, are also spoken of the same Spirit in relation to the Son ; and therefore there must be the same reason *presupposed* in reference to the Son which is *expressed* in reference to the Father.' In proof of this it is shown that the Holy Ghost is equally called the Spirit of *God* (e.g. 1 Cor. ii. 11, 12) and the Spirit of *Christ* (e.g. Rom. viii. 9). Again it is urged that the Holy Ghost is said to be sent by the Father (John xiv. 26) and by the Son (John xv. 26). Hence a parity of relation is said to follow. 'The Father is never sent by the Son, because He received not the Godhead from Him ; but the Father sendeth the Son, because He communicated the Godhead to Him. In the same manner neither the Father nor the Son is ever sent by the Holy Spirit, because neither of them received the divine nature from the Spirit. But both the Father and the Son sendeth the Holy Ghost, because the divine nature common to both the Father and the Son was communicated by them both to the Holy Ghost. As, therefore, the Scriptures declare *expressly* that the Spirit proceedeth from the Father, so do they also *virtually* teach that He proceedeth from the Son.'

[1] 'Creed,' Art. VIII.

PART II.

THE RULE OF FAITH.

ARTICLE VI.

Of the Sufficiency of the Holy Scriptures for Salvation.

Holy Scripture containeth all things necessary to salvation : so that whatsoever is not read therein, nor may be proved thereby, is not to be required of any man, that it should be believed as an Article of the Faith, or be thought requisite[1] necessary to salvation.

In the name of Holy Scripture we do understand those Canonical Books of the Old and New Testament, of whose authority was never any doubt in the Church.

Of the Names and Number of the Canonical Books.

Genesis,
Exodus,
Leviticus,
Numbers,
Deuteronomy,
Joshua,
Judges,
Ruth,
The I. Book of Samuel,
The II. Book of Samuel,
The I. Book of Kings,
The II. Book of Kings,

De divinis Scripturis, quod sufficiant ad salutem.

Scriptura sacra continet omnia, quæ ad salutem sunt necessaria, ita ut quicquid in ea nec legitur, neque inde probari potest, non sit a quoquam exigendum, ut tanquam Articulus fidei credatur, aut ad salutis necessitatem requiri putetur.

Sacræ Scripturæ nomine, eos Canonicos libros Veteris et Novi Testamenti intelligimus, de quorum auctoritate, in Ecclesia nunquam dubitatum est.

De nominibus et numero librorum sacræ Canonicæ Scripturæ Veteris Testamenti.

Genesis,
Exodus,
Leviticus,
Numeri,
Deuteron,
Josuæ,
Judicum,
Ruth,
Prior liber Samuelis,
Secundus liber Samuelis,
Prior liber Regum,
Secundus liber Regum,

---

[1] So in copy of 1571, collated by Hardwick. Some insert *as*; the common text inserts *or*.

The I. Book of Chronicles,	Prior liber Paralipom.,
The II. Book of Chronicles,	Secundus liber Paralipom.,
The I. Book of Esdras,	Primus liber Esdræ,
The II. Book of Esdras,	Secundus liber Esdræ,
The Book of Esther,	Liber Hester,
The Book of Job,	Liber Job,
The Psalms,	Psalmi,
The Proverbs,	Proverbia,
Ecclesiastes, or Preacher,	Ecclesiastes vel Concionator,
Cantica, or Songs of Solomon,	Cantica Solomonis,
IV. Prophets the greater,	IV. Prophetæ Majores,
XII. Prophets the less.	XII. Prophetæ Minores.

And the other Books (as *Hierome* saith) the Church doth read for example of life and instruction of manners; but yet doth it not apply them to establish any doctrine. Such are these following :

Alios autem libros (ut ait Hieronymus) legit quidem Ecclesia, ad exempla vitæ, et formandos mores : illos tamen ad dogmata confirmanda non adhibet, ut sunt

The III. Book of Esdras,	Tertius liber Esdræ,
The IV. Book of Esdras,	Quartus liber Esdræ,
The Book of Tobias,	Liber Tobiæ,
The Book of Judith,	Liber Judith,
The rest of the Book of Esther,	Reliquum libri Hester,
The Book of Wisdom,	Liber Sapientiæ,
Jesus the son of Sirach,	Liber Jesu filii Sirach,
Baruch the Prophet,	Baruch propheta,
The Song of the Three Children,	Canticum trium puerorum,
The Story of Susanna,	Historia Susannæ,
Of Bel and the Dragon,	De Bel et Dracone,
The Prayer of Manasses,	Oratio Manassis,
The I. Book of Maccabees,	Prior liber Machabeorum,
The II. of Maccabees.	Secundus liber Machabeorum.

All the Books of the New Testament, as they are commonly received, we do receive, and account them Canonical.

Novi Testamenti omnes libros (ut vulgo recepti sunt) recipimus, et habemus pro Canonicis.

Notes on the Text of Article VI.

1. The Latin text is in close accordance with the English and needs no elucidation.

2. The enumeration of the Canonical books in this Article is as distinct as the assertion that they are to be accepted as the sole ground for the belief of all Articles of the Faith. But when we proceed to the basis of their canonicity here stated, we find ourselves by no means free from difficulty. We cannot allow that any distinction is intended between those Canonical books which constitute Holy Scripture, and Canonical books generally, as some have suggested. Holy Scripture and the Canonical books are obviously one and the same. We have, therefore, as the definition of a Canonical book, one ' of whose authority was never any doubt in the Church.' How is this to be understood ? It is well known that doubts were entertained by some Churches in the first three centuries as to the canonicity of several books of the New Testament. Accordingly they have been divided into the two classes derived from a passage in Eusebius : ὁμολογούμενα, those generally received; and ἀντιλεγόμενα, those disputed by some Churches or individuals. The latter class consisted of the Epistle to the Hebrews, the Epistles of St. James, St. Jude, the Second of St. Peter, the Second and Third of St. John, and the Apocalypse. An account of this may be found in any introduction to the New Testament.[1] The distinction was equally familiar in the age of the Reformation. The Lutheran and Calvinistic divines freely discussed it; and in our own country Tyndale (to go no further) noticed it in his prologues. What, then, was meant by the definition of a Canonical book in our Article ? Some have thought that *the Church* here means the Church of England, as it does in some passages in the Formularies. This is scarcely probable, and leads to no result of any value. It seems more likely that our Reformers were distinguishing here between the Church Catholic, and particular portions or members of it. These last have often expressed doubts about

---

[1] See also Paley's ' Evidences,' c. ix. § 8.

the authority of certain portions of the Word; but the Church
as a whole, so far as its collective judgment and general
practice can be gathered, never doubted or varied the Canon.
If this be so, our Church has given us as exact a definition of
a Canonical book as probably could be conveyed in a few
words.   But the Church of the first three centuries never pronounced, or had an opportunity of pronouncing, its judgment
on the subject.   Hence the historical demonstration of the
Canon of Scripture consists, in point of fact, of a collection of
the testimony of individual divines and Churches to the reception of the several books from the first age of Christianity
downwards.   The hesitation of some as to a few of the books
has been always justly thought to give the greater value to the
final and all but general consent of the whole body.   So that
the less learned reader may rest satisfied with the result briefly,
and somewhat boldly, expressed in our Article, that there has
been unanimity from the first as to the authority of every portion
of Holy Scripture.   Not that every book came at once into
the possession of every *individual* Church with full evidence
as to its origin.   But that after due communication of the several
Churches which possessed the original apostolical writings,
the whole Church came to a complete and early agreement;
and the hesitation which lingered here or there was very
partial, arose out of imperfect information, and before long
merged in the general consent.   Paley remarks upon this:
' When that diversity of opinion which prevailed, and prevails
among Christians in other points, is considered, their concurrence in the Canon of Scripture is remarkable, and of great
weight, especially as it seems to have been the result of
private and free enquiry.'

    This subject may be illustrated by the following precept of
Augustine[1]:—' In Canonical Scriptures you must follow the
judgment of the majority of Churches.   You will prefer those
received by all Catholic Churches to those which are not
received by some; but in those which are not universally
received, you will prefer those which the major and graver
part receive to those which are received by fewer Churches

            [1] ' De Doctrinâ Christianâ,' ii. 8.

and those of minor authority.   And if you find some received by the majority, and others received by the more authoritative Churches (though I do not think this case will ever occur), you may regard them as of equal authority.'

3. For the history and meaning of the word *Canon* reference may be made to Appendix A., to Westcott ' On the Canon of the New Testament.'   Connected with a large family of words of which the English word *cane* is a member, it meant originally any kind of rule used in measuring.   It occurs rarely in the New Testament (Gal. vi. 16 and 2 Cor. x. 13–16). The word was used by the early Fathers loosely, and in the fourth century was applied especially (as it still is) to the enactments of Synods.   It is first found in the writings of Athanasius as applied to Holy Scripture.   Westcott assigns to it a twofold meaning in that connexion, viz. : (1) that the Canonical books may be taken as meaning those which are defined to be Holy Scripture by a canon or rule of the Church, or (2) those which themselves are the canon or rule of faith to the Church.

4. The use of the Apocryphal books is defined as being practical only, and not doctrinal.

5. The inspiration of Holy Scripture might have naturally found a place among the statements of this Article.   But there was no controversy on this head at the time of the Reformation, and thus all reference to it was omitted.   It is, however, necessarily implied and assumed throughout the Articles.   In particular, the expression ' God's word written' (Art. XX.) may be noted.

6. This Article has been considerably altered from the Fifth Article of 1552, which asserted the sufficiency of Holy Scripture for salvation, but did not enumerate or define the Canonical books.   The clause which defines the Canonical books was derived from the Wurtemburg Confession in 1563.

7. The Ten Articles of Henry VIII., 1536, had defined the rule of faith to be the Bible and the three Creeds, interpreted literally, and as ' the holy approved doctors of the Church do entreat and defend the same.'   We need scarcely say that this possesses no authority.   It has only *historical*

E

value, as showing the progress of doctrine during **the**
successive stages of the Reformation.

THE PROOF FROM SCRIPTURE.

Passages bearing on this Article may be arranged in the
following manner :—

1. *Texts which imply or assert the Inspiration of Scripture, such as these :*

' All Scripture is given by inspiration of God ' (2 Tim. iii. 16).

' Which He promised afore by His prophets in the Holy
Scriptures' (Rom. i. 2).

' The oracles of God ' (Rom. iii. 2).

' One jot or one tittle shall in nowise pass from the law,
till all be fulfilled ' (Matt. v. 18).

' The Scripture cannot be broken ' (John x. 35).

' In the words which the Holy Ghost teacheth ' (1 Cor. ii. 13).

' The Spirit of the Lord spake by me, and His word was in
my tongue' (2 Sam. xxiii. 2).

' Behold, I have put my words in thy mouth' (Jer. i. 9).

' Which the Holy Ghost by the mouth of David spake
before' (Acts i. 16).

' If any man shall add, . .   . and if any man shall take
away from the words of the book of this prophecy, God shall
take away his part out of the book of life,' &c. (Rev. xxii. 18,19).

' No prophecy of the Scripture is of any private interpretation : for the prophecy came not in old time by the will of
man : but holy men of God spake as they were moved by the
Holy Ghost ' (2 Pet. i. 20, 21).

2. *Texts appealing to the Scripture as authoritative ; for example :*

' What things soever the law saith ' (Rom. iii. 19).

' What saith the Scripture ? ' (Rom. iv. 3).

' The Scripture saith ' (Rom. ix. 17).

' The Scripture foreseeing ' (Gal. iii. 8).

' That the Scripture might be fulfilled ' (John xix. 28, 36).

' As the Scripture hath said ' (John vii. 38).

' This Scripture must needs have been fulfilled which the Holy Ghost by the mouth of David spake before ' (Acts i. 16)

' Wherefore as the Holy Ghost saith ' (Heb. iii. 7).

' David himself said by the Holy Ghost ' (Mark xii. 36).

3. *Forms perpetually recurring, such as these* :

' Thus saith the Lord ; ' ' The Lord hath spoken ; ' ' The voice of the Lord ; ' ' The word of the Lord by the mouth of ; ' &c.

4. *Duties which we owe to the Scripture.*

Search the Scriptures (John v. 39).

Meditation therein (Ps. cxix. 15).

Love (Ps. cxix. 97).

Obedience (Rom. xvi. 26).

They must be taught (Deut. vi. 7).

They must be used against our spiritual enemies (Eph. vi. 17).

5. *Effects of Scripture on the Believer.*

It makes wise unto salvation (2 Tim. iii. 15).

It perfects, thoroughly furnishing unto all good works (2 Tim. iii. 17).

It converts the soul (1 Pet. i. 23).

It causes growth in grace (1 Pet. ii. 2).

It sanctifies (John xvii. 17).

THE DOCTRINE OF THE ROMAN CHURCH.

The doctrine of the Roman Church on the authority of Scripture is laid down in the decree of the Fourth Session of the Council of Trent. The following extracts contain those portions which bear most closely on the present subject.

The Council declared that ' the truth and discipline ' given by Christ and His Apostles ' are contained in books written and in unwritten traditions, which having been received from the mouth of Christ Himself by the Apostles, or at the dictation of the Holy Ghost from the Apostles themselves, and transmitted as it were by hand, have come down to us.' That the Council, therefore, ' following the example of the Orthodox Fathers, receives and venerates with equal pious affection the books both of the Old and New Testament, and the traditions themselves, whether pertaining to faith or manners, as having been orally dictated by Christ or by the Holy Ghost, and preserved by continuous succession in the Church Catholic.'

An enumeration of the Canonical books follows, including a large portion of those which the Church of England pronounces apocryphal. The Council then decrees that the Vulgate shall be taken *pro authentica* in all public services, and that no one shall on any pretext presume to reject it. Further, that no one shall dare to interpret Scripture against that sense which holy Mother Church holds, or against the unanimous consent of the Fathers, even if the interpretation is not meant for publication. It next decrees restraints upon printers, and the necessity for an edition of the Vulgate to be printed *quam emendatissime*. With respect to the use of the Bible by private persons, the Council decreed (*De libris prohibitis*) that 'he who shall presume to read or to have a Bible without a license, may not receive absolution until he has surrendered the Bible.' Much stronger expressions have been used by individual popes or divines, but the above is sufficient as setting forth the unquestionable law of the Roman Church.

THE DOCTRINE OF THE ENGLISH CHURCH.

This Article draws a great distinction between things necessary for salvation, and things practically beneficial, but not essential. This distinction is the main subject of the second book of Hooker's ' Ecclesiastical Polity.' He defends it against some extreme Puritans, who demanded Scripture authority for every act of life, and for all the minutiæ of Church order. The concluding paragraph of that book draws the distinguishing line with admirable clearness :—' Two opinions there are concerning sufficiency of Holy Scripture, each extremely opposite unto the other, and both repugnant unto truth. The schools of Rome teach Scripture to be insufficient, as if, except traditions were added, it did not contain all revealed and supernatural truth, which absolutely is necessary for the children of men in this life to know, that

they may in the next be saved. Others, justly condemning
this opinion, grow likewise unto a dangerous extremity, as if
Scripture did not only contain all things in that kind necessary, but all things simply, and in such sort, that to do anything according to any other law were not only unnecessary,
but even opposite unto salvation, unlawful, and sinful.
Whatsoever is spoken of God, or things appertaining to God,
otherwise than the truth is, though it seem an honour, it is an
injury. And as incredible praises given unto men do often
abate and impair the credit of their deserved commendation ;
so we must likewise take great heed, lest, in attributing unto
Scripture more than it can have, the incredibility of that do
cause even those things which it hath most abundantly to be
less reverently esteemed.'

The sufficiency of Holy Scripture for salvation (as taught
in this Article) was a universal article of faith in the first four
centuries. This has been abundantly demonstrated by over-
whelming collections of quotations from all the primitive
writers. The citations in Paley's 'Evidences,' chap. ix. §§
1, 9, are naturally those which first come before the attention
of the student. And these will give him a fair impression as
to the usual manner in which the authority and use of the
Holy Scripture are handled by the Fathers. But a complete
and masterly investigation of this subject will be found in the
tenth chapter of the ' Divine Rule of Faith and Practice,' by
the late Dean Goode. The general result of that investigation
may be summed up in the following well-known quotation
from Augustine :—' If it is established by the clear authority
of the divine Scriptures, those I mean that are called Canonical
in the Church, it is to be believed without any doubt. But
other witnesses or testimonies which are used to persuade you
to believe anything, you may believe or not, just as you shall
see that they have or have not any weight giving them a just
claim to your confidence.' [1]

For a further declaration of the mind of the Church of
England on this subject the First Homily may be consulted.
It is in entire harmony with this Article, as may be inferred

[1] 'Ad Paulin.' Ep. 147.

from the following citation :—' Let us diligently search for the well of life in the books of the Old and New Testament, and not run to the stinking puddles of men's traditions, devised by men's imaginations for our justification and salvation.'

It is unnecessary to refer to the Confessions of other Protestant Churches, as they are notoriously one with the English Church on this head. Much obloquy has been thrown on the word *Protestant* of late, as if it were a mere negation implying no positive truth. It may, therefore, be useful as well as interesting to quote the following passage from the original Protest presented to the diet at Spires, 1529, by the Lutheran princes of Germany, from which the name Protestant was derived :—' Seeing that there is no sure doctrine but such as is conformable to the Word of God; that the Lord forbids the teaching of any other doctrine; that each text of the Holy Scripture ought to be explained by other and clearer texts; and that this holy book is, in all things necessary for the Christian, easy of understanding, and. calculated to scatter the darkness; we are resolved, by the grace of God, to maintain the pure and exclusive teaching of His only Word, such as it is contained in the Biblical books of the Old and New Testament, without adding anything thereto that may be contrary to it. This Word is the only truth; it is the sure rule of all doctrine and of all life, and can never fail or deceive us. He who builds on this foundation shall stand against all the powers of hell, whilst all the human vanities that are set up against it shall fall before the face of God.

' For these reasons we earnestly entreat you to weigh carefully our grievances and our motives. If you do not yield to our request, we PROTEST by these presents before God, our only Creator, Preserver, Redeemer, and Saviour, and who will one day be our Judge, as well as before all men and all creatures, that we, for us and our people, neither consent nor adhere in any manner whatsoever to the proposed decree, in anything that is contrary to God, to His Holy Word, to our right conscience, to the salvation of our souls, and to the last decree of

Spires.'   [This decree had given liberty of worship to each German State.]

Those who read this noble Protest and compare the doctrines of the Church of England and the Church of Rome on the rule of faith, as given above, can say whether the Church of England is Protestant or no.   They may also decide whether Protestantism is a bare negation or the assertion of a living principle, the absolute supremacy of the Word of God, and the right of all men to search that Word.   Other Articles protest against individual Roman errors.   This Article is the fundamental one which stamps the Church of England as essentially PROTESTANT.

THE HISTORY OF THE CANON.

The historical testimony to the Canon of the New Testament requires to be stated first.   The ninth chapter of Paley's ' Evidences' contains a clear summary of that testimony.   As this work is required to be read by nearly all theological students, it is judged inadvisable to burden them at this stage with any different arrangement.   Paley divides the proof under the following eleven sections:—

I. That the historical books of the New Testament, meaning thereby the four Gospels and the Acts of the Apostles, are quoted or alluded to by a series of Christian writers, beginning with those who were contemporary with the Apostles, or who immediately followed them, and proceeding in close and regular succession from their time to the present.

II. That when they are quoted, or alluded to, it is with peculiar respect, as books *sui generis* ; as possessing an authority which belonged to no other books, and as conclusive in all questions and controversies among Christians.

III. That they were, in very early times, collected into a distinct volume.

IV. That they were distinguished by appropriate names and titles of respect.

V. That they were publicly read and expounded in the religious assemblies of the early Christians.

VI. That commentaries were written upon them, harmonies formed out of them, different copies carefully collated and versions of them made into different languages.

VII. That they were received by Christians of various sects, by many heretics, as well as Catholics, and usually appealed to by both sides in the controversies which arose in those days.

VIII. That the four Gospels—the Acts of the Apostles, thirteen Epistles of St. Paul, the First Epistle of St. John, and the First of St. Peter—were received without doubt by those who doubted concerning the other books which are included in our present Canon.

IX. That the Gospels were attacked by the early adversaries of Christianity, as books containing the accounts upon which the religion was founded.

X. That formal catalogues of authentic Scriptures were published; in all of which our present sacred histories are included.

XI. That these propositions cannot be affirmed of any other books claiming to be books of Scripture; by which are meant those books which are commonly called Apocryphal Books of the New Testament.

These eleven ' allegations' are supported by copious quotations from the early writers of Christianity, which Paley has selected from the results of Lardner's investigations. Few memories can retain even specimens of such an array of citations. But Paley's admirable arrangement of the eleven allegations may be remembered. They are capable of being simply stated to any thoughtful person, as propositions capable of distinct historical proof. And the unprejudiced mind of such a person will usually acknowledge that if the history of the reception of the Canon of the New Testament rests on such a basis, partial objections and minor difficulties need not disturb his faith. For a more detailed discussion of the whole question, Westcott 'On the Canon of the New Testament' may be consulted.

The authority of the New Testament having been thus assumed, the authority of the Old Testament over Christians follows, as being proved from the New Testament. Our Lord and His Apostles quote it, and refer to it continually, as the one absolute authority in all controversy, and they treat it as wholly inspired. This will be found borne out by an examination of their modes of quotation and reference, and the names and epithets which they apply to the Old Testament. No portion is excepted or subordinated. The whole of what was then held by the Jews as Scripture is endorsed; indeed, all the books, except six, are expressly quoted or referred to.

To know, therefore, what are the Canonical books of the Old Testament thus received by our Lord, the simple historical enquiry is needed—What books were at that time included in the Jewish Canon? The evidence is most clearly presented in an ascending order :—

1. The Hebrew Canon of the Modern Jews is the same as ours.

2. The Talmud, which was in process of compilation from about A.D. 150 to A.D. 600, recognises the same. There are also Targums belonging to those and earlier times, of our Canonical books, and of no others.

3. In the fourth century Jerome enumerates the same books as belonging to the Hebrew Canon.

4. In the third century Origen does the same.

5. In the second century Melito, Bishop of Sardis, gives the same testimony.

6. Josephus, in the first century, speaks of the books as Jerome did. He, moreover, says (evidently alluding to the Apocrypha) that 'books written since Artaxerxes Longimanus had not the same credit as those before that time, because the succession of prophets had failed.'

7. Philo's testimony is similar, but not so precise in detail.

Hence it is concluded that what our Lord and the Apostles sanctioned as Holy Scripture was the Hebrew Canon of the Old Testament, as its books are enumerated in this Article.

But the version in almost universal use in the Early Church was that of the LXX.

This contained the Apocryphal books inserted by Alexandrian Jews.

There was scarcely any knowledge of Hebrew among Christians after the first century, and the *whole* of the LXX. was almost indiscriminately quoted by many early Christian writers. Yet it has been shown by many passages quoted in works on this subject that the Church in general, and her leading divines in particular, never lost sight of the distinction between the Canonical and Apocryphal books.

We may now thus sum up our reasons for rejecting the Apocrypha:—

1. We receive the Jewish Scriptures on the authority of Christ and His Apostles.

2. We have seen what books the Jewish Scriptures of that age included.

3. Therefore the Apocrypha stands excluded, as being outside that catalogue, and, therefore, destitute of that authority.

4. Also (though not without some confusion), it stands excluded by the testimony of the Early Church; and in particular by that of Melito, Origen, Athanasius, Hilary, Jerome, the Council of Laodicæa, &c.

Finally, if in the face of such a weight of primitive testimony the Council of Trent presumed to decree the reception of a large portion of the Apocrypha, it must be deemed the very arrogance of authority.

ARTICLE VII.

Of the Old Testament.

The Old Testament is not contrary to the New, for both in the Old and New Testament everlasting life is offered to mankind by Christ, who is the only Mediator between God and Man, being both God and Man. Wherefore they are not to be heard, which feign that the old Fathers did look only for transitory promises. Although the Law given from God by Moses, as touching Ceremonies and Rites, do not bind Christian men, nor the Civil Precepts thereof ought of necessity to be received in any commonwealth; yet notwithstanding, no Christian man whatsoever is free from the obedience of the Commandments which are called Moral.

De Veteri Testamento.

Testamentum Vetus Novo contrarium non est, quandoquidem tam in Veteri, quam in Novo, per Christum, qui unicus est Mediator Dei et hominum, Deus et homo, æterna vita humano generi est proposita. Quare male sentiunt, qui veteres tantum in promissiones temporarias sperasse confingunt. Quanquam lex a Deo data per Mosen (quoad cæremonias et ritus) Christianos non astringat, neque civilia ejus præcepta in aliqua republica necessario recipi debeant, nihilominus tamen ab obedientia mandatorum (quæ moralia vocantur) nullus (quantumvis Christianus) est solutus.

NOTES ON THE TEXT.

1. The Latin is very closely followed in the English version. In the Article of 1552, *non sunt audiendi* was read instead of *male sentiunt,* and the former is still to be seen in the English version, 'they are not to be heard.'

2. The Article obviously consists of two principal sections:—

I. What was the condition upon which salvation was obtained under the Law.

II. How far the Mosaic Law is binding upon Christians.

This question involves the distinction between moral commandments, and precepts ceremonial, ritual, or civil.

3. This Article combines with some modifications the Sixth and Nineteenth of 1552. As it will throw some light on the subsequent discussion of the doctrines involved, and the errors which our Reformers had in view, those Articles are subjoined.

ARTICLE VI. (1552).

The Old Testament not to be refused.

The Old Testament is not to be put away as though it were contrary to the New, but to be kept still; for both in the Old and New Testaments, everlasting life is offered to mankind by Christ, Who is the only Mediator between God and Man, being both God and Man. Wherefore they are not to be heard, which feign that the old Fathers did look only for transitory promises.

ARTICLE XIX. (1552).

All men are bound to keep the Moral Commandments of the Law.

The Law which was given of God by Moses, although it bind not Christian men as concerning the Ceremonies and Rites of the same: Neither is it required that the Civil Precepts and Orders of it should of necessity be received in any common weal: Yet no man (be he never so perfect a Christian) is exempt and loose from the obedience of those Commandments which are called Moral. Wherefore they are not to be hearkened unto, who affirm that Holy Scripture is given only to the weak, and do boast themselves continually of the Spirit, of Whom (they say) they have learned such things as they teach, although the same be most evidently repugnant to the Holy Scripture.

THE PROOF FROM SCRIPTURE.

For the first section of the Article :—

1. Such passages may be alleged from the Old Testament

as show that 'the old Fathers' had a hope reaching beyond the grave (e.g. Ps. xvi. 8–11).

2. Positive declarations made by our Lord about the hope of the Patriarchs (e.g. John viii. 56).

3. The demonstration of the doctrine of justification by faith drawn by St. Paul from the Old Testament (e.g. Rom. iv. ; Gal. iii).

4. The eleventh chapter of the Epistle to the Hebrews.

5. The frequent declarations of Christ and the Apostles as to the true bearing of the (Old Testament) Scriptures on gospel times and promises.

The second section of the Article may be dealt with scripturally under such an arrangement as follows :—

1. A consideration of the relation of the civil law to the theocracy of the Old Testament. It relates to a limited country, and to a past condition of a peculiar race. It is not possible for any nation at will to set up a similar theocracy. Therefore, the civil law which depends upon it cannot be re-enacted and enforced.

2. St. Paul teaches obedience to magistrates generally ; and to laws, irrespective of any revealed origin. The declaration of our Lord is express—'My kingdom is not of this world.'

3. St. Paul argues urgently not only that the Christian is free from the ceremonial law, but that he may not place himself under it. The Epistles to the Romans and Galatians may be freely quoted on this head. Gal. v. 3 is, in fact, a demonstration. The obligation of the Law is bound up with the rite of circumcision, and absolutely ceases with it.

4. The Epistle to the Hebrews asserts and argues in many places the transitory nature and the abolition of the sacrificial system (e.g. Heb. viii. 13).

5. To the moral law the above considerations will not apply, because it was antecedent to the peculiarities of the Jewish Law. It was adopted in the law, but was itself older than the law, and remains when the Mosaical super-addition has passed away.

Hence Christ and His Apostles recognise the Ten Com-

mandments as binding.   St. Paul refers to all of them (Rom.
xiii. 9), and to the Fifth expressly (Eph. vi. 2).   St. James
also speaks of them all (Jas. ii. 10).

OBSERVATIONS ON ARTICLE VII.

It will be sufficient to remind the student of the manner in
which the Gnostics and Manichees in the early days of Christianity dealt with the authority of the Old Testament.   It is
assumed that these portions of ecclesiastical history need not
be recapitulated.

The Articles of 1552, quoted above, make it abundantly
manifest that in framing this Article there was a reference to
the fanatical sects of that time.   Those who have read the
correspondence of the Reformers, printed in the 'Zurich Letters'
published by the Parker Society, know well how these hydra-
headed heresies embarrassed their work.

We may refer to Mosheim[1] for some account of those sects
which arose first in Germany.   But the following extract
from Hardwick's 'History of the Articles' (chap v.) will give
a general view of the heresies with which that stormy period
was rife, and will illustrate not only this Article, but several
others:—

'The ramification of these varied misbelievers may be
traced in many cases to the scene of the original collisions between the old and new learning.   One of their distinctive
errors, though not *the* grand characteristic of their system,
was the absolute rejection of infant baptism, and from this
peculiarity came the title " Anabaptists." . . . . . . But the
points at which they had departed from the ground of the
Reformers were not limited to infant baptism.   They proceeded to assail the Lutheran formula, in which salvation was
attributed to faith only, and in agitating this they fell into a
further question respecting the two natures of our blessed Lord
and His essential divinity.   John Denk and others now
affirmed that man may earn salvation by his own virtuous
actions, and regarded the Founder of Christianity chiefly in His

[1] ' Cent. XVI.' part ii. c. i. 25, 26, and c. iii.   .

character of Teacher and Exemplar. In Him, as one of the most spotless of our race, the Father was peculiarly manifested to the world, but to assert that Christ is the Redeemer, in the ordinary meaning of the term, was to convert Him into an idol. He was held to be a Saviour of His people, *because* He was the leader and forerunner of all who would be saved.'

'While notions of this kind were rapidly spreading on every side, a second school of " Anabaptists " were devising a very different creed. The tone of thought prevailing in the former school was strongly rationalistic: in the latter it was more entirely mystical. They introduced a dualistic (quasi-Manichean) distinction between the " flesh " and the " spirit ; " and instead of holding, like the former sect, that man, though fallen, may be rescued by his natural powers, they alleged that the " flesh " alone participated in the fall, and further that when the material element in him was most of all obnoxious to the indignation of God, the spirit still continued free and uncontaminated by the vilest of the outward actions. They attributed the restoration of harmony between these elements of our nature to the intervention of the Logos, but maintained that His humanity was peculiar, not consisting of flesh and blood which He derived from the substance of the Virgin. Not a few of these same Anabaptists afterwards abandoned every semblance of belief in the doctrine of the Holy Trinity, and so passed over to the Arian and Socinian schools, then rising up in Switzerland, in Italy, and in Poland.'

'In addition to these deadly errors, some of the original Anabaptists had insisted on the dogma of an absolute necessity. Others preached the restoration of all things and the ultimate conversion of the devil. Others fancied that the soul will sleep throughout the interval between death and judgment: while the great majority of them cherished the belief that in a kingdom (the millennial) to be speedily established, there would be no longer any need of an external magistracy, nor even of the guidance furnished by the written Word of God. In close connexion with this hope, they now asserted the community of goods. They censured military service of a merely secular kind, and steadily objected to the taking of an oath in their negotiations with the world in general. Some moreover held that the observance of the Lord's Day was anti-Christian ; others openly advocated a license of polygamy, and are even charged with holding that to those who had received the Spirit, or in other words had passed the Anabaptist ordeal of initiation, adultery was itself no sin. By all it was agreed that Anabaptists were at liberty to evade the jurisdiction both of civil and ecclesiastical tribunals, to denounce the latter as a grievous burden, and to aid in the emancipation of all Christians from the discipline as well as doctrine of the Catholic Church.'

' If we add to this imperfect sketch of continental Anabaptism one of the most prominent of its remaining features, we shall understand how formidable the system must have looked to all the sober and devout Reformers. It was advocated as a leading principle that every Anabaptist was not only able, but was *bound*, to execute the office of a teacher as soon as he perceived within his breast the motions of the Holy Spirit. The effect of this immediate inspiration also made the preacher independent of the sacred volume, which he sometimes ventured to denominate "mere dead letter," obsolete in itself, and in the course of its transmission falsified in such a manner as to be unworthy of the faith of full-grown Christians. Thus the last external check imposed on man's presumptuous speculations ran the risk of being summarily demolished ; and if Anabaptism had prevailed, it would have reared its throne upon the ruins of all ancient institutions, and have trampled under foot the Word of God itself.'

This account of the Anabaptist heresies will prepare the student for many passages in the Articles, doctrinal, ceremonial, and civil. A few observations may be necessary.

1. It will be seen that the general term 'Anabaptist' groups together a vast variety of opinions, from those which simply rejected infant baptism, to those which destroyed the very foundations of Christianity itself. Hence it will be seen how modern sects of various hues are more or less directly traceable to these ramifications. The *Baptist* of modern times springs directly from the moderate section of Anabap-

tists who retained the main doctrines of Christianity and faith in Holy Scripture. The mysticism, and claims to inspiration, and independence of Church order, and even of the Scripture itself, asserted by George Fox and the early Quakers, have also their manifest origin among some sections of continental Anabaptists. The *family of love* and other extravagances of the seventeenth century are also traced to their root in the more extreme of these fanatics of the previous age.

2. It is, however, needful to caution the student not to suppose that the monstrous evils pourtrayed above ever obtained deep hold of the English mind. They were sufficiently formidable; they distracted the attention of the Reformers; they caused a great reaction in favour of Romanism, if indeed they were not wilfully fomented by Romish agents, of which there is some evidence, but the mass of the English people rejected these impious absurdities.

3. It is just to the cause of the Reformation to note that fanatical opinions akin to those of the extreme Anabaptists had been secretly held for centuries, and had occasionally broken out, especially in Germany.[1]

4. Finally, to return more precisely to the Article before us, we may note among the successors of those against whom it was levelled, that the Brownists, the fathers of the Independents, and after them many of the Puritans, held that 'we are necessarily tied unto all the judicials of Moses.' Thomas Cartwright, Hooker's opponent, held that idolaters, among whom he included ' contemners of the Word and prayers,' should be put to death according to the Mosaic Law. Stubbs— 1585—speaking of blasphemers being stoned, adds, 'which law judicial standeth in force to the world's end.'[2] The Puritan colonists, commonly known as Pilgrim Fathers, enacted some portion of the Mosaic judicial Law in their new settlement in America, and put it in force with severity.

---

[1] See the account of 'The Beghards,' Gieseler, vol. iv. p. 220; or Mosheim, on 'The Brethren of the Free Spirit and kindred Sects in the Thirteenth Century,' ' Cent. XIII.' part ii. c. v. 9–15.

[2] See Rogers ' On the Articles.' Parker Society. Ar. VII. 4.

And, generally speaking, in the reasonings and policy of a large portion of the Puritans in the days of the Commonwealth there will be found a great confusion between their own condition and that of the Jews under the theocracy.

Turning to our own times, although Antinomian principles may be held directly or indirectly in many various quarters, no considerable section professing to belong to the Church of Christ is chargeable with the errors denounced in this Article.

ARTICLE VIII.

Of the Three Creeds.

The three Creeds, *Nicene* Creed, *Athanasius'* Creed, and that which is commonly called the *Apostles'* Creed, ought thoroughly to be received and believed : for they may be proved by most certain warrants of Holy Scripture.

De tribus Symbolis.

Symbola tria, Nicænum, Athanasii, et quod vulgo Apostolorum appellatur, omnino recipienda sunt, et credenda, nam firmissimis Scripturarum testimoniis probari possunt.

NOTES ON THE TEXT.

The Latin text calls for no special comment.

The word rendered Creed is *Symbolum*, the Greek derivation of which is obvious. Various suppositions rather than reasons have been given to explain the application of this particular name to the Creeds. The learned Bingham[1] thus enumerates some of these :—

1. *Symbolum* signifies a *collection*, so called because each Apostle contributed a clause to it.

2. The military sense of *Symbolum*, a *badge of distinction*, is suggested.

3. *Symbolum* signifies a *collection* or epitome of Christian doctrine.

4. The military oath of service, or

5. The password among the initiated into the ancient mysteries is alleged as a possible origin.

This diversity sufficiently shows that the origin of this

[1] 'Antiquities,' bk. x. ch. iii. 1.

appellation is unknown, nor is it of any real consequence. Bingham thinks the second suggestion the most probable.

Our English word *Creed* is an obvious corruption of the word *Credo*, the name usually given to it before the Reformation, from the word with which it begins in Latin.

OBSERVATIONS ON ARTICLE VIII.

We may here note the care with which the Reformers supplemented the Sixth Article with this. They had there laid down the doctrine that the Holy Scriptures are the sole rule of faith. They now took the further precaution to state that the Creeds themselves were no exception to this, for that they derived their authority wholly from the Bible. The necessity for this statement may have arisen from the fact, already noted, that the Ten Articles of Henry VIII. made the Creeds together with the Scriptures the rule of faith. This observation is of considerable value in the face of assertions, often freely made, that it is the Church which gives authority to the Bible as well as the Creed. It may also be remarked that the Church of England here claims the right of exercising an independent judgment even on the first two General Councils which sanctioned the Nicene Creed. This is in strict accordance with Article XXI.

HISTORY OF THE CREEDS.

I. *The Apostles' Creed.*

It has often been asserted that this Creed came from the Apostles themselves, and some have added various apocryphal stories to this assertion. Bingham [1] shows how baseless this notion is. His arguments may be thus summed up:—

1. The New Testament is silent as to the existence of such a document.

2. The ecclesiastical writers of the first three centuries are similarly silent.

[1] Bk. x. ch. iii. 4.

3. The ancient Creeds, although agreeing in the main, as setting forth the substance of the Christian faith, differ sufficiently in detail to show that there was no one acknowledged apostolical formula which none would have presumed to change.

4. The ancients call the Nicene and other Creeds apostolical as well as this. The epithet, therefore, referred to the subject-matter, not to the formula.

Unquestionably, however, a profession of faith was made in baptism from the very first (Acts viii. 37, and perhaps also 1 Tim. vi. 12 and 2 Tim. i. 13, 14), and it would naturally soon take a shape not very different from this Creed.

It is generally admitted, from a comparison of early Creeds, that the one which ultimately prevailed in the West, and which we call the Apostles', is that which was used in the fifth century in the Roman Church, though not in all other Italian Churches. The subsequent authority of Rome made it universal in the West.

Bingham [1] says that it does not appear that the Roman or Apostles' Creed was ever used in the Eastern Church. The latter section of the Church had several symbols resembling the Nicene, before that form was adopted.

II. *The Nicene Creed.*

It is assumed that the student has studied the history of the Councils of Nice and Constantinople, and the various phases of the Arian controversy.

Bingham [2] gives ancient Creeds used in different Churches of the East before the Council of Nice. They seem for the most part nearer to the elaboration of the Nicene than the simplicity of the Roman Creed.

The basis of the Nicene Creed is said to have been presented to the Council by Eusebius, Bishop of Cæsarea.[3] The Council modified this by inserting some expressions more distinctly anti-Arian.

The Creed so sanctioned terminated with the words 'I believe in the Holy Ghost.'

[1] Bk. x. ch. iv. 17.   [2] Bk. x. ch. iv. 1-11.
[3] Neander's ' Eccl. Hist.' ' Council of Nice.'

The clauses which now follow those words are to be found in Epiphanius about A.D. 373, and had been probably used for some time in some Churches. They were, however, adopted by the Council of Constantinople, A.D. 381; for which reason this Creed is sometimes called the Constantinopolitan Creed.

We must refer to ecclesiastical history for the introduction of the famous words *filioque* by the Western Church, and the bitter controversies which followed between the Greek and Roman Churches. Some reference has been made to this under Article V. (p. 40).

The practice of reciting the Creed in divine service dates from the middle of the fifth century in the Greek Church, and still later in the Latin Church. The early use of Creeds was for the instruction of Catechumens, and as a profession of faith in baptism, but not as a part of the ordinary service of the Church.

III. *The Athanasian Creed.*

This Creed probably received its name because it sets forth so fully the Athanasian doctrine of the Holy Trinity. In the middle ages, and until the seventeenth century, it was almost universally believed to be the work of Athanasius himself. The progress of historical criticism showed this view to be untenable. Gerard Vossius—1642—in his book ' De tribus Symbolis,' opened the controversy as to the origin of this Creed. Many learned critical treatises have since been written upon it. A compendious account of the criticism will be found in Bingham's ' Antiquities.' [1] But Waterland's learned ' History of the Athanasian Creed ' is the standard work on the subject, and some of his principal conclusions are subjoined:—

1. Setting aside quotations from spurious works, the most ancient testimony to the reception of the Athanasian Creed is stated to be a decree of the Council of Autun, about A.D. 670.

2. The most ancient comment on this Creed is ascribed to Venantius Fortunatus, Bishop of Poitiers, about A.D. 570.

[1] Bk. x. ch. iv. 18.

3. The earliest Latin MSS. of this Creed are ascribed to the seventh century. The Greek MSS. are much later, few, and disagreeing with each other.

4. This Creed was received in the Gallican Church in the seventh, or perhaps the sixth, century, and in the Spanish Church about the same time. Charlemagne held it in high esteem, and in his days its use extended into Germany, Italy, and England. It was probably received by the Roman Church early in the tenth century. Waterland thinks it has been only partially received by the Oriental Churches.

5. A careful comparison of the controversial modes of expression devised to meet the several heresies on the doctrine of the Holy Trinity in the fifth and sixth centuries leads to the conclusion that the Creed was composed after the Arian and Apollinarian heresies, and before the condemnation of the Nestorian and Monophysite opinions. It is also thought to have derived expressions from Augustine 'De Trinitate.' From these data, the years A.D 420–430 are assigned as including the probable date of its composition.

6. All the earliest notices of the Creed point to Gaul as the country in which it was written and obtained currency.

7. Out of the Gallic writers in that age, Hilary of Arles is selected as the most probable author of this Creed. What is known of his style, and his study of the works of Augustine, harmonises with this supposition. It is also affirmed by the writer of his life that he composed an admirable exposition of the Creed,[1] which probably refers to this very document. For it was rarely called in ancient times *Symbolum* (as not emanating from a Council), but rather *Expositio Catholicæ Fidei*, or some similar descriptive title. Upon the whole, Waterland concludes that this Creed was probably written in Gaul by Hilary, Bishop of Arles, about A.D. 430.

The controversy now pending questions the dates of Waterland's chief authorities, and wishes to reduce the document to the age of Charlemagne. It also raises questions as to the mode of stating the equality of the Persons, and the accuracy of the English translation.

[1] 'Symboli Expositio.'

PART III.

DOCTRINE.

ARTICLE IX.

Of Original or Birth sin.

Original sin standeth not in the following of *Adam*, (as the *Pelagians* do vainly talk;) but it is the fault and corruption of the nature of every man, that naturally is engendered of the offspring of *Adam*; whereby man is very far gone from original righteousness, and is of his own nature inclined to evil, so that the flesh lusteth always contrary to the Spirit; and therefore in every person born into this world, it deserveth God's wrath and damnation. And this infection of nature doth remain, yea, in them that are regenerated; whereby the lust of the flesh, called in Greek Φρόνημα σαρκὸς, which some do expound the wisdom, some sensuality, some the affection, some the desire, of the flesh, is not subject to the law of God. And, although there is no condemnation for them that believe and are baptized, yet the Apostle doth confess, that concupiscence and lust hath of itself the nature of sin.

De peccato originali.

Peccatum originis non est (ut fabulantur Pelagiani) in imitatione Adami situm, sed est vitium, et depravatio naturæ, cujuslibet hominis ex Adamo naturaliter propagati : qua fit, ut ab originali justitia quam longissime distet, ad malum sua natura propendeat, et caro semper adversus spiritum concupiscat, unde in unoquoque nascentium, iram Dei atque damnationem meretur. Manet etiam in renatis hæc naturæ depravatio. Qua fit, ut affectus carnis, Græce Φρόνημα σαρκὸς, (quod alii sapientiam, alii sensum, alii affectum, alii studium carnis interpretantur,) legi Dei non subjiciatur. Et quanquam renatis et credentibus nulla propter Christum est condemnatio, peccati tamen in sese rationem habere concupiscentiam, fatetur Apostolus.

Notes on the Text of Article IX.

The Latin text in this Article calls for particular notice. It is a link of connection with the scholastic phraseology of the Middle Ages, which must to some extent be understood by all who desire to appreciate the doctrinal position assumed by our Reformers. For they had been trained in the language, and now stood opposed to the system of the schoolmen. The following Latin and English equivalents may be especially noted :—

1. *In imitatione Adami*=' In the following of Adam.'

2. *Vitium et depravatio naturæ* = ' The fault and corruption of the nature.'

3. *Quam longissime distet* =' Very far gone.'

4. *In Unoquoque nascentium* = ' Every person born.' [Obs. : *nascentium* not *natorum*. This accurately implies *at*, not *after*, their birth.]

5. *Renatis* =' Regenerated.'

6. *Naturæ depravatio* =' Infection of nature.'

7. *Affectus carnis* =' The lust of the flesh.'

8. *Renatis et credentibus* =' For them that believe and are baptized.' [Obs.: though *renatis* is here used as an equivalent for *baptized*, it does not seem to imply full *spiritual* birth, because it is qualified by the word *believe*. All who have that true birth of the Spirit do believe. Faith is the element in which they live.]

9. *Peccati rationem* =' Nature of sin.'

N.B. *Peccatum originale* and *Peccatum originis* are equivalent expressions.

This Article has only some slight and verbal differences from the Eighth of 1552. The latter, however, added to the assertion about the Pelagians these words, ' which also the Anabaptists do now-a-days renew.' The notice of the Anabaptists under Article VII. will sufficiently illustrate this.

The Article is said by Bishop Browne and Archdeacon Hardwick to have been derived from the Augsburg Confession. This assertion can scarcely be maintained in any very exact sense, on a close inspection of the text of the two docu-

ments, as may be seen from the following English version of
the Second Article of the Augsburg Confession :—

'They also teach that since the fall of Adam, all men, naturally begotten, are born with sin, that is, without the fear of
God, without faith towards God, and with concupiscence;
and that this disease or fault of origin is truly sin, condemning,
and even now bringing eternal death to those who are not
born again by baptism and the Holy Spirit.

'They condemn the Pelagians and others who deny that the
fault of origin is sin, and in order to diminish the glory of the
merit and benefits of Christ, maintain that a man can be justified before God by the power of his own reason.'

The similitude between the English and Augsburg forms
does not seem much more than the general family likeness
which runs through all the Reformed Confessions.

THE MAIN DIVISIONS OF ARTICLE IX.

1. Original sin is defined (A.) negatively, (B.) positively.
2. Its universality and degree.
3. It is in itself deserving of the wrath of God.
4. It remains in the regenerate.
5. Nevertheless, true believers have no condemnation.
6. The indwelling sinful desire, irrespective of indulgence
or of action, has the nature or *ratio* of sin.

The student will do wisely if he carefully collects and considers passages of Scripture, proving these separate propositions. He will thus obtain clear doctrinal conclusions, instead
of confusedly gathering the general notion of man's sinfulness.

THE HISTORY OF THE DOCTRINE OF ORIGINAL SIN.

It is assumed that the student is familiar with the Oriental
notions of the Gnostics and Manichees of the first three
centuries, as to the connexion of moral and spiritual evil with
matter.

It is also assumed that the history of the Pelagian and
Semi-Pelagian controversies of the fifth century is sufficiently
known.

We omit, therefore, further notice of these. But in order to understand the phraseology of this Article and the questions really at issue, we must refer to the schoolmen of the Middle Ages and to the received Roman theology. For the position taken up in this and the following doctrinal Articles, although by no means merely negative, is to a great degree one of antagonism to Rome. These Articles are strongly and scripturally constructive and positive; but in their most definite statements the opposite Romish doctrine seems to be held in view. The schoolmen are named in Article XIII.; and indeed it will at once be seen that the Reformers, trained as they were in the scholastic theology, could scarcely avoid writing with a reference, direct or implied, to the terms and principles of that system.

The 'Summa Theologiæ' of Thomas Aquinas was dominant in the schools before the Reformation. His doctrine of original sin was more plainly expounded by the great Roman Catholic controversialist, Bellarmine, at the close of the sixteenth century; and we shall endeavour to give a simple account of it, as it lies at the basis of many ill-understood controversies.

It is the less difficult to do so, as those divines, whatever their errors may be, are generally very exact in their definitions. [The most accessible books on the subject will probably be Willet's 'Synopsis Papismi,' and Müller's ' Christian Doctrine of Sin,' Clark's translation.]

In order to arrive at a knowledge of the nature of original sin, these authors discuss what Adam lost by the fall. They assert that the original righteousness in which Adam stood was no part of his nature, but a supernatural gift superadded to it. They say that he was created mortal, but had the superadded gift of immortality. Hence the result of the fall was simply a withdrawal of the superadded gifts, and a reduction of man to the state in which he would have been without them. Bellarmine thus enunciates this theory :—' The state of man after the fall of Adam differs from the state of Adam in what was purely natural to him (*in puris naturalibus*) no more than a man who is stripped differs from a naked man. Nor is human nature worse, if you take away original sin, nor does it labour more with ignorance and infirmity, than it would be and would labour in what is purely natural as it was created.'

The singular comparison used above explains exactly the scholastic idea. Adam was originally (spiritually) naked. He was mortal. He was then clothed with the supernatural gifts of grace and immortality. Upon his fall he was stripped of these, and became spiritually naked and mortal, just as he was created; save that the Almighty now viewed him with displeasure, as a creature who had trifled with and lost precious gifts, and was destitute of that which he ought to have. Thus original sin is not a positive quality or inherent evil disposition, but simply an absence of the original righteousness.

How, then, do these divines deal with a more practical and more formidable question—the most conspicuous and most disastrous feature in man's history—his tendency to sin? On the above theory, this, to which they gave the name of *concupiscentia*, used also in our Article, was denied to be sin. For if fallen man stood as Adam stood, in all purely natural respects, and was only exposed to wrath as lacking the gifts he had trifled with, then the concupiscence, or tendency to sin, had in it no necessary guilt. For man was in this respect as God had made him, and that could not be a state of guilt.

It may now be seen in what respect baptism was held by these divines to put away original sin. It is manifest that it does not take away the *concupiscence*. But it was conceivable that it might restore the supernatural gifts lost by the fall. The gift of immortality, indeed, and exemption from earthly suffering were obviously excepted. But the Catechism of the Council of Trent [1] accounts for this by saying that the baptized members must not be in a more exalted condition than Christ their head was; and that infirmities and sufferings lead the Christian to greater heights of virtue and consequent glory than otherwise he could attain.

We are now in a position to refer to the dogma of the Council of Trent on original sin. There was too much divi-

[1] Part ii. c. ii. Q. 47.

sion of opinion in the Council to allow them to agree upon a definition of original sin itself. But the Fifth Session passed this decree, bearing on some of the principal points in the present Article:—

'If any one denies that through the grace of our Lord Jesus Christ, which is conferred in baptism, the guilt of original sin is remitted; or moreover asserts that the whole is not taken away of that which has the true and proper nature (*ratio*) of sin : but says that it is only cut down or not imputed ; let him be anathema. . . . . Nevertheless, this holy Council doth confess and is of opinion that concupiscence, or the fuel of sin, remaineth in the baptized; which being left for the purpose of trial, cannot hurt those who do not consent to it, but manfully through the grace of Christ resist it. . . . . The holy Council declares that the Catholic Church hath never understood that this concupiscence, which the Apostle some-times calls sin, is called sin because sin is truly and properly in the regenerate, but because it is of sin, and inclines to sin. If anyone hold a contrary opinion, let him be anathema.'

This doctrine is substantially that of Aquinas and Bellar-mine, but more cautiously worded.

Looking now at our Article, we see the full force of its several parts. . It first guards against Pelagianism. It then proceeds to define original sin in language intentionally op-posed to the Scholastic and Tridentine doctrine. It omits the question wherein the original righteousness of man con-sisted. It asserts that original sin is a *vitium et depravatio* of nature in every man. This must be widely different from the mere lack of superadded righteousness, the *privatio* of the scholastics. It says that man has departed in no slight degree, but *quam longissime*, from original righteousness. It says that this infection of nature remains in the regenerate. It further asserts, in opposition to the Roman dogma, that the *concupiscentia* itself, apart from indulgence, has the nature '*ratio*) of sin. It omits the doctrine of the imputation of Adam's guilt to his posterity, herein agreeing with the Confes-sion of Augsburg, as well as the Helvetic, Saxon, and Belgic Confessions. On the other hand, the Confession of Faith of

the Assembly of Divines at Westminster (which is the authorised Confession of the Established Church of Scotland) asserts
this plainly (c. vi. 3):

'They being the root of all mankind, the guilt of their sin
was imputed, and the same death in sin and corrupted nature
conveyed to all their posterity, descending from them by ordinary generation.'

The series of doctrinal discourses by Bullinger, known as
his Decades, were enjoined as a subject of study upon the less
educated clergy in Elizabeth's time.   From *Dec.* iii. s. 4 the
following passage is selected on the sinfulness of concupiscence:
' Concupiscence is a motion or affection of the mind, which of
our corrupt nature doth lust against God and His law, and
stirreth us up to wickedness, although the consent or deed
itself doth not presently follow upon our conceit. . . . Wherefore that evil and unlawful affection, which is of our natural
corruption and lieth hid in our nature, but betrayeth itself
in our hearts against the pureness of God's law and majesty,
is that very sin which in the tenth commandment is
condemned.   For although there be some which think that
such motions, diseases, blemishes, and affections of the mind
are no sins, yet God, by forbidding them in this law, doth
flatly condemn them.   But if any man doubt of this exposition, let him hear the word of the Apostle, who saith:
" I knew not sin but by the law; for I had not known lust
except the law had said, Thou shalt not lust.   Without
the law sin was dead: I once lived without law, but when the
commandment came, sin revived, and I was dead." And again:
" The affection of the flesh is death, but the affection of the
spirit is life and peace: because the affection of the flesh
is enmity against God: for it is not obedient to the law of
God, neither can be.   So then they that are in the flesh cannot
please God."   The affection of concupiscence, therefore, doth
condemn us; or, as I should rather say, we are worthily condemned by the just judgment of God for our concupiscence,
which doth every hour and moment bewray itself in the
thoughts of our hearts.'

The Homily ' Of the Misery of Mankind ' sets forth from

Scripture man's lost condition, and the imperfection of his best works, in·forcible language. But the style is popular, and does not enter into theological distinctions.

There is also a striking passage in Hooker's ' Discourse of Justification' (sec. 7). It does not speak expressly of the sinfulness of concupiscence, but, if it be not sin, the language has no force and the ideas are not true: ' If our hands did never offer violence to our brethren, a bloody thought doth prove us murderers before Him : if we had never opened our mouth to utter any scandalous, offensive, or hurtful word, the cry of our secret cogitations is heard in the ears of God. . . . Let the holiest and best things which we do be considered. We are never better affected to God than when we pray ; yet, when we pray, how are our affections many times distracted ! How little reverence do we show unto the grand majesty of God, unto whom we speak ! How little remorse of our own miseries ! How little taste of the sweet influences of His tender mercies do we feel ! . . . The best things which we do have somewhat in them to be pardoned. How, then, can we do anything meritorious or worthy to be rewarded ? . . . We see how far we are from the perfect righteousness of the law ; the little fruit which we have in holiness, it is, God knoweth, corrupt and unsound; we put no confidence at all in it, we challenge nothing in the world for it, we dare not call God to reckoning as if we had Him in our debt-books; our continual suit to Him is, and must be, to bear with our infirmities and pardon our offences.'

ARTICLE X.

Of free will.

The condition of man after the fall of *Adam* is such that he cannot turn and prepare himself, by his own natural strength and good works, to faith and calling upon God: Wherefore we have no power to do good works, pleasant and acceptable to God, without the grace of God by Christ preventing us, that we may have a good will, and working with us when we have that good will.

De libero arbitrio.

Ea est hominis post lapsum Adæ conditio, ut sese naturalibus suis viribus, et bonis operibus, ad fidem et invocationem Dei convertere ac præparare non possit. Quare absque gratia Dei (quæ per Christum est) nos præveniente, ut velimus, et cooperante, dum volumus, ad pietatis opera facienda, quæ Deo grata sunt et accepta, nihil valemus.

Notes on the Text.

1. The Latin text, as compared with the English, presents no peculiarity requiring special comment.

2. The student will have noticed that the word *Adam* is Latinized—either thus, *Adāmus, Adami,* as in Article IX.; or *Adam, Adæ,* as in this Article.

3. The ninth Article of 1552, 'of free will,' consisted of the latter half only of the present tenth Article. The opening clause was added in 1562, and is thought to have been derived from the Wurtemberg Confession of 1552, and the latter clause from Augustine 'De Gratia' (Hardwick, chap. vi.). In the Articles of 1552 this Article was followed by another, dealing with the same subject, which is here subjoined:

' *Of Grace.*

'The grace of Christ, or the Holy Ghost by Him given, doth take away the stony heart and giveth a heart of flesh. And although those that have no will to good things He maketh them to will, and those that would evil things He maketh them not to will the same; yet, nevertheless, He enforceth not the will. And, therefore, no man when he sinneth can excuse himself, as not worthy to be blamed or condemned, by alleging that he sinned unwillingly or by compulsion.'

The fatalist views held by some of the Anabaptists were, no doubt, the object at which that Article of 1552 was aimed. The Anabaptist excesses were less formidable ten years later; moreover, the doctrine of irresistible grace maintained by many of the Elizabethan divines probably rendered it desirable to strike out the Article in question.

THE PRINCIPAL TOPICS OF ARTICLE X.

1. Fallen man cannot of himself turn to God.

2. The prevenient or preventing grace of God is needful before our works can please God.

3. This *prevenient grace* gives us ' the good will.'

4. The *coöperating grace* is needful after the good will has been received.

The scriptural proof of this Article should be grouped round these main propositions.

OBSERVATIONS ON ARTICLE X.

The question of the Freedom of Man's Will is involved in philosophical as well as theological difficulties. All philosophical schools of thought—pre-Christian, Christian, and unbelieving—have discussed the various branches of this question. They have debated how far man is a voluntary agent, or the slave of circumstances, or in bondage to his own natural propensities, or the creature of the education to which he has been subjected.

Hence the difficulties belonging to the subject must not be deemed as peculiarly affecting its religious aspect. Whether the Christian solution be accepted or not, no thoughtful man can charge the difficulties on Christianity.

The limits of man's free will were debated before Christianity existed, and are now discussed outside its pale.

Hence also the history of the doctrine is too voluminous for our purpose.

The earlier Fathers, especially in their apologetic works, frequently touched on this doctrine. Their main object in such passages was to vindicate the holiness of God, lest He should be made the author of sin; or to repudiate the fatalism of most heathen systems, in order to uphold man's responsibility. They therefore frequently asserted the free will of man, but without discussing its limits or its relation to the doctrines of grace.

The Pelagian controversy first brought out all the points at issue between Christians on this subject into prominent relief. Pelagius, holding that each man was born untainted by Adam's fall, consistently maintained that he could rise to God by his own efforts.

The semi-Pelagians held that man was fallen and needed coöperating grace, but they did not teach the absolute necessity of prevenient grace for turning to God.

Augustine wrote at much length on all points of this controversy, in close accordance with the terms of our present Article. One of his treatises is entitled 'De libero arbitrio.'

The schoolmen discussed this doctrine, Thomas Aquinas taking the Augustinian view, Duns Scotus approximating rather to semi-Pelagianism.

In the age of the Reformation the question of free will was much debated. All orthodox branches of the Reformation were at first strongly attached to Augustine's doctrines, rejected the notion of the freedom of the will, and denied coöperation on the part of man in the work of conversion.[1]

The Council of Trent, in this as in other doctrines,

[1] For authorities on this point see Hagenbach's 'Hist. of Doctrines,' § 248.

endeavoured to mediate between Scotists and Thomists, Franciscans and Dominicans. It enacted the following canon (Session VI. canon 4):

'Whosoever shall say that the free will of man, moved and excited by God, does not at all coöperate with God when exciting and calling, that thus he may dispose and prepare himself for obtaining the grace of justification, and that he cannot dissent though he wills it, but, like something inanimate, does nothing at all, and holds himself merely passive, let him be anathema.'

Also (Session VI. canon 5): 'Whosoever shall say that the free will of man was lost and extinguished after Adam's sin, or that it is a thing of name merely, or a name without a thing, in short, a figment introduced into the Church by Satan, let him be anathema.'

Since the Reformation, the Augustinian views have been for the most part discouraged in the Church of Rome. The dominant Jesuit theology has been of a semi-Pelagian cast. In the Reformed Churches, whenever the great predestinarian controversy has been revived, the question of man's free will, of which it is a part, has necessarily been prominent. It was so in the seventeenth century, when the Puritans, who were usually strong predestinarians, frequently called their opponents *free-willers* as a term of reproach.

Having glanced at the historical aspect of the questions at issue in this Article, we turn to more explanatory matter. We have to deal with metaphysical ideas—the will and its liberty. We have happily some admirably clear comments of Hooker to guide us.[1] 'Man, in perfection of his nature, being made according to the likeness of his Maker, resembleth Him also in the manner of working; so that whatsoever we work as men, the same we do wittingly work and freely ; neither are we, according to the manner of natural agents, any way so tied but that it is in our power to leave the things we do undone. . . Choice there is not, unless the thing which we take be so in our power that we might have

[1] 'Ecc. Pol.' i. 7.

refused and left it. If fire consume the stubble, it chooseth not so to do, because the nature thereof is such that it can do no other. To choose is to will one thing before another; and to will is to bend our souls to the having or doing of that which they see to be good. Goodness is seen with the eye of the understanding, and the light of that eye is reason. So that two principal fountains there are of human action, Knowledge and Will; which Will, in things tending towards any end, is termed Choice.' Concerning Knowledge, 'Behold (saith Moses), I have set before you this day good and evil, life and death.' Concerning Will, he addeth immediately, ' Choose life; that is to say, the things that tend to life, them choose. . . The object of Appetite is whatsoever sensible good may be wished for ; the object of Will is that good which Reason doth lead us to seek. Affections, as joy, and grief, and fear, and anger, with such like, being, as it were, the sundry forms and fashions of Appetite, can neither rise at the conceit of a thing indifferent, nor yet choose but rise at the sight of some things. Wherefore it is not altogether in our power whether we will be stirred with Affections or no : whereas Actions which issue from the disposition of the Will are in the power thereof to be performed or stayed. Finally, Appetite is the Will's solicitor, and Will is Appetite's controller; what we covet according to the one, by the other we often reject; neither is there any other desire termed properly Will but that where Reason and understanding, or the show of Reason, prescribeth the thing desired.'

Hooker proceeds with a discussion of the numerous causes which pervert, enfeeble, and misguide the Will, making it in so many things subservient to the Appetites. But we have quoted enough for our present purpose.

The Will being thus that in us which has the power of determination to do or not to do any mental or corporal act, the question next before us is this : How far is it, in our present condition, actually free ? How far is the Will in a state of Liberty or Necessity, as the two opposite ideas of its condition are usually styled ?

It is probably a mode of expression liable to misapprehension to make our statements turn much on the freedom or bondage of the Will. Our Article does not so word it.

Our Will exercises its power of choice according to the tastes, feelings, knowledge, and, in a word, apprehension of what is desirable to, and relished by, the human nature of which it is the determining principle. If, therefore, the nature be angelic, the Will determines accordingly. If the nature be corrupt, and in whatever degree it is so, the Will determines and leads the life and thoughts corruptly.

This state, indeed, may be called one of bondage, and is so called in Scripture; but it is not so as being one of blind necessity, but as of inevitable consequence from a depraved condition.

The debate therefore seems more properly to belong to Art. IX., and to result from different views of man's inherent corruption since the fall. And indeed this Article will, on perusal, appear to be a necessary supplement to Art. IX., defining more precisely the helpless condition of fallen man.

The Roman doctrine of original sin as a state of privation only would naturally lead to the Tridentine assertions that man coöperates with grace in preparing himself for justification. On this the remarks of Calvin[1] are remarkably clear: 'We certainly obey God with a will, but it is with a will which He has formed in us. Those, therefore, who ascribe any proper movement to free will, apart from the grace of God, do nothing else than rend the Holy Spirit. Paul declares, not that a faculty of willing is given to us, but that the will itself is formed in us.' (Phil. ii. 13.)

Finally, Delitzsch[2] thus lays down the distinction of which we have treated :

' Since the fall, man is free to choose, and for that reason is accountable . . . He is free to choose, in so far as no foreign will can irresistibly constrain him to will against his own will. He is not free, in so far as within his own personality

---

[1] 'Antidote to Council of Trent.'   Tracts, vol. iii. p. 47.
[2] ' Bibl. Psychology,' p. 193.

the sin which has been allowed by himself rules and enslaves his will.'

In the practical work of the ministry a scholastic mode of treating this subject would be usually either unintelligible or repulsive. Yet a fairly accurate illustration of the meaning of this Article may be presented in a popular manner in this way. An appeal may be made grounded on the failure of good resolutions, and the utter breakdown of result from numerous wishes to serve God. The reason may be traced to the will, the determining power, remaining with its old bias. And this brings us to the very root of the matter, the absolute necessity for conversion.

It is an obvious but not an unnecessary caution to give, that before treating on this subject it should be carefully considered what is meant by the will, and in what respect either liberty or bondage is predicated of it.

ARTICLE XI.

Of the Justification of Man.

We are accounted right-eous before God, only for the merit of our Lord and Sav-iour Jesus Christ by Faith, and not for our own works or deservings. Wherefore, that we are justified by faith only is a most wholesome doc-trine, and very full of com-fort, as more largely is ex-pressed in the Homily of Justification.

De hominis justificatione.

Tantum propter meritum Domini ac Servatoris nostri Jesu Christi, per fidem, non propter opera, et merita nos-tra, justi coram Deo reputa-mur. Quare sola fide nos justificari doctrina est salu-berrima, ac consolationis ple-nissima, ut in homilia de justificatione hominis fusius explicatur.

Notes on the Text of Article XI.

The Latin text chiefly requires us to notice the prepositions in the following clauses: *for* the merit, *propter meritum*; not *for* our own works, *non propter opera*; *by* faith, *per fidem*; *propter* implies the meritorious cause, and *per* the medium of communication. This is changed in the last clause of the Article into the more direct ablative of the instrument *solâ fide.*

The first clause of this Article, compared with the Title and with the last clause, gives us this definition of *justification*: *the being 'accounted righteous.'* Since many controversies on this subject (as on others also) turn upon the definition of the terms used, this should be especially noticed.

The eleventh Article of 1552 was more brief than our present form; it was thus expressed : ' Justification by only faith (*ex sola fide*) in Jesus Christ, in that sense as it is declared in the Homily of Justification, is a most certain and wholesome doctrine for Christian men.'

It is well known that none of the homilies bears or has borne this title. Yet it would seem hardly possible, without disingenuity, to profess doubt which homily is meant. It cannot be seriously maintained that they who wrote both Articles and homilies, or who, in Elizabeth's time, revised and recast this Article, forgot or carelessly miscalled the title of the homily. They evidently chose to speak of the one in question, viz., the homily of ' *The Salvation of Mankind*,' by a shorter name, describing its main subject, and identifying it more closely with this Article.

THE CHIEF TOPICS OF ARTICLE XI.

1. The justification of the sinner is the same thing with God accounting him righteous.

2. The meritorious cause of justification is: A—positively, the merit of Christ; B—negatively, not our works or deservings.

3. The instrumental cause of justification in the sinner himself is faith.

4. Nothing is coupled with faith in this peculiar office which it has in justification.

5. The salutary and consoling nature of this doctrine.

The student will consider and carefully compare these five points with Holy Scripture. Especially he will repeatedly study the grand exposition of this doctrine in the Epistle to the Romans, until he has mastered its connection, and can quote and apply it readily.

OBSERVATIONS ON ARTICLE XI.

The doctrine of Justification has of necessity been dealt with more or less by every Christian writer from the first; for the salvation of man is the Gospel itself. The sentiments of writers of all ages might be alleged in a series of quotations,

in, which every shade of opinion might be found as to the
efficacy of faith and works, and as to the nature of Justification.   It is satisfactory to know that the very earliest
uninspired Christian writer is most distinctly in agreement
with our own Article.   Thus he writes :—' We, too, being
called by His will in Christ Jesus, are not justified by ourselves, nor by our own wisdom, or understanding, or godliness, or works which we have wrought in holiness of heart ;
but by that faith through which, from the beginning,
Almighty God hath justified all men.' [1]

For reasons already given in the Preface it is thought more
useful, instead of attempting any general discussion based on
a catena of authorities, to present to the student what may
be a sufficiently full view of the doctrine of Justification, as
held by the leading representatives of the schools of theology,
with which we are more immediately concerned.   The following may suffice for this purpose:

    I. The Scholastic Theology.

    II. The Decrees of the Council of Trent.

    III. Luther.

    IV. Calvin.

    V. The ' Homily of Justification.'

    VI. Hooker.

    VII. Bishop Bull.

The student who has fairly understood the position of
these representative men and documents will have an intelligent understanding of the subject, and will be able to
enlarge his reading according to his opportunities.

I. *The Scholastic Theology.*

An able and interesting account of the views upon Justification held by the great scholastic writers will be found in
Neander's ' History of the Church,' vol. viii. pp. 276–301
(Clark's Edition).   What the student will chiefly require
under this head will be the meaning of some scholastic and
metaphysical phrases.   A few notes of this kind are therefore
subjoined:

[1] Clemens Rom. Ep. i. 32.

1. Faith was classified under two heads—*Fides informis*, and *Fides formata*. *Fides informis* may be described as the bare admission of a thing as true, corresponding to what we call a dead faith, or bare historical faith. It was called unformed, being conceived of as the unorganised shapeless matter out of which true faith is to be shaped. When love, with its consequent life and action, was added to this it became *Fides formata*. It may be that what was meant by some of the best of these writers was not very different from what we call a living or divine faith, as distinguished from one which is merely human and dead. But what has been, and is now, meant by the term *Fides formata*, is not faith considered full of life, and with a capacity and necessity for producing good works—the *vera et viva fides* of Art. XII.— but faith together with love and works considered under one term. It will at once be seen that such a definition involves most important doctrinal and practical consequences. For justification by faith may thus be verbally asserted, and justification by works intended.

2. In order to the proper understanding of many expressions in our older divines (e.g., ' Pearson on the Creed,' Art. I. : ' Faith is a *habit* of the intellectual part of man ; ' ' The belief of the heart is the internal *habit* residing in the soul '), it may be desirable to add a few words on the scholastic use of the word *habit*. The difference between the scholastic use and the modern popular use of the word mainly lies in this. We usually mean by this word some action which by use and repetition has become familiar to us. The philosophy of Aristotle (which was also that of the schoolmen) meant by the word *habit*, not the action, but the acquired mental state or condition which has made such an action natural to us. Aristotle held the human soul to be naturally neutral with regard to virtue and vice, and therefore every *virtue*, as distinguished from *virtuous actions*, to be an acquired *habit*.[1] Virtue, therefore, he defines as a *habit*. A heathen could go no further. But Christian divines, adopting the same definition, saw in divine grace the power

[1] Ethics, ii. 5.

which could implant in the soul *at once* the facility and inclination to virtue, which otherwise could only come *gradually* and imperfectly by a repetition of virtuous actions. Hence Aquinas defines virtue as a *habit*, and a *habit* as 'a quality not easily removed, by which one acts easily and pleasantly.' And again he describes *grace* as a *habit* which is the principle and root of the virtues. Aristotle, then, held that the mental condition, which he styled *habit*, could be acquired. The schoolmen added that it could be *infused* or *implanted* at once by divine power, and that grace (according to their meaning of the term) was such an implanted *habit*. The student will now understand Bishop Pearson's definition of Faith as an 'internal *habit*,' and also the expression *habitual righteousness*, which he will meet with in 'Hooker on Justification.'

3. Since many causes usually contribute towards bringing about any result, there was in the schools a fourfold classification of causes derived from Aristotle:

(1.) *The material cause.*—That is, the matter, thing, or substance without the existence of which that which we are considering could not be—e.g. without clay, or something analogous, the work of the potter could not come into existence. Or, to take a different subject, the material cause of the Irish Church Disestablishment Act was the Parliament and that Church.

(2.) *The formal cause.*—The combination of all the necessary conditions which, being present, give that shape to the result which actually comes forth. In the above example the formal cause of the Act was the combination of all the political and social influences and usages which gave the ultimate shape to it.

(3.) *The efficient cause.*—The first mover in the transaction as far back as it requires to be considered. In the above example the efficient cause was the Prime Minister.

(4.) *The final cause.*—The real end, aim, or object for which the thing was done. In the example taken, it was said to be the pacification of Ireland.

This account of causes may be of some use to the student,

who may encounter such terms in the older theology, especially in treatises on Justification. In the subsequent account of Tridentine theology, the classification of causes is enlarged by the addition of *meritorious* and *instrumental causes.* They sufficiently speak for themselves. The former really belongs to the class called formal causes, being a necessary condition towards the justification of man in that mode in which it was to take place. The material cause there was no need to name, being man and his sinful state.

II. *The Council of Trent.*

The Council of Trent dealt with the question of Justification in its sixth session. It enacted a lengthy decree on this subject. The following extracts from it will illustrate the main points of the Roman doctrine. The fifth and sixth chapters speak of the necessity for a preparative work of divine grace on the heart. Then the seventh chapter proceeds thus: 'Justification itself follows this disposition or preparation; and justification is not remission of sin merely, but also sanctification, and the renewal of the inner man by the voluntary reception of grace and divine gifts, so that he who was unrighteous is made righteous, and the enemy becomes a friend, and an heir according to the hope of eternal life. The causes of justification are these: the final cause, the glory of God and of Christ, and life eternal; the efficient cause, the merciful God, who freely cleanses and sanctifies, sealing and anointing with the Holy Spirit of promise, which is the earnest of our inheritance; the meritorious cause, His well-beloved and only-begotten Son, Jesus Christ our Lord, who through His great love wherewith He loved us, even when we were enemies, merited justification for us by His most holy passion on the cross, and made satisfaction for us to God the Father; the instrumental cause, the sacrament of baptism, which is the sacrament of faith, without which no one can ever obtain justification; lastly, the sole formal cause is the righteousness of God, not that by which He Himself is righteous, but that by which He makes us righteous, with which, being endued by Him, we are renewed in the spirit of our minds, and are not only accounted righteous, but are properly called righteous, and are so, receiving righteousness in ourselves, each according to his measure.'

The tenth chapter asserts of the justified that ' by the observance of the commandments of God and the Church, faith coöperating with good works, they gain an increase of that righteousness which was received by the grace of Christ, and are the more justified.'

The fourteenth chapter says that ' those who by sin have fallen from the grace of justification received may be justified again when, moved by divine influence, they succeed in recovering their lost grace by the sacrament of penance, through the merits of Christ. For this method of justification is that recovery of the lapsed which the holy fathers have fitly called " the second plank after shipwreck " of lost grace.'

The sixteenth chapter teaches that, since the justified are united to Christ, ' it must be believed that they are in no respect deficient, but that they may be considered as fully satisfying the divine law (as far as is compatible with our present condition) by their works, which are wrought in God, and as really deserving eternal life, to be bestowed in due time if they die in a state of grace . . . . So that neither is our righteousness set up as if it were actually derived from ourselves, nor is the righteousness of God unknown or disallowed. For it is called our righteousness because we are justified thereby, through its in-dwelling in us ; and, at the same time, it is the righteousness of God, because it is infused into us by God, through the merits of Christ.'

It will be seen that the Roman doctrine, thus defined, stands in sharply marked contrast with the doctrine of the English Church. The Roman justification requires, indeed, as the Anglican does, a certain preparation of faith and repentance. But it is not a forensic act whereby God imputes or accounts righteousness to the sinner, but an act whereby God infuses *habitual* righteousness. So that the *habits* of faith, hope, and love are thenceforward in the soul ; and in respect of, and by reason of, these, God views the soul as in itself righteous. Justification is thus identified with sanctification. Not only so, but the sanctification itself is regarded as perfect to such a degree as to ensure acceptance with God. The Romanist is accustomed to sneer at the doctrine of imputed righteousness as an unreal mockery. But rightly viewed it unites these two great facts : God's willingness to save the penitent believer, and the believer's imperfect sanctification. Whereas, when we consider that the Roman doctrine holds that all persons are justified (in the sense above defined) in and by baptism, and that God accepts them accordingly on account of the *real*, and not *imputed*, holiness that is in them, it becomes very difficult to reconcile this with the obvious facts of the unholiness of the majority of the baptized. The charge of unreality applies more strongly to such a daring assumption than it can to the doctrine of an imputed right-eousness.

III. *Luther on Justification.*

First in order of time in the reformed theology we must place Luther's doctrine. The student may be reminded how the doctrine of justification by faith was to him the means of deliverance from his own spiritual difficulties, and the key to his teaching. His revulsion from the bondage of the Roman theology led him at times to use incautious language as to good works of which his enemies took full advantage, but no one has in other passages more carefully guarded against Antinomian excesses than he has done. It was Luther who propounded the celebrated maxim that justification by faith was the *articulus stantis aut cadentis ecclesiæ.* The following extracts from Luther's commentary on the Epistle to the Galatians will illustrate his views on the subject. 'This is the true mean of becoming a Christian, even to be justified by faith in Jesus Christ and not by the works of the Law. Here we must stand and not upon the wicked gloss of the school-men, who say that, faith then justifieth, when charity and good works are joined withal. . . . When a man heareth that he ought to believe in Christ and yet notwithstanding faith justifieth not, except it be formed and furnished with

H

charity, by-and-by he falleth from faith, and then he
thinketh : If faith without charity justifieth not, then is faith
in vain and unprofitable, and charity alone justifieth ; for
except faith be formed with charity it is nothing.' Then
follows a passage on the absolute necessity of good works and
their right time and place. He then proceeds thus: ' Christ is not
the law : he is not my work, or the work of the law, he is not
my charity, my obedience, my poverty : but he is the Lord
of life and death, a mediator, a Saviour, a redeemer of those
that are under the law and sin. In him we are by faith, and
he in us. The bridegroom must be alone with the bride in
his secret chamber, all the servants and the household being
put apart. But afterwards when the door is open, and he
cometh forth, then let the servants and handmaidens return
to minister unto them : then let charity do her office and let
good works be done. . . . . Christ is the Lamb of God,
that taketh away the sins of the world. This doth faith
alone lay hold of, and not charity, which notwithstanding, as a
certain thankfulness, must follow faith.' [1]

' These three things, faith, Christ, acceptation or imputation,
must be joined together. Faith taketh hold of Christ, and
hath him inclosed, as the ring doth the precious stone. And
whosoever shall be found having this confidence in Christ
apprehended in the heart him will God account for righteous.
. . . . . And this acceptation or imputation is very necessary ;
first, because we are not yet perfectly righteous. . . When
we have thus taught faith in Christ, then do we teach also
good works.' [1]

This was a theme of which Luther was never weary, Christ
dwelling in the heart by faith, the true righteousness of the
Christian, as opposed to the scholastic idea of the infused
righteousness of charity, as a *habit* of the spiritual nature of
man.

IV. *Calvin on Justification.*

Calvin has for three hundred years so deeply moulded the
theology of a large part of Christendom that his views may be

[1] Luther on Gal. ii. 16.

considered as *representative*, beyond those of any writer of his age. We shall first give several extracts from his ' Institutes.' ' I must refute the nugatory distinction of the Schoolmen between formed and unformed faith. For they imagine that persons who have no fear of God, and no sense of piety, may believe all that is necessary for salvation, as if the Holy Spirit were not the witness of our adoption by enlightening our hearts unto faith. . . . They insist that faith is an assent with which any despiser of God may receive what is delivered by Scripture. But we must first see whether any one can by his own strength acquire faith, or whether the Holy Spirit, by means of it, becomes the witness of adoption. . . . . We in one word conclude that they talk absurdly when they maintain that faith is formed by the addition of pious affection as an accessory to assent, since assent itself, such, at least, as the Scriptures describe, consists in pious affection. . . . . To express the matter more plainly, faith consists in the knowledge of Christ; Christ cannot be known without the sanctification of the Spirit; therefore faith cannot possibly be disjoined from pious affection.' [1]

Again, Calvin defines Justification ' as the acceptance with which God receives us into his favour as if we were righteous, and we say that this justification consists in the forgiveness of sins, and the imputation of the righteousness of Christ.' [2] He proceeds to argue that this is the proper and most usual signification of the term in Scripture.

In his ' Antidote to the Council of Trent' (sixth session), when discussing the Roman doctrine as laid down by that Council, Calvin thus writes : ' It is not to be denied that the two things, Justification and Sanctification, are constantly conjoined and cohere; but from this it is erroneously inferred that they are one and the same. . . . . There is no dispute as to whether or not Christ sanctifies all whom He justifies. It were to rend the Gospel, and divide Christ Himself, to attempt to separate the righteousness which we obtain by faith from repentance. The whole dispute is as to the cause

---

[1] Institutes, III. ii. 8. [2] Ibid. III. xi. 3.

of Justification. The Fathers of Trent pretend that it is
twofold, as if we were justified partly by forgiveness of sins
and partly by spiritual regeneration. . . . . I maintain that it
is one and simple, and is wholly included in the gratuitous
acceptance of God. I, besides, hold that it is without us,
because we are righteous in Christ only. . . . . I neither can
nor ought to let pass the very great absurdity of calling
baptism alone the instrumental cause. What then will
become of the Gospel? Will it not even be allowed the
smallest corner? . . . . Let them cease to sport with trifles
such as—man receives faith, and along with it hope and love;
therefore it is not faith alone which justifies. Because if eyes
are given us, and along with them ears and feet and hands,
we cannot, therefore, say that we either hear with our feet, or
walk with our hands, or handle with our eyes. Next follows
their worse than worthless distinction between an informal
and a formed faith. . . . . They are dreaming of that faith
devoid of charity which is commonly called by the Sophists
informal. For if the doctrine of Paul is true that Christ
dwells in our hearts by faith, they can no more separate faith
from charity, than Christ from His Spirit. . . . . It is, therefore, faith alone which justifies, and yet the faith which
justifies is not alone; just as it is the heat alone of the sun
which warms the earth, and yet in the sun it is not alone,
because it is constantly conjoined with light. Wherefore
we do not separate the whole grace of regeneration from faith,
but we claim the power and faculty of justifying entirely for
faith.'

V. *The Homily of the Salvation of Mankind.*

Passing from foreign to English theology, this document
first requires our attention.

The Article so distinctly refers us to this Homily for a
further explanation of the doctrine in question, that it becomes
of almost equal authority with the Article itself.

That this Homily is meant appears positively, because—

1. The reference being found in King Edward's Article

fixes it to the first book of Homilies only, excluding the
second book published in the reign of Elizabeth.

2. There are only twelve homilies in that book, and a
glance at the titles will show that this is the only one bearing
definitely on the subject.

3. In point of fact, Justification is by name the subject of
this Homily from beginning to end, as may be seen in every
page.

We subjoin an analysis of this treatise. All being
sinners, every man needs a ' righteousness of justification, to
be received at God's own hands, that is to say, the forgiveness
of his sins and trespasses in such things as he hath offended.
And this justification or righteousness which we so receive of
God's mercy and Christ's merits embraced by faith is taken,
accepted, and allowed of God for our perfect and full justification.'

Infants dying after baptism are by Christ's sacrifice accepted.

They who sin after baptism, on repentance are entirely
cleansed.

This justification is *free* to us. Yet by union of mercy
with justice a ransom was paid by Christ, who ' besides this
ransom, fulfilled the law for us perfectly.'

' So the grace of God doth not shut out the justice of God in
our justification, but only shutteth out the justice of man, that
is to say, the justice of our works, as to the merits of deserving
our justification. And, therefore, St. Paul declareth here
(Rom. iii. xii. x.) nothing on the behalf of man concerning
his justification, but only a true and lively faith, which nevertheless is the gift of God, and not man's only work without
God. And yet that faith doth not shut out repentance, hope,
love, dread, and the fear of God, to be joined with faith in
every man that is justified; but it shutteth them out from
the office of justifying. So that although they be all present
together in him that is justified, yet they justify not altogether;
neither doth faith shut out the justice of our good works,
necessarily to be done afterwards of duty towards God . . . .
but it excludeth them, so that we may not do them to this
intent, to be made just by doing of them.'

In consequence of their imperfection our good works cannot justify us.

Christ has fulfilled the law as well as paid the ransom, so that in Him we fulfil the law.

Three things are required in justification :

1. God's mercy.
2. Christ's justice.
3. A true and lively faith out of the which faith spring good works.

The way of Faith is the way of Grace.

Twelve ancient authors from Origen to Bernard are next quoted or referred to, as bearing out these statements.

' This saying that we be justified by faith only, freely, and without works, is spoken for to take away clearly all merit of our works, as being unable to deserve our justification at God's hands, and thereby most plainly to express the weakness of man and the goodness of God ; the great infirmity of ourselves, and the might and power of God ; the imperfection of our own works, and the most abundant grace of our Saviour Christ ; and, therefore, wholly to ascribe the merit and deserving of our justification to Christ alone, and his most precious bloodshedding.'

This is the doctrine of Scripture and antiquity. It exalts Christ, and lowers man. He who denies it is an adversary to Christ.

The importance of clearly holding this doctrine is urged, lest carnal men abuse it to live a worldly life, therefore a further explanation of it is added. ' Justification is not the office of man but of God. . . . . It is not a thing which we render to Him, but which we receive of Him, not which we give to Him, but which we take of Him by His free mercy, and by the only merits of Christ.'

Hence this doctrine ' is not that this our own act to believe in Christ, or this our faith in Christ which is within us, doth justify us, and deserve our justification unto us.' But that, although we have all virtues and good deeds, yet we renounce their merit as ' things far too weak and insufficient and imperfect to deserve remission of our sins and our justification,' and therefore we must trust only in God's mercy and Christ's sacrifice.

Faith, like John the Baptist, puts us away from itself to the Lamb of God.

Man's duty to God follows.

Not to strive how little good we may do, much less to live carnally. A faith that so acts is a counterfeit, dead and devilish.

For even devils believe the facts of Christ's life, &c. 'The right and true Christian Faith is, not only to believe that holy Scripture, and all the Articles of our Faith are true, but also to have a sure trust and confidence in God's merciful promises to be saved from everlasting damnation by Christ: whereof, doth follow a loving heart to obey His commandments.'

No devil or man living an ungodly life can have this faith.

These things rightly considered stir us up to good works.

VI. *Hooker on Justification.*

Hooker has been spoken of by so many divines of all shades of opinion as a true representative of the Reformed English Church after the first heat of controversy had passed, that his writings are generally supposed to carry more weight than those of other divines considered as individuals. We, therefore, next subjoin the following epitome of his opinions on this subject.

Analysis of Hooker's Discourse on Justification.

'The wicked doth compass about the righteous' (Hab. i. 4).

CHAPTER II.—All have sinned. No human being is naturally void of unrighteousness, not even the Blessed Virgin. We have, therefore, to show how Christ is made our righteousness.

CHAPTER III.—The different kinds of righteousness are thus defined:

1. The glorifying righteousness in the world to come which is both perfect and inherent.

. 2. The righteousness whereby we are here justified, which is perfect, but not inherent.

3. The righteousness whereby we are sanctified, which is inherent, but not perfect.

[N.B.—' Inherent,' from its derivation, implies that which abides in us so closely as to become part of ourselves and to belong to us. Accordingly, in other words, the justifying righteousness above spoken of, is the righteousness of Christ not in us or of us, as being or becoming part of our own nature, but as imputed to us *ab extra*, and appropriated to us by genuine justifying faith. But the sanctifying righteousness is that which is wrought in us by the Holy Spirit working in and with us. So far as this is the work of the Spirit it must be perfect; so far as it is the result of our co-operation with the Spirit, it must be imperfect. This righteousness is manifestly *ab intra*, inherent, abiding in us, and growing in us.]

CHAPTER IV.—How far we agree with Rome.

1. That infants, before actual sin, are by nature corrupt.

2. That in making men righteous none do efficiently work with God.

3. That none ever attained to righteousness but by the merits of Christ.

4. That Christ as God is the efficient cause, and as man the meritorious cause of our justification.

5. But that something is required by which his merits are to be applied to us for our justification.

CHAPTER V.—Where we disagree with Rome on justification.

' We disagree about the nature and essence of the medicine whereby Christ cureth our disease; about the manner of applying it; about the number and the power of means which God requireth in us for the effectual applying thereof to our soul's comfort.'

They say that justifying righteousness is a divine quality infused into the soul, capable of increase or diminution, so that we are more and more justified by receiving more of it. That the first justification takes place in baptism, and then by good works more grace is received, and the justification is increased, which they call the second justification. If the justification is diminished by venial sins, the decay may be repaired by holy water and the like. If it be lost by mortal sin, it may be restored by the sacrament of penance, howbeit, not so perfectly but that purgatorial pains are needful.

CHAPTER VI.—The error of the Romanists in their doctrine of justification is argued from the following passage, Phil. iii. 8, 9 : ' And be found in him, not having mine own righteousness which is of the Law, but that which is through the faith of Christ, the righteousness which is of God through faith.' ' Whether they speak of the first or second justification, they make the essence of it a divine quality inherent. They make it righteousness which is in us. If it be in us, then it is ours as our souls are ours.' . . . . But from the above passage it appears that ' the righteousness wherein we must be found, if we will be justified, is not our own ; therefore, we cannot be justified by any inherent quality. Christ hath merited righteousness for as many as are found in Him. In Him God findeth us if we be faithful, for by faith we are incorporated into Christ. Then although in ourselves we be altogether sinful and unrighteous, yet even the man who is impious in himself—full of iniquity, full of sin—him, being found in Christ through faith, and having his sin remitted through repentance ; him God beholdeth with a gracious eye, putteth away his sin by not imputing it, taketh quite away the punishment due thereunto by pardoning it, and accepteth him in Jesus Christ as perfectly righteous, as if he had fulfilled all that was commanded him in the Law. Shall I say more perfectly righteous than if himself had fulfilled the whole Law ? I must take heed what I say ; but the Apostle saith, " God made Him to be sin for us, who knew no sin, that we might be made the righteousness of God in Him." Such we are in the sight of God the Father as is the very Son of God Himself.'

Thus the Church of Rome in teaching justification by inherent grace, perverts the gospel.

The righteousness of sanctification is inherent, and cannot exist without works ; it is different in its nature from the righteousness of justification ; we are righteous the *one* way by

the faith of Abraham; in the *other* way, except we do the
works of Abraham, we are not righteous. Of the one, says
St. Paul (Rom. iv. 5), 'to him that worketh not, but
believeth, his faith is counted for righteousness.' Of the other,
St. John says (1 John iii. 7), 'he that doeth righteousness is
righteous.' Thus also St. Paul is reconciled with St. James,
if the former is speaking of justifying righteousness without
works, and the latter of sanctifying righteousness with works.

In Romans vi. 22, St. Paul distinguishes between these two
kinds of righteousness; 'being made free from sin'—this is
the righteousness of justification—'ye have your fruit unto
holiness'—this is the righteousness of sanctification.

CHAPTER VII.—The imperfection of sanctifying righteousness. All Christians have the title of saints, because it is
concluded that they are partakers of the sanctifying righteousness; some, however, have no more of this than the title, and
the best are very far from perfection, and dare not rely for salvation on their greatest advances in this inherent, sanctifying,
righteousness, but only on the *justifying* righteousness, whereby God does not impute their trespasses unto them.' [This
noble chapter should be thoughtfully read throughout for its
truly spiritual perception of the imperfection of man's highest
holiness.]

CHAPTERS VIII.-XX., inclusive.—The question is discussed
whether Roman Catholics can be saved, being in error on the
doctrine of justifying righteousness. Hooker concludes that
they may, through God's mercy, provided they hold fast by
the foundation of Christ crucified for our sins.

CHAPTER XXI.—'We have already showed that there be
two kinds of Christian righteousness; the one without us,
which we have by imputation; the other in us, which con-
sisteth of faith, hope, and charity, and other Christian virtues,
and St. James doth prove that Abraham had not only the
first, because his faith was counted to him for righteousness,
but also the second, because he offered up his son. God
giveth us both the one justice and the other; the one by
accepting us for righteous in Christ; the other by working
Christian righteousness in us.'

The efficient cause of the righteousness of sanctification is the spirit of adoption in our hearts; it consists of the infused virtues proper to saints, love, faith, hope, &c., which the Spirit brings with it from the first moment of its abode; the effects of it are good works, fruits of the Spirit.

We may therefore divide the righteousness of sanctification into two kinds, analogous to the root and the fruit; these are called *habitual* and *actual*.

First, *habitual*;[1] the inward graces of holiness, with which the soul is imbued when it becomes a temple of the Holy Ghost. This we hold the thief on the cross possessed.

Second, *actual*; that which comes out in act, and adorns the life. This the thief on the cross could scarcely possess.

The question may be asked, which do we first receive? It is answered, the imputed righteousness of Christ to our justification, and the *habitual* righteousness of sanctification we must receive at one and the same time, when we are made temples of the Holy Ghost; but though we receive them at the same time, they are not one and the same thing.

But the *actual* righteousness of sanctification must of necessity follow afterwards in point of time.

So far a perfect identity of doctrine on the essential point of justification will have been seen in the reformed theology. With very slight variation of language, Luther, Calvin, our Homily, and Hooker are at one with each other and with our present Article. Justification is kept distinctly apart, as a theological term and spiritual fact, from sanctification. The essence of the latter is habitual holiness inherent in the soul, and infused into it by the Holy Spirit, and capable of many degrees. Justification, on the other hand, is 'not the office of man, but of God.' It is the act of God towards us, by which He not only forgives our sins, but also accounts us righteous. This, considered as a *spiritual fact*, is quite distinct from the former. Therefore to confuse justification with sanctification is not a pardonable blunder in mere theological phraseology, but it mistakes two distinct spiritual processes upon and in the soul of man. It therefore destroys the clearness of the anatomy of the divine life in the soul, and proportionally renders less certain the Christian hope. Yet the other point, brought out

[1] See Note on Habits, p. 93.

no less distinctly in the above extracts, is of equal importance.
Justification cannot be divorced from Sanctification for a *moment*.
As Hooker says, they 'are received at one and the same time.'
As Calvin tersely expresses it: ' It is faith alone which justifies,
and yet the faith which justifies is not alone.' It is with
these as with the great doctrine of the Incarnation. Separate
the two natures in Christ, and we have lost our One Saviour.
Confuse them, and we have another, who is not He. So
fundamental is this difference of definition which separates us
from the doctrine of Rome in the great fact of our justification.
The doctrine of the Reformation, thus defined, continued to be
held with none but insignificant variations until the reign of
Charles I. was well advanced. Nor had there even then arisen
any other defined school of theology on this head. To this
Bishop Bull may himself be called as a witness, 'that we fall
not into the same error as Luther, and most of our own divines
after his time.'[1] But in the year 1669, Bull, afterwards
Bishop of St. David's, published his ' Harmonia Apostolica,
or Agreement of St. Paul with St. James on Justification.'
This was the legitimate fruit and consequence of much of the
English theology of the preceding forty years. A large part
of the English clergy no longer used the language of the
Reformation on this doctrine, and was ripe to receive Bull's
teaching. Its publication was an era in English theology.
The following sketch is meagre, but the work itself does not
possess the fulness and richness of our previous authorities,
and we can do no more than attempt fairly to exhibit its
main positions.

It is divided into two dissertations. The first is on
St. James ii. 24, and the second on Romans iii. 28. The
object of the whole work is to reconcile these two statements,
which is done by accommodating the second to the first.

Dissertation I.

'Ye see then how that by works a man is justified, and not by faith
only ' (James ii. 24).

CHAPTER I.—The word *justify* is defined in a legal sense, as

[1] Justif. I. iii. 3.

'meaning to acquit or pronounce guiltless.' This would appear to fall short of the definition in Article XI. But it is supplemented (Ch. i. § 5) by the further statement that 'the word *justify* both with St. Paul and St. James has exactly the same force as *to impute a reward, to impute righteousness, and to impute for righteousness*. Now it is well understood that *imputation* denotes the act of God regarding a man as just, not making him just.' It follows that the word justify is used in the sense of our Article, and of the Protestant writers. It is taken to be equivalent to forgiveness of sin, and *accounting* (not *making*) the sinner righteous.

The preposition *by* in the passage from St. James is further defined as taken in a lower sense, as signifying the means or condition, not the meritorious or principal cause. Since neither faith nor works can be a principal cause or a cause at all, unless inaccurately speaking. The true cause is the grace of God, obtained through the merits of Christ.

In the remaining five chapters of this dissertation the author argues in favour of the absolute and unqualified acceptation of the passage from St. James, as a distinct theological proposition, setting forth the true Christian doctrine, that a Christian ' is justified by works and not by faith only.' The following is a sketch of his argument.

CHAPTER II.—Bishop Bull alleges those numerous passages of Scripture ' which speak generally of good works, of piety, sanctity, and obedience (all which have the same meaning) as the conditions necessarily required that anyone should be acceptable unto God to salvation, i. e. be justified, for these are synonymous terms.' Accordingly, whatever is said in Scripture to be necessary to *salvation* he takes to be equivalent to being necessary to *justification*. He denies to faith any special and peculiar force as an instrument in justification, urging that repentance, which includes at least eleven works (e. g. contrition, humiliation, confession, supplication, love of God, &c.), is equally necessary. [It is hoped that the student will see what a doctrinal confusion this is. Repentance can conduce to justification only in so far as it brings to Christ, at which moment it passes into the substance of faith, and this uniting the sinner to Christ, he is justified according to the words of our Saviour (John iii. 18).]

CHAPTER III.—Sets forth the Decalogue, as explained and perfected by Christ, as the law by which Christians will be acquitted or condemned, and concludes that by faith without works no one is justified.

CHAPTER IV.—Faith is analysed into its three acts of knowledge, assent, and confidence. Each of these is asserted to be possible to evil men, and to have no necessary justifying power.

CHAPTER V.—The future judgment is said by Scripture to be according to our works. It is inferred that justification now must follow the same law.

CHAPTER VI.—It is argued that Protestant divines confess that the faith which justifies must be a living faith, that is, productive of good works. Therefore, on their own showing, good works are necessary to salvation, or in other words, are necessary to justification.

The foregoing reasoning of Bishop Bull seems to reduce theology into a hopeless chaos. In Holy Scripture the words justify, sanctify, save, faith, works, obedience, salvation, &c., are not used indiscriminately. Each has its own place and degree of necessity in the great and complex work of the sinner's salvation. This, as applied to the soul, is the work of the Holy Ghost, convincing the soul of sin, revealing to it Christ with a peculiar and distinct perception of the necessity and sufficiency of all that He has done, and all that He is, in order to the salvation of that soul for ever. This work is not one that terminates. The Holy Spirit, which has wrought this, continues to dwell in that soul, which is now a ' temple of the Holy Ghost.' Consequently, though with a sad residue and admixture of the fallen nature which remains beside it, good thoughts, words, and works of necessity flow forth from that pure fountain. Salvation, therefore, is one work and act of the great vivifying and renewing Spirit. But viewed in its complex action upon man, it is susceptible of a great number of divisions. Repentance, faith, obedience are all necessary to it. To say otherwise were, in Calvin's words, before quoted, 'nothing else than to rend the Spirit,' who is One. But they are not all necessary precisely in the same office. And for the work of Justification it has pleased God to set apart faith, 'that it might be by grace,' and that the sinner may learn that union with Christ is the sure and only condition of the life of the saved.

The second dissertation takes for its text Romans iii. 28: 'Therefore we conclude that a man is justified by faith without the deeds of the law.' It is much longer than the first. Its object is to bring the meaning of St. Paul to a coincidence with the doctrine laid down in the first dissertation as the right interpretation of St. James.

The first three chapters discuss some of the principal modes for reconciling the conflicting passages in St. Paul and St. James, which have been given by different divines, and are here rejected.

The fourth chapter sets out with the principle that 'the words of St. James being express, clear, and evident' . . . . 'whatever obscurity there is must be attributed to the Epistles of St. Paul.' It is then decided that the ambiguity lies not in the word *justifies*, but in the words *faith* and *works*, which ' St. Paul uses with a different meaning upon different occasions.'

The following definition is then laid down. 'Faith, to which justification is attributed by St. Paul, is not to be understood as one single virtue, but denotes the whole condition of the Gospel covenant ; that is, comprehends in one word all the works of Christian piety.' It is added somewhat naïvely, 'If we prove this point, we shall find less difficulty with the other passages of St. Paul.' The general method used to establish this sweeping assertion is to allege such passages as these—'But they have not all obeyed the Gospel, for Esaias saith, Lord, who hath believed our report.' On which Bishop Bull thus comments, 'Who does not here perceive that to "believe" and to "obey" the Gospel, signify the same thing with St. Paul ?' It is a strange mode of reasoning to confuse the *result*, *obedience*, with the *ground* of it, which is *faith*. Such a theology cannot be safe to follow.

This meaning of the word faith having been further pressed in the fifth chapter, Bishop Bull proceeds in the sixth chapter to St. Paul's use of the word *works*.

The sixth chapter begins thus: 'There is another difficulty in the word *works* as used by St. Paul, and this is indeed the consequence of what we have already proved; namely, that Faith in St. Paul's Epistles means all the works of Christian piety. This being allowed, it is certain that the works which St. Paul excludes from justification are not all kinds of works, but of a certain description only. Distinctly to explain of what kind these are is a matter of no little labour, and we have now arrived at the chief difficulty of our work.' This 'difficulty' is solved by pronouncing the *works* excluded by St. Paul to be 'the works prescribed in the Mosaic law' in the case of a Jewish convert; and in the case of Gentile converts to be the works done by the light of natural conscience, and by human strength only.

A discussion of this view of *works* from various passages and in various lights occupies the greater part of the remainder of the work. The argument by which he seeks to evade what the Apostle says of boasting being excluded by the law of faith, though not by the law of works (Rom. iii. 27), is the same as that of the Romanists. 'Those good works which we perform, are not so much ours, as those of God within us. But no man can properly boast before God of that which is owing to God.' The student will discern the fallacy of this, and the contrast with Hooker's doctrine on the same subject (p. 105). At the same time Bishop Bull protests warmly against the Roman doctrine of the *merit* of good works, since 'the right which the good works of the just have to eternal life is founded only in the Gospel covenant and promise.'

The Eleventh Article is disposed of in this summary manner. 'Although other virtues are no less necessary to justification than faith, and faith in reality has no more effect in it than any other virtue; but yet of all the virtues faith is that one by which we embrace the Gospel promise, by which promise we are justified: therefore by a convenient phrase, our justification may be and is usually attributed to faith only.' If the solemn statements of our Articles may be passed over as 'convenient phrases,' any lengthened commentary on them would be superfluous. In this case we have the comment on this phrase furnished by the homily to which the Article itself refers us for further explanation of its meaning. 'Faith doth not shut out repentance, hope, love, dread, and the fear of God to be joined with faith in every man that is justified; but it shutteth them out from the office of justifying.'

Lastly, Bishop Bull cautions the reader to distinguish between the first and second justification. 'It must be understood that only the internal works of faith, repentance, hope, charity, &c., are absolutely necessary to the first justification; but the other external works, which appear in outward actions, or in the exercise of the above-named virtues, are only the signs and fruits of internal piety, being subsequent to justification, and to be performed provided opportunity be given.'

Nelson, in his 'Life of Bishop Bull,' says of the controversy raised by this publication, that 'in a very few years the strife ceased, forasmuch as the victory was so complete, as none were found able to rally their forces in this cause against our judicious harmoniser.' This is true, though it was by no means due entirely to Bishop Bull. The nonjurors and high churchmen of William's and Anne's days belonged to the Laudian and Sacramental School, to which this view of justification was exceedingly congenial. The other chief section of the clergy, comprising such men as Tillotson and Burnet, was called the Latitudinarian party. In their efforts for comprehensiveness they were only too much inclined to break down the barriers of doctrine. How far Burnet sympathised with such views as those of Bishop Bull may be judged from his definition of *faith*, when writing on the Eleventh Article. 'Faith, in the New Testament, stands generally for the complex of Christianity in opposition to the Law.'

Such doctrines easily led to the condition of semi-

Socinianism and apathy into which the Church of England lapsed under the first Georges. And when the great Reformation doctrine of justification by faith was again preached by the forerunners of the Evangelical revival in the last century, it was received by the mass of the so-called orthodox divines, as though some new and strange heresy were promulgated. A few concluding notes and cautions may be added.

1. Holy Scripture and our Church know nothing of any justification but one. Before this no works acceptable to God are done (Art. XIII.), and after it the Christian is fruitful in good works (Art. XII.). It is not possible, unless by arbitrary assertion, to distinguish the justification in the Eleventh Article from that in the Twelfth and Thirteenth. The Romanist distinction of a first and second justification being repudiated, many evasions of the Eleventh Article fall away at once.

2. Romanist divines and their followers in attacking the doctrine of justification by faith have always found it convenient to strip faith as far as possible of every moral attribute, and to reduce it as nearly as may be to a bare assent of the understanding and the will. They also omit what we consider the essence of the doctrine, that the faith which justifies, is not alone in the heart, but is joined with contrition and other graces, and is the direct gift of the Holy Spirit to the heart in which it abides.

We always distinguish it, therefore, from that faith which is the act of the human reason and will.

3. Protestant divines, who have not accepted this doctrine simply understood, enlarge the idea of faith so as to make it include the whole or a large part of Christianity, instead of perceiving that where faith in its true sense is, there the Holy Spirit dwells, and therewith all of Christianity must be associated. It may not be necessary for all minds to grasp the distinction. But there can be no clear theology, and therefore no clear and salutary teaching, unless the Christian minister discerns it plainly.

4. As a test of Bishop Bull's exegesis of the word *faith* as used by St. Paul, the test of substitution may be applied

Occasionally, no doubt, this word is used objectively of the thing believed, as all words of this class are (e.g. Gal. i. 23). But it is most commonly used subjectively, and it occurs (it must be remembered) sometimes in the form of the verb, sometimes in the form of the noun. We may give two instances which may be multiplied to any extent. St. Paul perceived that a certain cripple 'had *faith* to be healed' (Acts xiv. 9). Did he perceive that he had 'the complex of Christian graces,' or 'all the works of Christian piety'? Again he said to the jailor at Philippi, 'Believe on the Lord Jesus Christ, and thou shalt be saved' (Acts xvi. 31). Is it possible to substitute for the word believe any such complexity of periphrasis? or was it not a single spiritual act to which the man was called?

Again, with regard to the use of the word works in the Epistles to the Romans and Galatians; were the works of the ceremonial and strictly Mosaic law those which were repudiated as capable of justifying the sinner, or was it not rather the moral law, whether written in the conscience, or enjoined in the Mosaic law (Rom. iii. 10–18)? This subject should be carefully studied with a very close examination of those epistles, ' calling no man master ' in this vital matter.

5. He who would form a scriptural system of doctrine, on which he might feel that he could rely, should frame for himself a tabulated system of passages with the help of a Greek concordance. An English one will not suffice, because our translators have not adhered to one rendering of the same word.

Such a table would include these words: $\delta i \kappa a \iota o \varsigma,$ $\delta i \kappa a i \acute{o} \omega,$ $\delta i \kappa a i \omega \sigma \iota \varsigma,$ $\delta i \kappa a i o \sigma \acute{v} \nu \eta,$ $\delta i \kappa a i \omega \mu a,$ $\pi i \sigma \tau \iota \varsigma,$ $\pi i \sigma \tau \epsilon \acute{v} \omega,$ $\pi \epsilon \pi o i \theta \eta \sigma \iota \varsigma,$ $\lambda o \gamma i \zeta o \mu a \iota.$

It need scarcely be noted how very rarely this is done; in other words, how rarely our divines make a thorough examination of Scripture for themselves.

6. It may be useful to bring together some of the principal methods of interpreting St. James ii. 24.

(1.) Bishop Jewel and others held that St. James refers to evidential justification; i.e. to justification, as it may be manifested to man, which cannot be without works (Matt. vii. 16), inasmuch as faith is invisible; while St. Paul speaks of justification before God.

(2.) Hooker, as we have seen, holds that St. James means the righteousness of sanctification. But it may be asked if the New Testament anywhere else uses the word justify in this sense.

(3.) Bishop Bull and others take St. James absolutely, and stretch St. Paul's use of the word faith so as to include works.

(4.) Many hold that St. James is arguing with false professors on their own grounds; and, taking up their own word *faith* in their sense of it, shows that on their meagre notion of faith, justification by faith only would not convey the meaning of Scripture.

ARTICLE XII.

Of Good Works.

Albeit that Good Works, which are the fruits of Faith, and follow after Justification, cannot put away our sins, and endure the severity of God's Judgment: yet are they pleasing and acceptable to God in Christ, and do spring out necessarily of a true and lively Faith; insomuch that by them a lively faith may be as evidently known as a tree discerned by the fruit.

De bonis operibus.

Bona opera, quæ sunt fructus fidei, et justificatos sequuntur, quanquam peccata nostra expiare, et divini judicii severitatem ferre non possunt; Deo tamen grata sunt, et accepta in Christo, atque ex vera et viva fide necessario profluunt, ut plane ex illis, æque fides viva cognosci possit, atque arbor ex fructu judicari.

Notes on the Text of Article XII.

The following phrases may be noticed on comparing the Latin with the English: '*justificatos sequuntur*' stands for ' follow after justification.' ' *Expiare peccata* ' presents a more definite idea than the English ' put away sins.' ' *Viva* ' is rendered ' lively,' as in 1 Pet. i. 3. It will be observed that in the Eleventh Article *Faith* is used without any qualifying epithet, but there can be no reasonable doubt of the identity of the *Faith* spoken of in both these Articles, and, therefore, this epithet *lively* must be understood as equally qualifying the word Faith in both.

This Article was added in 1562, not having been one of the Forty-two Articles of 1552. It is said by Archdeacon Hardwick[1] to have been adapted from the Wurtemberg Con-

---

[1] ' History of the Articles,' p. 379.

fession, but the resemblance is rather slight, and the language of Augustine has been probably the common basis. The Elizabethan divines no doubt had in view the Antinomian Anabaptists as well as the Romanists in the statements of this Article.

THE MAIN DIVISIONS OF ARTICLE XII.

1. The imperfection before God of the good works of men faithful and justified.

2. The nature and ground of the regard God has to such works.

3. The relation of good works to faith.

The Scripture proof may conveniently and clearly be grouped round these principal divisions.

OBSERVATIONS ON ARTICLE XII.

The Pelagian and Semi-Pelagian controversies of necessity involved the question of the value of the good works of the Christian. We do not recur to the history of those controversies. The teaching of the scholastic divines on the merit of good works is deferred until we come to the Thirteenth Article. We pass on to the Council of Trent (Session VI. canon 32), 'Whosoever shall say that the good works of a justified man are in such a sense the gifts of God that they are not good merits of the justified man himself, or that a justified man by good works which are done by him through the grace of God, and the merits of Jesus Christ, of whom he is a living member, does not truly merit increase of grace, eternal life, and the actual attainment of eternal life if he die in grace, together with increase of glory, let him be anathema.'

It will scarcely be necessary to produce authorities in addition to those already brought forward under the Eleventh Article. The passages from the Homily, from Hooker, and from Bull sufficiently cover the ground of this Article also. The student who desires to read more on the Roman opinions of merit in the good works of the justified will find ample information in that treasure-house of learning, 'Field Of the Church.' [1]

This Article sets the seal on the preceding, inasmuch as good works are said to follow justification, and cannot therefore concur to obtaining it. Bishop Bull, and others of his school, evade this difficulty by their doctrine of the first and second justification. He says that eleven works of repentance are necessary with faith to the first justification, and that to the second justification, many more works are necessary and that of these this Article speaks.

Bishop O'Brien well observes: [2] 'What foundation does this Article or any other Article supply for this distinction of a first and second justification? . . . If there be another justification the Articles do not speak of it, or even glance at it. They tell us, indeed, of a justification before which no good works are done (Art. XIII.), and after which all good works are done (XII.). But they do not intimate to us, in any way, that this is but inchoate, and that there is another justification to the obtaining of which all these good works are necessary.'

It may be further noted that as good works are said in this Article to be the fruits of faith, they are distinguished from faith as the fruit is distinguished from the tree. Does not this cut up by the roots the attempt to explain faith in Art. XI. as including works? Or can *faith* in Art. XI. be taken in one sense as faith together with works, and in Art. XII. in another sense as distinguished from the works which it produces?

[1] Book iii. Appendix, chap. xii.
[2] 'Nature and Effects of Faith,' p. 422.

ARTICLE XIII.

Of Works before Justifica-
tion.

Works done before the
grace of Christ, and the Inspiration of his Spirit, are not
pleasant to God, forasmuch as
they spring not of faith in
Jesus Christ, neither do they
make men meet to receive
grace, or (as the School-
authors say) deserve grace of
congruity: yea rather, for
that they are not done as God
hath willed and commanded
them to be done, we doubt not
but they have the nature of
sin.

De operibus ante justifi-
cationem.

Opera quæ fiunt ante gra-
tiam Christi, et spiritus ejus
afflatum, cum ex fide Jesu
Christi non prodeant, minime
Deo grata sunt, neque gratiam
(ut multi vocant) de congruo
merentur. Immo cum non
sunt facta ut Deus illa fieri
voluit et præcepit, peccati
rationem habere non dubita-
mus.

Notes on the Text of Article XIII.

The Latin word here used for inspiration is '*afflatus.*'
Where the English says 'School-authors,' the Latin, less
precisely, has '*multi.*' The technical phrase '*de congruo*'
answers to the English 'of congruity.' 'The nature of sin'
is in this Article, as in the ninth, '*peccati rationem.*'

The Schoolmen asserted two modes of meriting reward, '*de
congruo,*' and '*de condigno.*' Man may merit at the hands of
God in the former mode before grace has been received, in the
latter mode after the reception of grace. Dr. Hey [1] gives this
illustration to explain the distinction: 'A servant deserves

---

[1] 'Lectures on the Articles,' xiii. 14.

his wages ' *ex condigno* ; ' he may deserve support in sickness or old age, ' *ex congruo*.' Sometimes, instead of ' *ex congruo*,' the phrase ' *ex proportione* ' is used.'

Beveridge [1] quotes from De Soto: 'A work is *congruous*, to which a reward is not due from justice, but from a certain fitness;' and from Romæus: ' That is said to be merit " *de condigno*," to which a reward must be rendered according to the requirement of justice, so that between the merit and the reward equality of quantity holds, according to the principles of mutual justice. But one is said to deserve " *de congruo*," when between the merit and the reward there is a parity not of quantity but of proportion.' In plain English, the merit of condignity is such that there is an absolute failure of justice if it receive not recompense. This agrees with the doctrine of the Council of Trent noticed in Article XII. on works after justification, and will explain our allusion there to the scholastic doctrine of merit. And though the principle of *congruity* claims less at the hands of strict justice, yet it amounts to an equal certainty, inasmuch as the Most High must be conceived as always and without fail doing that which is congrous and proportional to His perfection and the nature of things to do.

Thus if man can ensure the bestowal of grace on the principle of *congruity* when still in his natural condition ; and can claim it, after grace received, on the principle of *condignity*, or strict right and justice, we are brought round by a circuitous path, and in spite of many words about grace, to much the same result as that which follows from the doctrines of Pelagius, namely that man by working in a particular manner ensures his own salvation.

This is one of the original Articles of 1552. No source is suggested for its expressions.

OBSERVATIONS ON ARTICLE XIII.

The Fathers were naturally led to discuss the nature of heathen virtues, but this question was scarcely within the view

---

[1] Art. xiii. note.

of the writers of the Article, although, no doubt, it comes within its terms. What has been already said of the doctrine of congruity will explain what the Reformers really had in view in this Article.

The Council of Trent avoided the terms *condignity* and *congruity*, to which some of its divines were much opposed; but its decisions seem to adopt both principles. The following canon bears most directly on the subject before us: 'Whosoever shall say that all the works which are done before justification, on whatsoever account they may be done, are truly sins, and deserve the hatred of God, or that the more vehemently a man tries to dispose himself for grace, the more grievously he sins, let him be anathema.'[1] To which Calvin replied, after quoting other passages: 'Let them anathematize the Apostle, who declares that without faith it is impossible to please God (Heb. xi. 6). Let them anathematize Christ and Paul, who declare that all unbelievers are dead, and are raised from death by the Gospel (John v. 24, Eph. ii. 1).'

It is obvious that in this and other Decrees and Canons the Council of Trent chose to state the condemned doctrine in the most offensive terms, and in words which (however susceptible of right interpretation) would not be deliberately adopted in the formal utterance of accredited divines. The doctrine of the present Article presents considerable difficulties to every mind which is not fully enlightened as to the true nature and abode of sin. There are few subjects, consequently, with respect to which a delicate discrimination and careful handling are more necessary. While the truth should be firmly held, broad assertions readily misunderstood should be sedulously avoided. The following quotation from Bishop Beveridge on this Article is clear in its distinctions, and carefully discriminative in its language: 'Though we have power to do such things as in themselves are pleasing to God, yet we have not power so to do those things that our doing them should be pleasing to Him. The matter of the actions we do may be accepted, but our manner of doing them is still rejected. Because though we do the thing that God

[1] Session VI. Canon 7.

commands of ourselves, yet we can never do it in the way that God commands.'

The truth is that the world, for the most part, never looks beyond the outer act. Some actions are sinful, some are virtuous. It can say little more. But the theologian cannot stop there. He knows that the real goodness of an action lies in the relation of the act to the mind which inspired it. One man from love, another from ostentation, another from covetous ambition, may perform some splendid act of public benefit. Outwardly, the transaction is identical in all these cases. The moral value of the act to the individual himself varies in each case from high virtue to absolute turpitude.

It is just this principle which is applied according to the rules of Scripture morality in the Article before us. That spiritual condition which can alone deliver a human being from the state of sin and condemnation being absent, whether we view it on the side of justification or sanctification, there must be the taint of sin unremoved in all the actions. We do not herein confuse virtue with vice. We do not lose sight of the truth that there are many degrees in sin and in consequent responsibility (Luke xii. 47, 48). But as in the Ninth Article we confessed that the *concupiscentia* remaining in the regenerate had, according to the Scripture standard, 'the nature of sin;' so now we are sadly obliged to own that the best actions of the unregenerated have 'the nature of sin' likewise. Not that the action itself loses its right description as a virtue, but that in its origin and outcoming from the heart, in its relation to the spiritual nature of the doer of it, it could not fail to partake of the sinfulness which was in him.

The scriptural treatment and proof of this Article may be most soundly constructed upon the above line of argument.

ARTICLE XIV.

Of Works of Supererogation.

Voluntary Works besides, over and above God's commandments, which they call Works of Supererogation, cannot be taught without arrogancy and impiety. For by them men do declare, that they do not only render unto God as much as they are bound to do, but that they do more for his sake, than of bounden duty is required; whereas Christ saith plainly, When ye have done all that are commanded to you, say, We be unprofitable servants.

De operibus supererogationis.

Opera quæ supererogationis appellant, non possunt sine arrogantia et impietate prædicari. Nam illis declarant homines, non tantum se Deo reddere, quæ tenentur, sed plus in ejus gratiam facere, quam deberent, cum aperte Christus dicat; Cum feceritis omnia quæcunque præcepta sunt vobis, dicite, Servi inutiles sumus.

Notes on the Text of Article XIV.

The derivation and use of the word supererogation may be thus traced: *Rogare* was the technical word used for proposing a law to the Roman people assembled in Comitia (Anglicè *to bring in a bill*). Erogare was similarly applied if the decree was one for paying money out of the treasury. Hence Supererogare easily came to mean to pay over and above the amount granted.

The word is used in the Vulgate and also in the Rhemish version in Luke x. 35, " quodcunque supererogaveris "—whatever thou shalt supererogate, Greek ' προσδαπανήσῃς.' The comment of the Rhemish Testament is this: ' It is manifest there are such works.' It ought rather to be said 'It is manifest there is such a word.' Its meaning is another question.

The history of the text of the Article presents no point of interest. It was retained from the Articles of 1552 with the slight change of the word 'impiety' instead of 'iniquity.'

OBSERVATIONS ON ARTICLE XIV.

The rise of the doctrine of supererogation is assigned by Mosheim to the thirteenth century. By this may no doubt be understood, not that there are no traces of the name and idea before that time, but that it then assumed form and consistency. Gieseler[1] thus writes: 'The Aristotelian divines of the 13th century readily entered on the task of vindicating dogmatically this most monstrous of all papal pretensions. Alexander of Hales and Albertus Magnus invented the doctrine of the *Thesaurus supererogationis perfectorum*, out of which, by virtue of the power of the keys, not only the temporal penalties of the living for sin, but agreeably to the extension of the power of the keys over the dead long ere now established, the penalties also of men suffering in purgatory were discharged. Thomas Aquinas completed this theory.' Gieseler adds this extract in a note; it will illustrate the teaching which first fashioned into a system the Roman dogmas: 'Indulgences hold good both ecclesiastically and in respect of the judgment of God, for the remission of the residuum of punishment after contrition and absolution and confession. The reason why they hold good is the unity of the mystical body in which many have supererogated in works of penitence beyond the measure of their debts, and have patiently endured many unjust tribulations, by which a multitude of punishments could have been discharged, had they been owing. Of whose merits so great is the abundance, that they exceed the punishment now due to the living, and especially by reason of the merit of Christ. . . But it has been said above that one man can satisfy for another. But the saints, in whom a

---

[1] 'Eccl. Hist.' 3rd Period, Div. III. c. 6, § 84.

superabundance of works of satisfaction is found, wrought not works of this kind definitely for him who needs remission (otherwise he would obtain remission without an indulgence), but in common for the whole Church . . . . and so the aforesaid merits are the common property of the whole Church. But that which is the common property of a number is distributed to individuals of that number, at the will of him who presides over it.'[1]

Such was the teaching which formed the Tridentine divines. The student will understand with what a revulsion of disgust the Reformers shrank back from these scholastic theologians; and will comprehend the feeling which prompted the epithets which they often applied to them.

The Council of Trent handled this subject very briefly. The subject of Indulgences was treated in the final session, which was exceedingly hurried. We have therefore only this general decree on indulgences (Session XXV.): 'Since the power of conferring indulgences has been granted by Christ to the Church, and since the Church from the earliest times has used a power of this kind, divinely given, this holy Council teaches and enjoins, &c.' (The remainder of the decree forbids the abuses of the improper vending of indulgences.) We have not, therefore, a decree of the Council of Trent directly on the subject of supererogation.

But Leo X. wrote thus: 'The Roman Pontiff may for reasonable causes, by his apostolical authority grant indulgences out of the superabundant merits of Christ and the saints to the faithful who are united to Christ by charity, as well for the living as the dead.'

Bellarmine[2] defines this matter more precisely. 'There is an infinite treasure of the satisfaction purchased by the passion of Christ extant in the Church . . . The price of Christ's blood hath not been applied to all, the most part of men being subject to condemnation; there remaineth then a great deal of the price of Christ's death to be applied'—and the bull of

---

[1] Thomas Aquinas, ' Comm. in Sent.' lib. iv.
[2] Willett, vol. ix. pp. 243–245.

Clement VI. says 'to the heap of which treasure the merits of the blessed mother of God and of all the saints add support.'

To one knowing the New Testament it is sufficient refutation to state the doctrine thus fully and broadly. But we add the following observations:

1. If Christ's merits are infinite, how can finite additions increase them? Infinity plus worlds is still only infinity.

2. The root of the error lies in the fundamental heresies noted under the previous Articles, relating to the nature of original sin; salvation by grace; the state of the justified; the works of the justified, &c.

3. The full antidote is to be found in the relation of the Christian to God. Reconciled in Christ he is a son, not a servant. His good works are the outflowing of filial affection, not works of a servant wrought for wages. So far as they are otherwise they are not *in him* good works at all.

4. The Twelfth Article has taught us that the good works of the justified cannot endure the severity of God's judgment. They can still less supply the deficiencies of other men, even if God had anywhere promised to accept such a substitution.

5. They who scoff at the imputation of Christ's righteousness as an unreal mockery of goodness have accepted the most unreal mockery of all, namely the merits of one sinner applied to the redemption of another sinner, neither being in the least cognisant of the transaction (see Aquinas above).

ARTICLE XV.

Of Christ alone without Sin.

Christ in the truth of our nature was made like unto us in all things (sin only except), from which he was clearly void, both in his flesh, and in his spirit. He came to be the Lamb without spot, who, by the sacrifice of himself once made, should take away the sins of the world, and sin (as St. *John* saith), was not in him. But all we the rest, (although baptized, and born again in Christ), yet offend in many things; and if we say we have no sin, we deceive ourselves, and the truth is not in us.

De Christo, qui solus est sine peccato.

Christus in nostræ naturæ veritate, per omnia similis factus est nobis, excepto peccato, a quo prorsus erat immunis, tum in carne, tum in spiritu. Venit ut agnus, absque macula, qui mundi peccata per immolationem sui semel factam tolleret, et peccatum (ut inquit Johannes) in eo non erat: sed nos reliqui etiam baptizati, et in Christo regenerati, in multis tamen offendimus omnes. Et si dixerimus, quia peccatum non habemus, nos ipsos seducimus, et veritas in nobis non est.

Notes on the Text of Article XV.

The Latin title is slightly more definite than the English, ' *qui solus est sine peccato.*' ' Clearly void' is in the Latin ' *prorsus immunis.*' ' Clearly ' must therefore be understood not in the sense of *manifestly*, but *so as to be clear*, ' entirely void.'

There are only one or two very slight verbal differences between this Article and the fourteenth of 1552. The history of the text presents no feature of special interest.

The Chief Divisions of Article XV.

1. That Christ was '*very man*' has been already demonstrated under Article II.   This is reasserted, with the addition of the absolute sinlessness of our Lord both in flesh and spirit.

2. This sinlessness made Him the perfect and sufficient sacrifice.

3. No other human being is free from sin.

The proofs from Scripture may be directed to establish these several propositions.

Observations on Article XV.

We have noticed already (p. 63) the presumption of some of the Anabaptists, who asserted that they had attained a sinless condition.   This will further come under notice in the next Article.   Neither need we comment further on the Pelagian notion of the possibility of a man leading a perfectly holy life. The history of the Article will mainly centre in the dogma of the immaculate conception of the Virgin Mary.   In Field's learned book, ' Of the Church,' [1] there will be found a full exposition of the novelty of this opinion.   It was first definitely discussed by the schoolmen.   About A.D. 1300, Duns Scotus made it part of his system, and thenceforward the Scotists and Franciscans upheld it.   On the other hand, the Thomists and Dominicans, following Thomas Aquinas, opposed it.

Early in the sixteenth century, the imposture practised by some Dominicans at Berne on the young monk Jetzer made this contest notorious.[2]   In the age of the Reformation the Roman Church was about equally divided on the subject. Cardinal Cajetan, well known in the history of Luther, presented a treatise to Leo X., controverting the doctrine as novel and untrue.   From this treatise, Field (*ut supra*) gives the following extract:

' St. Augustine, writing upon the thirty-fourth Psalm, saith

---

[1] Append. III. 6.   [2] See D'Aubigné, ' Hist. of Ref.' viii. 2.

that " Adam died for sin ; that Mary who came out of the
loins of Adam died for sin; but that the flesh of the Lord,
which He took of the Virgin Mary, died to take away sin."
And in his second book, " De Baptismo Parvulorum," " He
only, who ceasing not to be God became man, never had sin,
neither did He take the flesh of sin, or sinful flesh, though
He took the flesh of His mother that was sinful." And in his
tenth book, " De Genesi ad literam," he saith : " Though the
body of Christ were taken of the flesh of a woman that was
conceived out of the propagation of sinful flesh, yet because
He was not so conceived of her as she was conceived, therefore
it was not sinful flesh, but the similitude of sinful flesh." And
St. Ambrose, upon those words, *Blessed are the undefiled*,
hath these words : " The Lord Jesus came ; and that flesh
that was subject to sin in His mother performed the warfare
of virtue." And St. Chrysostom, upon Matthew, saith :
" Though Christ was no sinner, yet He took the nature of
man, of a woman that was a sinner." And Eusebius Emis-
senus (about 350), in his second sermon upon the Nativity,
hath these words : " There is none free from the tie and bond
of original sin, no, not the mother of the Redeemer."
St. Remigius (about 850) saith : " The blessed Virgin Mary
was made clean from all stain of sin, that the man Christ
Jesus might be conceived of her without sin." ' St. Maximus,
St. Bede, St. Bernard, and other Romish saints, are in like
manner quoted.

Scotus himself propounded the doctrine of the immaculate
conception cautiously, whilst Thomas Aquinas, following
Lombard and the earlier doctors of the Church, absolutely
denied it.

At the Council of Trent the two conflicting doctrines on the
immaculate conception came into open collision.

The matter was referred to the Pope, who suggested a
middle course. There was therefore the following rider attached to the first decree of the fifth Session :—

' This Holy Council, however, declares that it is not their
intention to comprehend in this decree, where it treats of
original sin, the blessed and immaculate Virgin Mary, the

mother of God, but that the constitutions of Pope Sixtus IV., of happy memory, are to be observed, under the penalties contained in these constitutions, which the Council renews.'

These constitutions also were neutral. In 1476 Sixtus IV. forbad the Franciscans to be accused of heresy on this point. But though he favoured the Franciscans, he did not pronounce any decision on the doctrine.

Since the era of the Reformation, mainly perhaps through the dominant influence of the Jesuits, the belief in the immaculate conception has more and more widely prevailed in the Roman Church. Finally (December 9, 1854), Pius IX. issued his bull, declaring the belief in that doctrine to be a matter of faith, almost without opposition.

The notion of the sinlessness of the Virgin Mary will be found in an earlier form than that which has ultimately prevailed in the Roman Church. Many who held that she was conceived in sin, thought that she was either sanctified *in* the womb, or at least *from* her birth, so as to be without sin. These ideas will be found in some of the quotations in the extract given above from Cajetan.   Augustine thought it more reverential to abstain from discussing the question.   Origen and Chrysostom, commenting on her history in the Gospels, distinctly attribute sin to her. For fuller details on this subject the student is referred to Field (*ut supra*).

ARTICLE XVI.

Of Sin after Baptism.

Not every deadly sin willingly committed after Baptism is sin against the Holy Ghost, and unpardonable. Wherefore the grant of repentance is not to be denied to such as fall into sin after Baptism. After we have received the Holy Ghost, we may depart from grace given and fall into sin, and by the grace of God we may arise again, and amend our lives. And therefore they are to be condemned which say, they can no more sin as long as they live here, or deny the place of forgiveness to such as truly repent.

De peccato post Baptismum.

Non omne peccatum mortale post Baptismum voluntarie perpetratum, est peccatum in Spiritum Sanctum, et irremissibile. Proinde lapsis a Baptismo in peccata, locus pœnitentiæ non est negandus. Post acceptum Spiritum Sanctum possumus a gratia data recedere atque peccare, denuoque per gratiam Dei resurgere ac resipiscere; ideoque illi damnandi sunt, qui se, quamdiu hic vivant, amplius non posse peccare affirmant, aut vere resipiscentibus veniæ locum denegant.

NOTES ON THE TEXT OF ARTICLE XVI.

The Latin text presents no important matter for comment as compared with the English, unless perhaps the phrase '*locus pœnitentiæ*' for 'grant of repentance.'

The expression '*peccatum mortale*,' or 'deadly sin,' may require a few words, inasmuch as our Church has been censured for using it, both here and in the Litany, as seeming to favour the Roman distinction of mortal and venial sin, whereas all sin is deadly or deserving of death.

But we observe that in fact our Church has avoided any such classification, and has nowhere assigned any marks or gradations by which sins might be distinguished into classes.

It is difficult to produce a clear and authoritative Roman definition of the distinction in question. The Council of Trent[1] decrees that all mortal sins must be confessed, but that ' venial sins, by which we are not excluded from the grace of God, may be concealed without fault, and expiated by many other remedies.' For a more exact account we must refer to the casuistical writers of the Roman Church. And here we find that practically the casuists of the Jesuit school have for the most part prevailed in modern Romanism. This brings us to such definitions as those of Bellarmine: ' Mortal sins are those which cast men out of God's favour, and deserve eternal damnation; venial sins do somewhat displease God, yet deserve not eternal death, but are pardonable of their own nature.' Further, venial sins are described as being involuntary and sudden passions—or voluntary sins of a light amount, such as stealing small coins, &c.

The essence of sin consists in its relation to the spiritual condition of the sinner. The very same act committed by two different individuals entails widely different measures of guilt. Any classification, therefore, such as those of Jesuit casuists, which only or chiefly takes account of the measure or even nature of the outward act, must be fundamentally unsound and untrue.

All sin is deserving of death; nevertheless, some sins committed in some states of mind have a peculiar heinousness as being more directly against grace. Sins of presumption, sins against light, are manifestly most deeply injurious to the soul, and may be so even when they injure our neighbour little or scarcely at all: Without defining these more exactly, our Church here distinguishes them by the epithet ' deadly ' from the ordinary sins of infirmity, which were spoken of more particularly in the last Article.

The present wording of the Article is very slightly varied from the Fifteenth Article of 1552. Archdeacon Hardwicke[2] says that it is borrowed chiefly from the Augsburgh Confession. Bishop Browne also adopts this opinion. But a

---

[1] Session XIV. c. 5.　　　[2] ' Hist. of Articles,' chap. v.

close comparison of this Article with the twelfth of the Confession of Augsburgh will hardly bear this out. There is
scarcely any verbal coincidence between the two.

THE CHIEF DIVISIONS OF ARTICLE XVI.

1. Even heinous sin after baptism is not necessarily unpardonable.

2. The nature of the sin against the Holy Ghost.

3. The liability of the regenerate to fall from grace, and
the possibility of their restoration.

4. The condemnation of two classes of opponents.

A scriptural exposition and proof of the Article may follow
this arrangement.

THE ROMAN DOCTRINE ON SIN AFTER BAPTISM.

The Fourteenth Session of the Council of Trent dealt with
Penance, and therefore with the present subject. The following extract from the second chapter of the decree of that
session may suffice for the purpose of the present Article:
'If the baptized afterwards defile themselves by any trans-
gression, it is not the will of Christ that they should be cleansed
by a repetition of baptism, which is on no account lawful in
the Catholic Church, but they should be placed as offenders
before the tribunal of penance, that they may be absolved by
the sentence of the priests, not once only, but as often as they
penitently flee thereto, confessing their sins.'

OBSERVATIONS ON ARTICLE XVI.

Early writers expressed themselves with various degrees of
severity on the subject of sin after baptism. The practice of
the Church in the second and third centuries exacted prolonged periods of penitence (the 'godly discipline' of our
commination service) before flagrant transgressors, and more
especially apostates, were restored to Communion. Yet the
Church Catholic always held the duty of restoring peni-
tents, and it was reserved for the sects of the Montanists
in the second century, or the Novatians in the third,

and their successors, to maintain the harsher practice in this matter.

The present Article would assure us that these rigid ideas were revived at the time of the Reformation. And we find that it was so. That this was one of the many forms of Anabaptist excess we learn from Calvin :[1] 'Our age also has some of the Anabaptists not very unlike the Novatians. . . . For they pretend that the people of God are regenerated in baptism into a pure and angelical life. . . . But if any man fail after baptism they leave nothing to him but the inexorable judgment of God.' Bishop Hooper[2] speaks in similar terms : 'A man, they say, who is thus regenerate, cannot sin. They add that all hope of pardon is taken away from those who, after having received the Holy Ghost, fall into sin.' It is of some importance thus distinctly to identify the contemporary errors which were before the writers of this Article. In this point of view the quotation from Calvin is the more important, especially as a learned writer of the present day presses the supposed Lutheran origin of the Article to do dogmatic duty in his interpretation of it. In this Article neither Luther nor Calvin speaks individually. It is the earnest protest of the Church against the fanatical sectaries who narrowed the pale of salvation. It is the voice equally of Luther, of Calvin, of the Church of England; all in this matter at one.

Bishop Browne, in treating on this Article, discusses at length the doctrine of final perseverance of the elect, which he thinks it was intended to controvert. Other writers, however, though of different theological schools, do not seem to notice it under this Article, to which indeed it can scarcely belong. The most extreme Calvinists would admit that the truly regenerate may and do fall into sin—but (they would add) not finally.

They would not, therefore, recognise the doctrine of final perseverance as being even touched upon here. And it is certain that some of those who had much to do with framing the Articles held that doctrine. It is, therefore, omitted here, as not coming within the scope of this Article.

[1] Institutes, IV. i. 23.   [2] Original Letters, Parker Soc. p. 65.

The Sin against the Holy Ghost.

The Article now under consideration was followed in the
Articles of 1552 by another, there ranking as the sixteenth,
which is here subjoined :—

'Blasphemy against the Holy Ghost.

'Blasphemy against the Holy Ghost is, when a man of
malice and stubbornness of mind doth rail upon the truth of
God's word manifestly perceived, and being enemy thereunto,
persecuteth the same. And because such be guilty of God's
curse, they entangle themselves with a most grievous and
heinous crime, whereupon this kind of sin is called and
affirmed of the Lord unpardonable.'

It was, probably, a wise exercise of discretion in Elizabeth's
divines to strike out this Article, and to abstain from an
attempt to define authoritatively the sin against the Holy
Ghost. At the same time we may note that the Anabaptist
extravagances occupy much less space in the thirty-nine than.
they did in the forty-two Articles. Those sects had declined
in the intervening ten years, or it had become manifest that
their adherents were of less consequence than had been supposed. And as the Article quoted above was, doubtless, intended to meet the case of consciences disturbed by the
Anabaptist denial of '*a place of repentance*' noted in the
foregoing Article, the partial subsidence of the error allowed
the Elizabethan divines to determine on its omission.

The doctrine of the Sin against the Holy Ghost has been
the subject of many anxieties and much reasoning. Bishop
Burnet at once dismisses its present possibility by limiting it
to the original occasion recorded in the Gospels. Bishop
Beveridge [1] thus deals with it : 'It shall therefore only never
be pardoned by God, because never repented of by us. For
if it could be repented of by us it could not but be pardoned
by God, the promise of pardon to repentance running in
general terms, that if a man do confess his sins to God, God
will pardon his sins to him.'

[1] Article XVI.

This seems the only treatment of the subject in harmony with the whole of Scripture. When we have marshalled and considered the grand array of Gospel promises, and asked ourselves what it is which excludes from a share in them, the answer cannot well be any other than this. It must be a spiritual state incompatible with the conditions of those promises. In other words, it must be a finally impenitent state, since the promises to repentance are so full and free. And since the Holy Ghost is the source of all true spiritual life and feeling, we may well understand why such a desperate condition is described as the result of the sin against the Holy Ghost.

ARTICLE XVII.

Of Predestination and Election.

Predestination to Life is the everlasting purpose of God, whereby (before the foundations of the world were laid) he hath constantly decreed by his counsel secret to us, to deliver from curse and damnation those whom he hath chosen in Christ out of mankind, and to bring them by Christ to everlasting salvation, as vessels made to honour. Wherefore, they which be endued with so excellent a benefit of God be called according to God's purpose by his Spirit working in due season: they through Grace obey the calling: they be justified freely: they be made sons of God by adoption: they be made like the image of his only begotten Son Jesus Christ: they walk religiously in good works, and at length, by God's mercy, they attain to everlasting felicity.

As the godly consideration of Predestination, and our Election in Christ, is full of sweet, pleasant, and unspeak-

De prædestinatione et electione.

Prædestinatio ad vitam, est æternum Dei propositum, quo ante jacta mundi fundamenta, suo consilio, nobis quidem occulto, constanter decrevit, eos quos in Christo elegit ex hominum genere, a maledicto et exitio liberare, atque (ut vasa in honorem efficta) per Christum, ad æternam salutem adducere. Unde qui tam præclaro Dei beneficio sunt donati, illi spiritu ejus, opportuno tempere operante, secundum propositum ejus vocantur, vocationi per gratiam parent, justificantur gratis, adoptantur in filios Dei, unigeniti ejus Jesu Christi imagini efficiuntur conformes, in bonis operibus sancte ambulant, et demum ex Dei misericordia pertingunt ad sempiternam felicitatem.

Quemadmodum prædestinationis et electionis nostræ in Christo pia consideratio, dulcis, suavis, et ineffabilis consolationis plena est vere piis, et his qui sentiunt in se vim spiritus Christi, facta

able comfort to godly persons, and such as feel in themselves the working of the Spirit of Christ, mortifying the works of the flesh, and their earthly members, and drawing up their mind to high and heavenly things, as well because it doth greatly establish and confirm their faith of eternal salvation to be enjoyed through Christ, as because it doth fervently kindle their love towards God: so, for curious and carnal persons, lacking the Spirit of Christ, to have continually before their eyes the sentence of God's Predestination, is a most dangerous downfall, whereby the Devil doth thrust them either into desperation, or into wretchlessness of most unclean living, no less perilous than desperation.

Furthermore, we must receive God's promises in such wise, as they be generally set forth to us in holy Scripture: and, in our doings, that Will of God is to be followed, which we have expressly declared unto us in the Word of God.

carnis, et membra, quæ adhuc sunt super terram, mortificantem, animumque ad cœlestia et superna rapientem ; tum quia fidem nostram de æterna salute consequenda per Christum plurimum stabilit atque confirmat, tum quia amorem nostrum in Deum vehementer accendit : ita hominibus curiosis, carnalibus, et spiritu Christi destitutis, ob oculos perpetuo versari prædestinationis Dei sententiam, perniciosissimum est præcipitium, unde illos diabolus protrudit, vel in desperationem, vel in æque perniciosam impurissimæ vitæ securitatem ; deinde promissiones divinas sic amplecti oportet, ut nobis in sacris literis generaliter propositæ sunt, et Dei voluntas in nostris actionibus ea sequenda est, quam in verbo Dei habemus, diserte revelatam.

Notes on the Text of Article XVII.

1. The Latin and English versions of this Article correspond very closely.

2. ' *Wretchlessness* ' signifies *carelessness*, the Latin equivalent being *securitas*. It is an antiquated form of the word *recklessness*, the older spelling of which was *reche* or *recche*. It is found in Hooker's second Sermon on Jude 17–21, § xxxiii:

' It is want of faith in ourselves, which makes us wretchless in building others.'

3. ' *We must receive God's promises in such wise as they be generally set forth to us in Holy Scripture ;* ' Latin, ' *ut nobis in sacris literis generaliter propositæ sunt.*' The word *generaliter* here requires special notice. It can hardly be necessary to observe that in a document of this character, written by men versed in technical phraseology, the popular or more modern usage of a word cannot be thought of; although probably in this case it would not lead us very wide of the mark. *Generalis* signifies that which relates to the *whole genus*. Hence in respect to the genus under consideration it is equivalent to *universal*; and is opposed to *singulus, specialis*. There are two modes of viewing the corresponding adverb *generaliter* in the clause under consideration. First we may take it in relation to the whole *genus* of promises. In this case we are admonished to take the whole of God's promises together, without selecting special ones here or there. It is the manner of Scripture to give a promise without condition in one place and with a condition in another (e.g. compare John xiv. 13 with 1 John v. 14). The Christian knows well how this manner conduces to a profitable searching of Holy Scripture and to a more accurate and balanced knowledge of the will of God.

Secondly, we may take the word *generaliter* in relation to the whole genus of those to whom the promises were given. There is some contemporary authority for so understanding it. The *Reformatio Legum Ecclesiasticarum* was prepared under the close superintendence of Archbishop Cranmer contemporaneously with the Articles. If Edward VI. had lived a year longer it would probably have become law. The language of the Articles is reproduced either literally or with some slight paraphrase in many of the corresponding portions. The twenty-second chapter, ' *de predestinatione* ' of the section ' *de hæresibus* ' is an expanded statement of the warning in the present Article against the peril of the doctrine of reprobation, and of the advantage of a pious reception of the doctrine of election. It frequently uses the very words of the Article, and it concludes with this admonition, 'Wherefore all should be admonished, that in their actions they should have no reference to decrees of predestination, but should adapt the whole course of their life to the laws of God ; since they see that promises to the good, and threatenings to the bad, are in Holy Scripture generally set forth (*generaliter propositas*). For in respect of the worship of God we ought to enter those ways, and dwell in that will of God, which we see manifested to us in Holy Scripture.' In this strictly parallel and contemporaneous passage, proceeding from the same authority, the word *generaliter* manifestly refers to the whole *genera* severally of the good and the bad.

Again in the controversies which led to the ill-omened attempt to lay the yoke of ultra-Calvinism on the Church of England in the days of Archbishop Whitgift, this expression of the Article was used in controversy. Dr. Baro, the Lady Margaret Professor of Divinity in Cambridge, dissented in some points from the extreme Calvinism then in vogue. The University authorities involved him in vexatious proceedings which ultimately led to his resignation.

Strype[1] gives an account of these troubles. In a discourse *ad clerum* (1595) Dr. Baro had maintained that 'the promises of God made to us, as they are generally propounded to us, were to be generally understood : as it is set down in the Seventeenth Article.'

The meaning of this is sufficiently plain from the doctrine of his opponents immediately subjoined—viz. that God did on purpose create the greatest part of men to destruction ; that Christ did not die for all ; and 'for the same cause they would not have the promises to be general, but extended them to those few persons alone who were created by God to be saved.' It appears, therefore, that the second is the more correct interpretation of this part of the Article, although the first is unquestionably true. And it seems also correct to identify this with the expression of Melancthon, ' and if other points about election are susceptible of subtle disputation, yet it is profitable to the godly to hold that *the promise is universal.*' But

[1] Whitgift, iv. 17, 18.

having admitted this, it will not do straightway to qualify it or recal it by limiting it to the baptized, or any other *class* in the human race, in order to deduce a theory of election. We must hold that the promises apply to the *genus*, and not to any *species* of the *genus* Man.

Finally, Bishop Beveridge well observes on this part of the Article:—' It is here very opportunely added, that we must receive God's promises as they be generally set forth in the Holy Scripture. Though they are but some that God hath elected, yet His promises are made to all: Come unto me all ye that are weary and heavy laden, and I will give you rest (Matt. xi. 28): and Whosoever believeth in Him shall not perish, but have everlasting life (John iii. 16). In the application of which and the like promises, we must not have respect to the eternity of God's purpose, but to the universality of His promise. His promises are made to all, and therefore are all bound to lay hold upon His promises ; and as we are to receive His promises, so are we also to obey His precepts as made to all. So that in all our doings the will of God is to be followed as we have it expressly declared to us in His word: not considering whether God elected me from eternity, but whether I obey Him in time: if I obey Him in time, I may certainly conclude that He elected me from eternity.'

In short, that God's promises are 'generally set forth,' is the very nerve and sinew of gospel preaching; as it is also the delight and confidence of the pious soul to think that God hath chosen it, rather than that it chose God.

4. There are only one or two unimportant verbal differences between the present Article and the corresponding form of 1552. It does not appear that the language of this Article was borrowed from any special theological source.

The Principal Divisions of Article XVII.

There are three principal divisions of this Article, corresponding to the three paragraphs which it contains.

I. The definition of predestination to life, its origin in the secret purpose of God, its manifestation, working, and final issue in the elect. To a great extent, this paragraph is a compendium of Rom. viii.

II. The blessedness of this doctrine to those who, by God's grace, have grasped His promises. The extreme peril of the opposite doctrine of reprobation to the unconverted.

III. A caution against partial dealing with God's word, whether by selecting special passages to build up a compact system ; or by limiting the wide scope and comprehensiveness of God's offer of mercy through Christ.

OBSERVATIONS ON ARTICLE XVII.

The purport of our observations upon this Article will be not so much to advocate any particular system as to introduce the student to the subject generally, and to give him a fair acquaintance with the chief phases of those controversies about it which are now happily dormant.

Before we enter upon the history of the doctrine of this Article, it is exceedingly important to note that difficulties about predestination are not peculiar to Christianity ; do not, in point of fact, arise out of it, and are not escaped by disbelieving the Scripture. The Fate of the Greek mythology was superior to Zeus himself. The Stoics among Greek philosophers were rigid fatalists. Some account of the disputes of Greek philosophers on this subject may be found in Cicero, ' De Fato.'

According to Josephus,[1] the Pharisees held that ' all things were done by Fate,' yet with a reservation of the freedom of the will. It is well known that Mahomedans are strict fatalists. An interesting account of the Mahomedan idea of the unity of God will be found in Palgrave's ' Journey through Central Arabia,' ch. viii. According to this statement, God is one, not only numerically and without plurality of nature or person, but as the only Agent, the only Force, through the universe, leaving nothing to any other beings but unconditional passiveness. The sole power, motor, energy, is God. Neither loving nor enjoying, He is thought of as an

[1] 'Antiquities,' XVIII. i. 3.

absolute, lonely Despot, dispensing felicity or damnation according to his will, and alike unsympathizing with either fate.

A subject like this, touching theology with one hand and philosophy with the other, as well as deeply rooted in Holy Scripture, was of necessity handled by the Early Fathers of the Church. Quotations from their writings may be seen in Bishop Browne, or other of the longer treatises on the Articles. It was reserved for Augustine in the fifth century to discuss systematically the doctrine of predestination. The following passage from his treatise 'De Prædest. Sanctorum,' ch. xviii., may illustrate his views:—'God hath chosen us in Christ before the foundation of the world, predestinating us to the adoption of sons: not because we were going to be *holy and spotless* of ourselves, but He elected us, in order that we might be such. He did this according to the pleasure of His will, in order that no man might boast of his own will, but of the will of God towards him.'

Augustine did not understand by *reprobation* a decree or purpose of damnation, but a leaving of the ungodly to the just consequences of their sins.

Since the time of Augustine, all sections of the Church have been more or less divided on this subject. The school-men discussed the subject of predestination with their usual minuteness. Aquinas and his followers adhered to Augustinian views. Scotus, in this, as in other doctrines of grace and merit, approached nearer to Pelagianism.

We come next to the age of the Reformation. The most has been made of supposed differences between Luther and Melancthon on the one hand, and Calvin on the other, in respect of this doctrine. But the Reformers of all countries were strong Augustinians, and, with some modifications, held the same general cast of doctrine on election. Dr. Macbride on this Article quotes Melancthon as saying that 'though he speaks less harshly and less like a Stoic, he knows that Luther substantially agrees with him. To Calvin he says, I am satisfied our views agree, only mine are stated in a less refined manner.' This may qualify assertions often made on a supposed serious difference between Luther, Melancthon, and

Calvin, on this point. Still it remains that Melancthon avoided the subject for popular treatment, gave it no place in the Confession of Augsburg, and would have shrunk from the harsh unqualified statements of Calvin; while the latter gave great prominence to it in every part of his teaching. In his 'Institutes' he laid down absolute definitions on all the points of election, and these became to a large portion of the Protestants tests of orthodoxy. Since his days the name of Calvinism has been generally given to opinions on election agreeing with, or even approximating to, those which he held. It is even probable that, if the tenets of Arminius on this doctrine were preached plainly from a London pulpit, the preacher would be called a Calvinist by the ordinary hearer; to such a degree has Calvinism become popularly synonymous with a belief in election. A few extracts from Calvin's 'Institutes' will illustrate his doctrine on matters lying within this Article[1] :—'By prescience we mean that all things always were and ever continue under God's eye. . . By predestination we mean the eternal decree of God, by which He determined with Himself whatever He willed to happen with regard to every man. All are not created on equal terms, but some are preordained to eternal life, others to eternal damnation.'

'We say, then, that Scripture clearly proves this much, that God by His eternal and immutable counsel determined once for all those whom it was His will one day to admit to salvation, and those whom on the other hand it was His will to doom to destruction.'[2]

'The first man fell because the Lord deemed it meet that He should; why He deemed it meet, we know not. It is certain, however, that it was just, because He saw that His own glory would thereby be displayed. When you hear the glory of God mentioned, understand that His justice is included. For that which deserves praise must be just. Man, therefore, falls, divine providence so ordaining, but he falls by his own fault.'[3]

These extracts sufficiently set forth the nature of Calvinism

Calvin, 'Instit.' Lib. III. xxi. 5.　　[2] Ibid. xxi. 7.　　[3] Ibid. xxiii. 8.

L

proper on the subject before us. It is not too much to say
that the leading theologians of Switzerland, Western Germany,
Holland, Scotland, and England,[1] during the reign of Elizabeth,
held views closely akin to those of Calvin. In the inevitable
flux and reflux of human opinion a reaction set in, the leading
spirit in which was Arminius. He was educated at Geneva,
and became professor of divinity at the University of Leyden.
He died A.D. 1609. After his death the celebrated Grotius,
Episcopius, and others maintained his opinions. So far as
our present Article is concerned, it is only necessary to quote
the first of the five Articles which the Arminians at first
maintained against the current theology in Holland :—[2]

'God, from all eternity, determined to bestow salvation on
those who, He foresaw, would persevere unto the end in their
faith in Jesus Christ : and to inflict everlasting punishments
on those who should continue in their unbelief, and resist unto
the end His divine succours.' We must refer for the history
of the Arminians, as a sect, to Mosheim as above.

We are now in a position to define the terms usually
employed by English divines in writing on the doctrine of
this Article.

1. Calvinism holds the absolute election to eternal life of a
certain limited number of individuals ; and that this election
is entirely irrespective of anything which God foresaw in them,
and proceeds from the exercise of His will alone. Calvin
himself taught also the predestination to damnation of the
residue of mankind. But the greater part of those commonly
called Calvinists do not hold the doctrine of *reprobation*.
They usually approach nearer to the doctrine of St. Augustine,
and are content to say that God simply leaves the impenitent
to the inevitable consequences of their sins—a doctrine known
technically as *præterition*.

There are, however, two distinct sections among Calvinists,
known as *Supralapsarian* and *Sub* or *Infralapsarian*, from the
opinion they hold about the fall of man in connection with the

---

[1] See Dean Goode on 'Infant Baptism,' chap. iii.
[2] Mosheim, 'Cent. XVII.' sect. ii. part ii. 3.

decrees of God. The *Supralapsarian* holds that God from all eternity decreed the fall of Adam, and the salvation or damnation of all men.

The *Sublapsarian* deems election to have taken place subsequently to, or at least on the supposition of, the fall of Adam, who sinned freely and not by the decree of God. He holds that all who have been elected in pursuance of this merciful interference of God will have the grace of final perseverance. With regard to the rest of mankind he usually holds the doctrine of præterition. It is obvious from the extracts given above that Calvin himself was a Supralapsarian. In our own country and Church few of those ordinarily called Calvinists follow him in the peculiarities of supralapsarianism.

2. Arminianism holds election to be contingent upon the foreknowledge of God as to the use which individuals will make of grace given. It does not hold the doctrine of final perseverance.

It is needful to caution the student as to the use of the terms *Calvinist* and *Arminian*, as popularly used in this country. The names are frequently given to those who have very little in common with either Calvin or Arminius, as those who are acquainted with the works of either of those great divines well know. To a great extent these two names are used simply to express the two antagonistic opinions as to the ground upon which the Almighty proceeds in His mysterious operation of *election*. The Calvinist holds that God elects (so to speak) *arbitrarily*, and that the subsequent salvation and sanctification of the elect are a consequence simply of their election, and necessarily follow from it.

The Arminian holds that God in His infinite foreknowledge, seeing the use which different persons will make of His grace given, determines and predestinates their eternal position accordingly.

Such is the established use of these words in England. It is obvious that there have been in this sense *Calvinists* and *Arminians* long before Calvin was born. They have existed in every section of the Christian Church, even in that Roman Church which would shrink from the names of Calvin and

Arminius with horror. It may illustrate the subject to add that in the great Methodist movement of the last century, Wesley took the Arminian and Whitfield the Calvinistic hypothesis. Their respective followers are still divided on this point, and the Wesleyans are reputed Arminians.

There have been some other opinions on the subject of election, which either evade its difficulties, or else attempt to modify or combine the two antagonistic doctrines.

Among the former of these may be named the opinion of those who hold election or predestination to life as simply implying that God calls certain nations to the knowledge of His saving truth, or certain persons to be members of His Church in which salvation is to be found. In other words, that He elects masses of men to privileges, but not individuals to salvation. It must be obvious at a glance that this evades, without solving, the difficulty. For there is just as much that is *arbitrary* (to our ideas) in placing some persons in a position where they may be saved, and omitting others, as there is in other views of election.

Among modifications or combinations of the two great antagonistic doctrines on election, that of Baxter may be mentioned, as illustrated by the following quotation from his 'God's Goodness Vindicated' (ii. 13). 'All have so much grace as bringeth and leaveth the success to man's will' (i.e. allows the possibility of salvation to all), and moreover there is 'a special decree and grace of God, which with a chosen number shall antecedently infallibly secure His ends in their repentance, faith, perseverance, and salvation. Is this any detraction from His universal grace, or rather a higher demonstration of His goodness? As it is no wrong to man that God maketh angels more holy, immutable, and happy.'

The history of this doctrine in our own Church may be briefly sketched thus:—Until the time of Laud the Calvinistic doctrine prevailed. In connection with this the student may refer to the Lambeth Articles and the Synod of Dort. In the time of Laud, and mainly through his influence, a predominance of Arminian doctrine was established. The reaction from the Puritanism of the Commonwealth, which was strongly

Calvinistic, further strengthened Arminianism, which thence‑
forward obtained a firm hold of the Church of England.

The opinion of an independent thinker like Coleridge may
be interesting to some readers, we therefore add the following
from his 'Aids to Reflection'[1]:—'No impartial person, com‑
petently acquainted with the history of the Reformation, and
the works of the earlier Protestant divines at home and abroad,
even to the close of Elizabeth's reign, will deny that the doc‑
trines of Calvin on redemption, and the natural state of fallen
man, are in all essential points the same as those of Luther,
Zuinglius, and the first Reformers collectively. These doctrines
have, however, since the re-establishment of the Episcopal
Church at the return of Charles II., been as generally ex‑
changed for what is commonly styled Arminianism, but
which, taken as a complete and explicit scheme of belief, it
would be both historically and theologically more accurate to
call Grotianism, or the Gospel according to Grotius. The
change was not, we may readily believe, effected without a
struggle.'

In the religious revival of the last century many of the
most devoted leaders held strong Calvinistic opinions. The
consequence was a renewal of controversy, often carried on
with great bitterness. But the example of Simeon, and other
leaders of the rising Evangelical body in the Church, led to
the abandonment of the controversy on the more speculative
points of the Calvinistic doctrine. It may be useful to the
student to be enabled to form some opinion on the existing
state of thought on this subject in the Church of England. If
it be possible to give a probable account of the present posi‑
tion of the bulk of that which is commonly called the Evan‑
gelical section of the Church in respect of this doctrine, there
can scarcely be found a more typical name in the general es‑
timation than that of Simeon. It may be well, therefore, to
give some extracts illustrating his views. In the preface to
his 'Horæ Homileticæ' he explains at some length his posi‑
tion as being in some respects midway between Calvinism and

---

[1] Aphorism II. 'On that which is indeed spiritual religion.'

Arminianism. But this is more tersely expressed in the 'Recollections of Simeon,' by the Rev. A. W. Brown, chap. xiii:—'Calvinists affirm the doctrine of free election apart from any excellence in man, of utter helplessness in our nature, of salvation entirely by faith, and that not of ourselves. This is all right and scriptural. On the other hand, the Arminians affirm that we shall be saved according as we do good or evil, that man is a free agent, that he is wholly responsible for his actions, that he must work out his own salvation. This also is all right and scriptural. But as soon as either party makes use of its own half of these doctrines to disprove those of its opponents, it is wrong. What though these doctrines are irreconcileable by us; does God require us to reconcile them? . . . . Election of the redeemed is made by God's sovereignty, quite irrespective of any good in them : if there turn out good in them, it is the consequence, not the cause, of their election. For the nature of man is wholly corrupt, and any good in it is put there by God. So far I agree with the Calvinists. But rejection or reprobation is not irrespective of evil in those who are rejected, because in that case God would *will the death of a sinner*, and would take pleasure in his death, and not that he should turn to God and live . . . I will never agree with the Calvinists, that both election and rejection are irrespective of man's character; nor with the Arminians, that they are both dependent on it.

'Christ died for the sins of the whole world. The Bible says so in many passages. What have we to do to judge God's revelation by metaphysical deductions and supposed consequences? Men say, Then some of the blood of Christ proved inefficacious. Scripture does not say so; and yet Scripture says, "And so the weak perish for whom Christ died" (1 Cor. viii. 11).

'Saints shall be preserved to the end, not because they cannot fall, for they may; but because God will uphold them. There is nothing in the saint that makes his salvation certain, yet God hath decreed that he shall not perish. He is preserved by God, but not by anything which God hath put into him.'

On comparing these statements with that which is properly called Calvinism, it will be found that they assert unconditional election by God's sovereign will, and the preservation of the elect to the end ; but they reject the doctrine of reprobation, and they assert that Christ died for all men.   This will bear out a previous statement that in point of fact the bulk of those in the Church of England who are usually styled Calvinists, are more properly Augustinians, for in those points in which Calvin went beyond Augustine they will be found generally agreeing with the latter.   It is difficult, if not impossible, to give an equally probable account of the state of opinion on the doctrine of this Article in other sections of the English Church.   It is, however, a probable supposition that the majority may be Arminian upon the whole, since denunciations of Calvinism are so frequently heard.

In the midst of this disunion of opinion as to the deep things of God's will, a point of agreement may be found for men of humble piety.   They will acknowledge that if they have found God, it was because God sought and found them.   State the alternative : Did you choose God, or did God choose you ? And who that knows his own heart will hesitate as to the answer ?   If they have the love of God in their hearts, and they are asked whether there was any distinguishing goodness in them for which they were chosen of God, they will unfeignedly deny it, and be the first to own that all was of God's free grace in bringing them to Him from first to last.

Turning next to the Church of Rome, we observe that the Tridentine divines were too much divided in their opinions to deal with the subject of election in general.   They did, however, negative the doctrine of reprobation[1]:—' If any one shall say that the grace of justification belongs to none but those predestined to life, but that all the rest who are called, are called, but do not receive grace, as being predestined by the divine power to evil, let him be anathema.'   Upon the whole, the section of the Roman Church which, since the Reformation, has upheld the doctrines of St. Augustine, has been the weaker.   This may be seen in the history of the

[1] Sess. vi. can. 17.

Jansenists in France in the latter part of the seventeenth century, and may be also inferred from the dominant influence of the Jesuits, whose theology has been of a more Pelagian cast.

For convenience of reference the following documents are subjoined :—

A Translation of the Lambeth Articles, as approved by Arch-bishop Whitgift and other bishops.[1]

I. God from eternity has predestined some to life, and some He has reprobated to death.

II. The moving or efficient cause of predestination to life is not the foresight of faith, or of perseverance, or of good works, or of anything which is in the persons predestinated, but it is the sole will of God who is well pleased.

III. The number of the predestinated is predefined and certain, it can be neither increased nor diminished.

IV. Those who are not predestinated to salvation, of necessity will be damned on account of their sins.

V. True, living, and justifying faith, and the sanctifying Spirit of God, is not extinguished, falleth not away, vanisheth not away in the elect, either finally or totally.

VI. A man truly faithful, i.e. endued with justifying faith, is certain with the full assurance of faith, of the remission of his sins, and his eternal salvation through Christ.

VII. Saving grace is not given, is not communicated, is not granted to all men, by which they may be saved if they will.

VIII. No man can come unto Christ unless it shall have been given to him, and unless the Father shall have drawn him. And all men are not drawn by the Father, in order that they may come to the Son.

IX. It is not placed in the will or power of each man to be saved.

[1] Strype's 'Whitgift.'

An abstract of the Five Points of Arminianism, condemned by the Synod of Dort.[1]

I. That God from all eternity decreed the salvation of all those whose faith in Christ He foresaw would endure to the end ; and the everlasting punishment of those whose ultimate unbelief He foresaw.

II. That Jesus Christ made a full atonement for all; which, however, must be appropriated by faith.

III. That true faith cannot be the growth of our natural free will; that, therefore, regeneration and renewal, the operation of the Holy Ghost, are necessary.

IV. That this divine grace is the source of all which is good in man ; but that it may be resisted by the sinful will, and be ineffectual.

V. That those who are endued with true faith have sufficient grace to give them final victory ; but that the question whether they may, nevertheless, fall away finally, has not yet been sufficiently cleared up from Holy Scripture.

This last question was afterwards answered by the Arminians in the affirmative. The Third Article was also taught in a manner that approached to Pelagian opinions.

[1] Mosheim, 'Cent. XVII.' sec. ii. pt. ii. c. iii. 4.

ARTICLE XVIII.

Of obtaining eternal Salvation only by the Name of Christ.

They also are to be had accursed that presume to say, that every man shall be saved by the Law or Sect which he professeth, so that he be diligent to frame his life according to that Law, and the light of Nature. For holy Scripture doth set out unto us only the Name of Jesus Christ, whereby men must be saved.

De speranda æterna salute tantum in nomine Christi.

Sunt et illi anathematizandi, qui dicere audent unumquemque in lege aut secta quam profitetur esse servandum, modo juxta illam et lumen naturæ accurate vixerit, cum sacræ literæ tantum Jesu Christi nomen prædicent, in quo salvos fieri homines oporteat.

NOTES ON THE TEXT OF ARTICLE XVIII.

They also are to be had accursed : Latin, ' Sunt illi anathematizandi.' The mode of expression is derived from the ancient usage of synodical condemnation by the word *anathema.*

The copulative particle *also* involves some little grammatical difficulty. But it seems to connect this Article with the Sixteenth. The text remains scarcely varied from the Forty-two Articles.

The Article consists of a proposition which is condemned, to which is added a clause indicating the reason of that condemnation, and the Scripture ground on which it is based. Hence the mode of dealing with this Article by Scripture proof will be manifest.

OBSERVATIONS ON ARTICLE XVIII.

This Article is not in debate between ourselves and any section of the Christian Church. Latitudinarians may call it in question ; but no sect can deny it which believes in the efficacy of the death of Christ.

It is manifest that the Article had in view some unbelievers of the age of the Reformation. That this was so appears from the contemporary ' Reformatio Legum ' (ch. xi.): —' Horrible and vain is the audacity of those who contend that men may hope for salvation in every religion and sect which they may profess.'

The subject of the possibility of salvation for a heathen is generally noticed under this Article. Most of the commentators seem to agree that the Article does not absolutely pronounce upon that point. It asserts that none can be saved but by Christ. But it is silent on the question which was touched upon with some degree of hope by some of the early Fathers, how far it may be conceivable that some who have never heard of Christ may be saved *by Him*. The first two chapters of the Epistle to the Romans will naturally be referred to on this subject. The ' Judge of all the earth ' has himself assured us that there will be discrimination at the last between the ignorant and the enlightened sinner. He tells us that eternal justice will not involve all in one *indiscriminate* ruin. 'That servant, *which knew his Lord's will*, and prepared not himself, neither did according to His will, shall be beaten with many stripes. But *he that knew not*, and did commit things worthy of stripes, shall be beaten with few stripes.' Consistently with that absence of detail and circumstantiality which it has been the will of God should characterise all revelations of the course of His final justice, what more distinct utterance could we have? We may add, what further revelation are we entitled even to desire ?

PART IV.

THE CHURCH.

ITS SACRAMENTS AND ITS MINISTERS

ARTICLE XIX.

Of the Church.

The visible Church of Christ is a congregation of faithful men, in the which the pure Word of God is preached, and the Sacraments be duly ministered according to Christ's ordinance in all those things that of necessity are requisite to the same.

As the Church of *Jerusalem*, *Alexandria*, and *Antioch*, have erred; so also the Church of *Rome* hath erred, not only in their living and manner of Ceremonies, but also in matters of Faith.

De Ecclesia.

Ecclesia Christi visibilis est cœtus fidelium, in quo verbum Dei purum prædicatur, et sacramenta, quoad ea quæ necessario exigantur, juxta Christi institutum recte administrantur. Sicut erravit Ecclesia Hierosolymitana, Alexandrina, et Antiochena; ita et erravit Ecclesia Romana, non solum quoad agenda, et cæremoniarum ritus, verum in his etiam quæ credenda sunt.

NOTES ON THE TEXT OF ARTICLE XIX.

The following Latin equivalents may be noted:—' Congregation,' Latin, *cœtus*; ' Duly,' Latin, *recte*; ' In their living,' Latin, *quoad agenda*; ' Matters of faith,' *quæ credenda sunt*.

The Article remained unchanged in the revision in Elizabeth's reign.

The Seventh Article of the Confession of Augsburg was manifestly the origin of the first clause, now before us. ' The Church is a congregation of saints, in which the Gospel is rightly (*recte*) taught, and the Sacraments are rightly administered.'

THE PRINCIPAL DIVISIONS OF ARTICLE XIX.

1. The word 'visible,' as it is used here, necessarily implies the existence of its opposite, 'invisible.' Otherwise the word 'Church,' unqualified by an epithet, would have sufficed. Hence the student must consider in accordance with well-arranged Scripture proofs—

A. The nature and privileges of the Church visible.

B. The nature and privileges of the Church invisible.

2. An assertion historically demonstrable is made that certain ancient Churches have erred. The general Scripture mode of dealing with this will be a consideration of the question whether a promise of inerrancy was left by the Saviour to the Church under any definition of that term. And whether, in point of fact, any Church in New Testament times, and the Roman Church in particular, proved itself inerrant.

THE DEFINITION AND NOTES OF THE CHURCH VISIBLE.

The early Christian Fathers often urged the name and authority of the Church Catholic against heretics. The thoughtful student will, however, perceive a very important distinction between our position and theirs, which may materially affect, not the truth and point of their assertions, but their application to the changed circumstances of the Church. We have arrayed against us the bulk of the Western Church, which has overlaid, added to, and corrupted the ancient Faith, and abandoned the rule of Faith in Scripture. We are severed by almost as serious differences from the varied sections of the Eastern Church. And there have grown up amongst us communities of Christians, differently organised, and often opposing our action, and yet for the most part readily acknowledging the same creeds and doctrinal articles. There is no parallel to this state of things in antiquity. Hence, in many things the voice of antiquity fails practically to teach us. The dictum of some ancient sage and Father of the Church, wise and true in its first application to the Church, as it was, may fail in point, or even in truth, if applied to the Church as it is. Ignatius might truly say,[1] speaking of the three orders of bishop, presbyters, and deacons, 'Apart from these there is no Church.' It was, doubtless, an unquestionable fact in that age. Apart from them there might be Jew, Heathen, or Gnostic, but not the Church. But to take these sayings of old, and to force their application dogmatically to a condition of the Church of which the venerable martyr had not the faintest glimpse, must surely be unjust to his memory and untrue to the facts.

Bishop Browne on this Article has collected a series of definitions of the Church from the writers of the first four centuries. They will be found to be very closely in accordance with our present Article, and to have little in them that is hierarchical and sacerdotal. But it was not until the great disruption of the Western Church at the Reformation that the question of the true definition of the Church acquired great importance. The claims of the popes, on the one hand, to universal dominion ; and of the reforming bodies, on the other, to an independent constitution of their Churches, raised the question of the true nature of the Church.

The technical phrase in use among divines to express the essential qualities which mark the true Church is *Notes of the Church.*

Hence these *Notes of the Church* have been hotly debated between Romish and Protestant controversialists, and again between the Church of England and rival sects.

In the definition before us in the present Article we have the following notes :—

1. The Church is a society of believers.

2. In it the pure word of God is preached.

3. In it the sacraments are duly ministered in all essentials of Christ's institution. The confession of Augsburgh in the clause quoted above contains precisely the same definition.

In pursuance of the plan of this work to introduce the student to recognised English theology, in further illustration of this Article we shall refer to the works of three writers who stand in

---

[1] Ep. ad Trall. 3.

M

the foremost rank—Bishop Pearson's ' Exposition of the Creed,'
Hooker's 'Ecclesiastical Polity,' Field's ' Of the Church.'

I. As Pearson's great work on the Creed will always be
minutely studied, it is not necessary in this place to notice it
at much length. The first part of Article IX. in that work
contains an exposition of the words, ' The Holy Catholic
Church.' The general method and results of that exposition
may be thus set forth. There is first a full discussion of the
use of the word *Church* in the New Testament, which is
obviously the prime essential in dealing with this subject, and
ought thoroughly to be mastered. ' Next the unity of the
Church visible is considered, and shown (from Acts ii. 41, 42,
44, 47) to consist in believing and baptized persons professing
the same faith, receiving the same sacraments, performing the
same devotions. The following six particulars are noted as
belonging to this unity: Christ as the one foundation, the
unity of faith, the reception of the same sacraments, the partaking of one hope, the bond of love, the unity of discipline
and government, through which Christ rules over all. Bishop
Pearson does not further define what he deems essential to
such unity of government. But the following remark may be
permitted. The divisions among Christians, not separated
essentially on any of the five previous points, will be found to
lie, not in their repudiation of this last note of unity ; but in
their opinion as to what is, or is not, essential to the unity of
discipline and government under Christ—whether a universal organisation of the whole Church, whether episcopacy
or presbytery, or some less organised and uniform constitution.
In the midst of the great dissensions which prevail, and which
are so great a stumbling-block to many, it is most desirable
thus to define and limit the degree in which unity, as defined
by this great divine, has been broken.

The holiness of the Church comes next for consideration.
Bishop Pearson shows in what respects it may be attributed
to the Church, whether considered in its visible aspect, or
with respect to those in it who ' are efficaciously called, justified, and sanctified.' But this, not belonging to our present
Article, need not be further noticed here.

A dissertation follows on the origin and early uses of the word Catholic; and it is concluded that Catholicity is an attribute of the Church in regard of these four particulars— its *diffusiveness*, as being spread through the whole world; because it holds the *whole* truth; because it requires the obedience of *all* men to *all* its precepts; and lastly, by reason of *all* saving graces being given in it. The studious moderation of this great divine in dealing with a subject round which so much heat of party zeal has gathered, cannot escape notice.

II. The third book of Hooker's 'Ecclesiastical Polity' discusses the nature of the Church, and how far *Church polity*, as distinguished from *matters of faith and salvation*, is to be found in Scripture. Some portions, which seem most directly to illustrate the present Article, are here epitomised.

The Church invisible, or mystical body of Christ, is partly in heaven and partly on earth. 'They who are of this society have such marks and notes of distinction from all others as are not objects unto our sense; only unto God, who seeth their hearts; unto Him they are clear and manifest.'

The everlasting promises belong to the mystical Church: the duties belong to a visible body. This also is one from the beginning of the world to the end; but the moiety since the coming of Christ is more properly the Church of Christ.

The unity of this body consists in these three things. Its members own one Lord, profess one faith, and are initiated by one baptism.

'In whomsoever these things are, the Church doth acknowledge them for her children: them only she holdeth for aliens and strangers in whom these things are not found.'

Hooker proceeds further to insist on the importance of distinguishing between the Church visible and invisible, and the manifold errors arising from confusing them. Among other things, he answers the taunting query, where our Church was before Luther, by the consideration that the Church visible may be overlaid with corruptions. This Church is 'divided into a number of distinct societies, every one of which is termed a Church within itself.' A Christian assembly may be called a Church, but *the Church* 'is not an assembly, but a society,' and remains when all assemblies are dispersed. The communion its members enjoy consists in the public exercise of such duties as those mentioned in Acts ii. 42 : 'Instruction, breaking of bread, and prayer.'

In the subsequent sections of this book Hooker passes to the controversy with his Puritan opponent, who contended that no form of church polity was lawful unless it were derived from Holy Scripture. This discussion would seem to lie outside our present Article. The question of Episcopacy will arise under Article XXIII., and is therefore omitted for the present.

III. A work second only to Hooker's, as in many respects representing English theology on such questions as that before us, is that of Field, ' Of the Church.' The author was Dean of Gloucester in the time of James I. From this learned work some selections are here presented which seem most directly to illustrate the Article now before us.

In book i. chap. 10, the distinction between the visible and invisible Church implied in this Article is thus explained. ' Hence it cometh that we say there is a visible and an invisible Church, not meaning to make two distinct Churches, as our adversaries falsely and maliciously charge us, though the form of words may serve to insinuate some such thing, but to distinguish the divers considerations of the same Church; which, though it be visible in respect of the profes- sion of supernatural verities revealed in Christ, use of holy sacraments, order of ministry, and due obedience yielded thereunto, and they discernible that do communicate therein ; yet, in respect of those most precious effects, and happy bene- fits of saving grace, wherein only the elect do communicate, it is invisible ; and they that in so happy, gracious, and desirable things have communion among themselves, are not discern- ible from others to whom this fellowship is denied, but are known only to God.'

The second book bears more directly on this Article. It is a discussion of the ' notes of the Church ' which Field states, and maintains in opposition to the Roman controversialists,

Stapleton and Bellarmine. It is therefore controversially very valuable on this fundamental question.

Book ii. chap. 2 : ' The proper and peculiar ' notes which absolutely ' distinguish the true Catholic Church ' are stated to be these three :—

1. ' The entire profession of those supernatural verities, which God hath revealed in Christ His Son.

2. ' The use of such holy ceremonies and sacraments as He hath instituted and appointed to serve as provocations to godliness, preservations from sin, memorials of the bene-fits of Christ, warrants for the greater security of our belief, and marks of distinction, to separate His own from strangers.

3. ' An union or connexion of men in this profession and use of these sacraments, under lawful pastors and guides, ap-pointed, authorised, and sanctified, to direct and lead them in the happy ways of eternal salvation.'

Having stated these *notes*, he proceeds in subsequent chap-ters to examine the objections of Bellarmine and Stapleton to them.

Book ii. chap 5 : We have these five *notes of the Church* propounded by Bellarmine, ' antiquity, succession, unity, universality, and the very name and title of Catholic ex-pressing the universality.' Field proceeds to show the un-certainty of these, and their failure as true notes of the Church.

We are now in a position to gather together briefly the statements of these writers, and to show their substantial agreement, and the unity of true English theology on the point now before us. Where it is requisite, the order of the *notes*, as arranged by the authors, is transposed, to bring them all into the same arrangement which is used in the Article.

Notes of the Church.

ARTICLE XIX.	BISHOP PEARSON.
1. A congregation of faithful men, or cœtus fidelium.	1. The unity of discipline and government under appointed pastoral guides.
2. The preaching of the pure Word of God.	2. The unity of Christ the foundation —the one faith, the one love, the one hope.
3. The due administration of the sacraments.	3. The reception of the same sacraments.

HOOKER.	FIELD.
1. ' The Church is . . . a visible society.'	1. A union of Christians under lawful pastors.
2. ' One Lord and faith.'	2. The profession of all the revealed word.
3. ' One baptism.' ' Instruction, breaking of bread, and prayers.'	3. The use of the sacraments.

Before leaving the subject it may be needful to observe that by *notes of the* Church is intended not simply things desirable for the completeness of the Church—gifts, graces, organisations, which may be useful, usual, or even apostolical, but, as Field words it, ' notes which are inseparable, perpetual, and absolutely proper and peculiar, which perpetually distinguish the true Catholic Church from all other societies of men, and professions of religion in the world.'

The absence from these notes of any special mode of organising the Church, or apostolical and necessary form of government, must already have struck the attention. It is obvious that such a necessity may lurk unexpressed in the Article under the words ' those things that of necessity are requisite to the same.' It may equally be supposed to lie concealed in the other authorities under the words, ' lawful pastors,' &c. How far this may be so in recognised English theology will be investigated under the Twenty-third and Thirty-sixth Articles.

The last clause of this Article asserts historically the fact that the Churches of Jerusalem, Antioch, Alexandria, as well as Rome, have erred not only as to the *agenda*, but also the *credenda*. It is obvious why these are selected. Rome,

Antioch, and Alexandria were the three great patriarchates recognised in the sixth canon of the Council of Nice. The seventh canon reserves the next place of precedence to the Bishop of Jerusalem. The patriarchate of Constantinople was not recognised until the second General Council. We need not particularly specify the errors of the Church of Rome. And without going back to the controversies of the fourth, fifth, and sixth centuries, in which Arian, Nestorian, and Monophysite errors in various degrees affected the Oriental Churches, it is well known that they now have many of the corruptions of the Roman Church, such as the worship of saints, transubstantiation, and other erroneous doctrines

ARTICLES XX. AND XXXIV.

ARTICLE XX.

Of the Authority of the Church.

The Church hath power to decree Rites or Ceremonies, and Authority in controversies of Faith: And yet it is not lawful for the Church to ordain any thing that is contrary to God's Word written, neither may it so expound one place of Scripture that it be repugnant to another. Wherefore, although the Church be a witness and a keeper of Holy Writ, yet, as it ought not to decree any thing against the same, so besides the same ought it not to enforce any thing to be believed for necessity of Salvation.

De Ecclesiæ auctoritate.

Habet Ecclesia ritus sive cæremonias statuendi jus, et in fidei controversiis auctoritatem; quamvis Ecclesiæ non licet quicquam instituere, quod verbo Dei scripto adversetur, nec unum Scripturæ locum sic exponere potest, ut alteri contradicat. Quare licet Ecclesia sit divinorum librorum testis et conservatrix, attamen ut adversus eos nihil decernere, ita præter illos nihil credendum de necessitate salutis debet obtrudere.

ARTICLE XXXIV.

Of the Traditions of the Church.

It is not necessary that Traditions and Ceremonies be in all places one, or utterly like; for at all times they have been diverse, and may be changed according to the diversity of countries, times,

De traditionibus Ecclesiasticis.

Traditiones atque cæremonias easdem, non omnino necessarium est esse ubique, aut prorsus consimiles. Nam ut variæ semper fuerunt, et mutari possunt, pro regionum, temporum, et morum diversi-

and men's manners, so that nothing be ordained against God's Word.. Whosoever through his private judgment, willingly and purposely, doth openly break the traditions and ceremonies of the Church, which be not repugnant to the Word of God, and be ordained and approved by common authority, ought to be rebuked openly, (that other may fear to do the like,) as he that offendeth against the common order of the Church, and hurteth the authority of the Magistrate, and woundeth the consciences of the weak brethren. Every particular or national Church hath authority to ordain, change, and abolish ceremonies, or rites of the Church ordained only by man's authority, so that all things be done to edifying.

tate, modo nihil contra verbum Dei instituatur.

Traditiones, et cæremonias ecclesiasticas, quæ cum verbo Dei non pugnant, et sunt auctoritate publica institutæ atque probatæ, quisquis privato consilio volens, et data opera, publice violaverit, is ut qui peccat in publicum ordinem Ecclesiæ, quique lædit auctoritatem Magistratus, et qui infirmorum fratrum conscientias vulnerat, publice, ut cæteri timeant, arguendus est.

Quælibet Ecclesia particularis, sive nationalis, auctoritatem habet instituendi, mutandi, aut abrogandi cæremonias, aut ritus ecclesiasticos, humana tantum auctoritate institutos, modo omnia ad ædificationem fiant.

NOTES ON THE TEXT OF THESE ARTICLES.

In Article XX. we may observe that the Latin equivalent for ' *keeper* of *Holy Writ* ' is ' *conservatrix divinorum librorum.*' The idea of the *keeper* is, therefore, one who *preserves*, not one who *reserves*, the Scriptures.

In Article XXXIV. the text calls for no special comment.

The Twentieth Article is identical with the nineteenth of 1552, excepting the first clause ascribing to the Church authority in controversies of faith, which was an addition in Elizabeth's reign. The history of that clause is singularly obscure. It does not exist in the copy of the Articles preserved among the Parker MSS. in the library of Corpus Christi College, Cambridge, which bears the autograph signatures of ten prelates. Archbishop Laud was accused of forging it. However, it appears in some, though not in all, of the printed copies in Elizabeth's reign. Laud defended himself by appealing to four editions of the Articles, printed during the reign of Elizabeth and containing the clause. He further produced an attested copy of the Article from the records of the province of Canterbury, which also contained it. Those records have since perished in the great fire of London, 1666. It is thus sufficiently proved that the clause, as it stands, was a part of the Twentieth Article, as finally ratified in the reign of Elizabeth. The Parker MS. must therefore be, as Strype suggests,[1] an early draught, and not the final record of the Thirty-nine Articles.

The question is now scarcely more than one of literary curiosity, inasmuch as the copy of the Articles enforced by the existing Act of Uniformity (that of 1662) contains the clause in question.

With regard to Article XXXIV. the text of the former portion, with a slight exception, stands as it did in 1552. The last clause on 'particular or national Churches' was added in Elizabeth's reign.

THE PRINCIPAL DIVISIONS OF ARTICLES XX. AND XXXIV.

1. The Church (i.e. each national Church) has power to decree and alter rites and ceremonies.

2. Those ceremonies need not be uniform in different countries.

3. The wilful schismatic should be 'rebuked openly.'

4. The Church is a judge in controversies of faith.

5. The legislative and judicial power of the Church is limited by the word of God.

6. The relation of the Church to the Scriptures is that of a 'witness and keeper.'

In dealing with these points out of Scripture, after alleging such individual passages as may seem to bear upon them, the most convincing method will be to point out that the New

---

[1] Strype's Parker, iv. 5.

Testament contains few express rules on Church Polity. It contains, however, many *principles* which are to guide the Church in all its proceedings. It follows, therefore, that the details of its polity must be more or less variable, and must be worked out by the Church in accordance with those principles. This is susceptible of copious illustration from the Epistles.

OBSERVATIONS ON THESE ARTICLES.

These two Articles are thus grouped because the Twentieth speaks of the power of the Church over both ceremonial and doctrine; and the Thirty-fourth deals more explicitly with its power over ceremonial. It follows that the one must illustrate the meaning of the other.

This will immediately appear when the first question arises which meets us on the face of Article XX. What is this Church to which such power is ascribed? It must be the Church visible. But does it mean that whole Church in its Catholic character, and acting in a corporate manner? If the Article stood alone, this might be maintained with some show of argument. But the Thirty-fourth Article here comes in to clear up the meaning. There we find ' *the Church*' used in the title, and in the first part of the Article, in the same general and indeterminate manner.

But the latter part claims for every ' *National* Church' authority (the same word as in Article XX.) ' to ordain, change, and abolish rites or ceremonies of the Church.' It appears, therefore, that *the Church* and a *National Church* are used convertibly in Article XXXIV. Taking the two Articles together it would, therefore, seem to be intended that every duly constituted and orthodox National Church, being an integral portion of the Church visible, has in itself, as such, the authority spoken of in the two Articles. Or, in other words, that the Church of England, in particular, claims that authority. As regards rites and ceremonies, the thirty-fourth Article asserts this in the plainest manner. A little consideration of a few matters of fact will serve to establish

that she means in the Twentieth to claim for herself the like
authority in matters of doctrine; and that this Article is not
the expression of a belief in General Councils or other
conceivable utterance of the Church Catholic.

For, in point of fact, the Reformed Church of England has
framed these Thirty-nine Articles, and did, by Royal Commissioners and in Convocation, mould, remould, and modify them.
She also requires the assent of her clergy to them, and in her
Ecclesiastical Courts exercises full jurisdiction over any diver-
gence from the standard of doctrine so laid down. To this
' authority,' in both these Articles, she acknowledges only
one limitation—the paramount authority of Holy Scripture.
These considerations seem to make clear in what sense the
word Church is used in these two Articles. It is the Church
considered in the free and independent action of its several
parts, but held together in practical and essential uniformity
by the common bond of allegiance to Holy Scripture.

These Articles, as originally intended, pointed two ways—
against the Romanists, who denied the sole authority of
Scripture, and the competence of a National Church to act
for itself,—and also against the Puritans, who, in their zeal
against some ceremonies retained at the Reformation, denied
the authority of the Church to decree anything which was not
explicitly or implicitly laid down in Scripture.

The whole of Hooker's 'Ecclesiastical Polity' may be
appealed to as bearing out the last assertion. One passage only shall be quoted, which will substantially cover
the ground so far taken under this Article.[1] 'The several
societies of Christian men, unto every of which the name of a
Church is given, with addition betokening severalty, as the
Church of Rome, Corinth, Ephesus, England, and so the rest,
must be endued with correspondent general properties
belonging unto them as they are public Christian societies.
And of such properties common unto all societies Christian,
it may not be denied that one of the very chiefest is Ecclesiastical Polity. . . . To our purpose the name of Church-
Polity will better serve, because it containeth both govern-

[1] Book iii. 1.

ment, and also whatsoever besides belongeth to the ordering of the Church in public.'

The student may be reminded that in the first three centuries there was in many respects a considerable degree of provincial variety and independence in the Churches. There were differences in Creeds and Liturgies; differences about Easter and various other matters. In the following centuries the action of the great Councils and of the Patriarchal jurisdictions was exercised strongly in favour of uniformity; and subsequently the papal despotism almost crushed out the local varieties of rite and discipline. The result may tend to show that probably there is more security for purity of faith in variety than in uniformity.

It need scarcely be observed to those who have read the history of the Church of England under the Tudor Sovereigns that the Thirty-fourth Article was very far from acknowledging the liberty of sects to organise themselves. The liberty which was claimed for the English State to organise the English Church was as freely granted to Scotland, Saxony, or Geneva; but more licence than this was not recognised in that age. Accordingly the *open rebuke*, as interpreted by the practice of the Tudors and Stuarts with regard to schismatics, included certain very severe personal results. Happily the Article itself is no warrant for these proceedings, and without difficulty adapts itself to the usage of a more tolerant age.

The relation of the Church to the Scriptures recognised in the latter part of Article XX. is one of great importance, whether considered with reference to the Roman Catholic controversy, or to recent discussions among ourselves. Extreme views have been put forth, to the following effect. The Church possesses the authentic Catholic tradition, and by this interprets Scripture. A part of this tradition is the authenticity of Holy Scripture, which is therefore received at the hands of the Church, and because we believe the Church. Further, private persons may not search Scripture independently of external help.[1]

---

[1] On this see Goode's ' Divine Rule of Faith and Practice,' chap. ii.

We have already dealt with this question under Article VI. But we may observe in addition that the office of the Church in relation to the Scriptures in Article XX. will not permit such a comment as the one noticed above. The Church is 'testis et conservatrix' of Holy Scripture. She is not the judge, far less the giver of Scripture. From age to age she has witnessed to each successive generation, 'these are the books which I have received, and these I have sedulously preserved.' The proof of the Canon consists, in fact, chiefly of the witness of members of the Church to the Canonical books, and of their reception by the Church, from the first ages until now—chiefly, but not only; for heathen, and heretic too, bear weighty testimony, and are also compelled to be witnesses of Holy Writ.

ARTICLE XXI.

Of the Authority of General Councils.

General Councils may not be gathered together without the commandment and will of Princes. And when they be gathered together, (forasmuch as they be an assembly of men, whereof all be not governed with the Spirit and Word of God,) they may err, and sometimes have erred, even in things pertaining unto God. Wherefore things ordained by them as necessary to salvation have neither strength nor authority, unless it may be declared that they be taken out of Holy Scripture.

De auctoritate Conciliorum Generalium.

Generalia Concilia sine jussu et voluntate Principum congregari non possunt; et ubi convenerint, quia ex hominibus constant, qui non omnes spiritu et verbo Dei reguntur, et errare possunt, et interdum errarunt etiam in his quæ ad Deum pertinent; ideoque quæ ab illis constituuntur, ut ad salutem necessaria, neque robur habent, neque auctoritatem, nisi ostendi possint e sacris literis esse desumpta.

OBSERVATIONS ON ARTICLE XXI.

The text of the Article remains as it stood in 1552, with the exception of a verbal omission of no great consequence. The Latin and English versions are in close agreement and require no special comment.

The first clause, on the legality of assembling General Councils, would seem to us to represent a mere matter of fact. A Council must be held in the territory of some State, and must consist of the subjects of some States. It must, therefore, be dependent on the civil laws permitting such meetings and the movements of individual subjects. The clause, however, was really directed against the claim of the Pope to have the power of summoning and dismissing such Councils.

In dealing with this subject we shall first follow the guidance of Dr. Barrow, in his 'Treatise on the Papal Supremacy,' for the historical facts as to the summoning General Councils. Then we shall point out the basis on which the popes have founded their claim.

Dr. Barrow[1] thus writes, 'There was no general synod before Constantine; and as to the practice from that time, it is very clear that for some ages the popes did not assume or exercise such a power, and that it was not taken for their due. Nothing can be more evident; and it were extreme impudence to deny that the emperors, at their pleasure and by their authority, did congregate all the first general synods; for so the oldest historians in most express terms do report, so those princes in their edicts did aver, so the synods themselves did declare. The most just and pious emperors, who did bear greatest love to the clergy, and had much respect for the pope, did call them without scruple; it was deemed their right to do it; none did remonstrate against their practice; the Fathers in each synod did refer thereto, with allowance, and commonly with applause; popes themselves did not contest their right, yea commonly did petition them to exercise it.'

Dr. Barrow proceeds to establish this by the express statements of Eusebius, Socrates, Sozomen, and the other ecclesiastical historians of the fourth and fifth centuries, setting forth the facts as to the actual mode of summoning the first Councils. It will be seen, on examining those statements, that it is impossible for historical facts to be more clearly ascertained than these are.

Dr. Barrow next shows that the popes themselves, when they desired the settlement of an important point of doctrine or discipline, petitioned the emperors again and again for the assembling of a General Council. Such Councils were generally held in the East. Pope Leo I. was exceedingly anxious that one should be held in Italy, and addressed the Emperor Theodosius in these words: 'All the Churches of our parts, all bishops, with groans and tears, do supplicate your grace, that you would command a general synod to be held in Italy.'

[1] Supposition VI.

This entreaty is not an exceptional instance, but a specimen of the ordinary course of proceeding.

Not only so, but it is next shown that the popes did not preside in the early Councils : St. James presided at Jerusalem; Constantine at Nice ; Nectarius and Gregory Nazianzen at Constantinople ; Cyril of Alexandria at Ephesus.

At Chalcedon, it is said that Pope Leo's legates presided, though Dr. Barrow shows, from the record of the transactions, that the Emperor's commissioners really controlled and conducted the proceedings.

In the fifth General Council the Patriarch of Constantinople presided ; and in the sixth 'the Emperor in each act is expressly said to preside, in person or by his deputies ; although Pope Agatho had his legates there.'

The historical facts being so clear, the next inquiry is upon what basis the popes have founded their exclusive claim to summon, to preside over, to dismiss, a General Council. The answer is, that they founded their claim upon those elaborate forgeries and falsifications of ancient documents, commenced by a writer under the name of Isidore in the middle of the ninth century. He produced what purported to be a collection of about a hundred decrees of the earliest popes, together with spurious writings of other prelates, and Acts of Synods. These decretals reigned unquestioned until the fifteenth century, and are the real basis of the papal claims.

There were other fabrications about the time of Gregory VII. In the middle of the twelfth century all these, with some additions, were engrafted into Gratian's *Decretum*, which became thenceforward the fundamental authority on Canon Law.

In the middle of the thirteenth century a Catena of spurious passages of Greek Fathers and Councils was presented to Pope Urban IV., containing a basis for the papal claims. The contemporary Thomas Aquinas, unacquainted with Greek, received these forgeries, and adopted them all into his system of theology, which, as is well known, has been since the great authority on dogmatic divinity in the Roman Schools. This is the basis on which the papal claims have been established, and in reliance upon which Leo X. and other popes have issued their bulls claiming absolute jurisdiction in the matter of General Councils.

Some account of these forgeries (especially of the Isidorian decretals) will be found in the ordinary Church histories ; but the most complete summary is contained in the recent work, entitled ' The Pope and the Council,' by Janus.

The next point arising under this Article is to what extent the authority of General Councils is recognised by the Church of England. The student will be reminded that so far [1] Holy Scripture has been laid down as the sole rule of faith. The creeds themselves [2] are received, not as the definitions of Councils, but as being in accordance with Holy Scripture. National Churches [3] may 'ordain, change, and abolish ceremonies, or rites of the Church, ordained only by man's authority;' the only restraints and limits assigned to this power being God's word, and the condition of edifying. It appears, therefore, that there is scarcely any place left for the superior restraining power of a General Council. Accordingly, the Article before us simply asserts the fallibility of all such Councils, and the actual failure of some in their definitions of Divine truth. It refuses to recognise any authority in their dogmatic decrees apart from that of Holy Scripture from which they must be derived. The ground upon which the fallibility of such Councils is argued is peculiarly important. If admitted, it utterly destroys the theory on which their infallibility has been based. The general argument for their infallibility has been to this effect. Christ left to His Church the promise that ' the gates of hell should not prevail against it.' This is assumed to imply that the Church visible (as a whole) shall be preserved from error in doctrine. It is further assumed that the whole visible Church may be represented in a General Council, and in point of fact has been so represented. From these premises it is deduced that a genuine General Council has the promise of inerrancy from Christ. It must be readily seen how weak every step of the argument is—that the exposition of the text is doubtful—that the possibility of a really General Council has hitherto been a very questionable thing—and that the (so

---

[1] Art. vi.   [2] Art. viii.   [3] Art. xxxiv.

called) General Councils have been summoned in a very arbitrary and partial manner; some of them, indeed, with the most indecent partisanship. But assuming the supposed fact of the Council being really General, and under the express guidance of the Holy Ghost, its decrees are further assumed to be infallible, whatever may be the individual characters of the members of the Council.

It will be seen from these considerations how entirely the Church of England repudiates the *inherent* authority of the Councils; for she takes into account the characters of the members composing them, instead of regarding any supposed sacred inspiration of the assembly as a whole.

Thus the Article declares that they 'may err and sometimes have erred,' because 'they be an assembly of men, whereof all be not governed with the Spirit and Word of God.'

A question of considerable importance remains. Although the *inherent* authority of the Councils has been thus rejected by the Church of England, it may be asked whether she has not acknowledged the validity of some of their decisions. In other words, whether she has not exercised her independent and co-ordinate authority [1] and decided that the dogmatic decrees of certain Councils are in accordance with the word of God, and therefore binding upon herself. To this it must be replied that there is no ecclesiastical formula of the Church of England, now in force, containing such a decision. The first Article of Henry VIII. (1536) recognised the judgments of the first four Councils against heresies. But that document, as it is well known, has no authority, and is in many respects in direct opposition to the Thirty-nine Articles. The Reformers of Edward's reign spoke with great respect of the four great Councils. The 'Reformatio Legum Ecclesiasticarum' declares that we reverently accept the four great Œcumenical Synods; but this document also has no authority. All this, then, and more which might be quoted, falls short of recognition by our Church. There was, however, in addition to this, a recognition to a certain extent of the four Councils in the Act of Parliament [2] which

---

[1] Arts. xx. and xxxiv.   [2] 1 Eliz. cap. i. 36.

restored the supremacy over the Church to the Crown. Authority having been given to the Crown by that Act to exercise its supremacy by means of commissioners appointed by letters patent under the great seal of England, the proviso was added that such commissioners should 'not in any wise have authority or power to order, determine, or adjudge any matter or cause to be heresy, but only such as heretofore have been determined, ordered, or adjudged to be heresy by the authority of the Canonical Scriptures, or by the *first four General Councils*, or any of them, or by any other General Council wherein the same was declared heresy by the express and plain words of the said Canonical Scriptures, or such as shall be ordered, adjudged, or determined to be heresy by the High Court of Parliament of this realm with the assent of the clergy in their convocation.'

This proviso of the Act was evidently intended to be a check on an undue exercise of the royal prerogative. The dogmatic decisions of the first four Councils relate to the doctrine of the Holy Trinity only, as it is professed in the Creeds, and these were adopted by Parliament as a guide to the Royal Commissioners. The majority of the canons of those Councils refer to matters of organisation and discipline, and are wholly omitted in the clause of the Act just quoted, which refers to judgments on questions of *heresy*, not of *discipline*. To this extent, therefore, the doctrinal, but not the disciplinary canons of the four Councils appear to have been legally binding as a limitation to the judicial authority of the Crown in questions of heresy. But the abolition of the High Commission in 1641 seems to have annulled this also. Vain, then, is the assertion in a recent edition of the canons of the four Councils that ' the decrees of the first four General Councils are declared as authoritative by Act of Parliament;' whereas several of the disciplinary decrees will be found in direct collision with the usages and organisation of the Church of England.

It will be manifest from what has been said, that we must look later than those four, for the General Councils which ' have erred in things pertaining to God.' If we include those of the middle ages, which have been commonly so styled, there will be no lack of unscriptural doctrine in their decrees. The second Council of Nice decreed the veneration of images; the Papal Councils (as those of the Lateran and others) sanctioned transubstantiation and other errors condemned by our Church.

For further information on the subject of General Councils reference may be made to Field ' Of the Church.' [1] According to Bishop Browne, the Greek Church acknowledges eight General Councils, including the second Council of Nice, 787, and the fourth of Constantinople, 869. To these the Roman Church has added many more. But the answer of the Patriarch of Constantinople to the pope's invitation to the Vatican Council of 1869, admits only seven General Councils. The Patriarch is reported to have spoken thus: ' According to an Œcumenical Council, the Œcumenical Church and true Catholicity is, and is defined to be, that holy, undefiled body, in which (independently of its material extent) the sum of the pure teaching of the Apostles is held, and the faith of the whole Church on earth, as it was established and thoroughly tried for the first eight centuries after the foundation of the Church, during which period the Fathers both of the East and West, and the seven and only Œcumenical and most holy and inspired Councils speak one and the same heavenly utterance of the Gospel.'

In the midst of this uncertainty about the true constitution, lawful assembly, and validity of the Acts of Councils assuming to be *general*, we may hail with gladness the wisdom of our Church, the most free upon earth as touching things not essentials to the Gospel. The difficulty of the subject is acknowledged in a document of 1536, signed by Archbishop Cranmer and many other bishops and clergy in the name of convocation.[2] In this paper, Gregory Nazianzen, who had seen more of Synods than most men, is quoted as writing thus: ' I think this, if I should write truly, that all assemblies of bishops should be eschewed; for I have seen a good result of no Synod, but an increase rather than a solution of evils; for love of controversy and ambition overcome reason (think not that I write maliciously).'

[1] Book v. 48–53.   [2] Burnet's ' Hist. Reform,' App. iii. 5.

ARTICLE XXII.

Of Purgatory.	*De Purgatorio.*
The Romish doctrine concerning purgatory, pardons, worshipping and adoration, as well of images as of reliques, and also invocation of saints, is a fond thing vainly invented, and grounded upon no warranty of Scripture, but rather repugnant to the word of God.	Doctrina Romanensium de purgatorio, de indulgentiis, de veneratione, et adoratione, tum imaginum tum reliquiarum nec non de invocatione sanctorum, res est futilis, inaniter conficta, et nullis Scripturarum testimoniis innititur: immo verbo Dei contradicit.

NOTES ON THE TEXT OF ARTICLE XXII.

The following equivalents may be noticed. Romish doctrine, Latin, *Doctrina Romanensium.* Pardons, Latin, *Indulgentiæ.* In Chaucer the seller of indulgences is called *the Pardoner.* Worshipping, Latin, *veneratio.* A fond thing, Latin, *res futilis. Fond* in the sense of *foolish* is familiar to every reader of Shakspeare. Vainly invented, Latin, *inaniter conficta.*

The Article of 1552 read 'the doctrine of school authors' instead of 'the Romish doctrine,' which was substituted in 1562. The latter phrase is more popularly intelligible.

OBSERVATIONS ON ARTICLE XXII.

As the *Romish* doctrine is here specifically condemned, it becomes necessary to obtain distinct statements of that doctrine; and this the more, because the celebrated Tract XC.

played upon this distinction. It urged, first, that doctrine on these subjects which might be shown to be not simply *Romish*, but also prevalent for many ages through the greater part of Christendom, and from early times, could not be styled distinctly 'Romish,' and might therefore be held; and, secondly, that doctrines which might differ some shades from the received Romish view were not inconsistent with this Article.

That Tract also argued that by 'the Romish doctrine' is not meant the Tridentine statement, because this Article was drawn up before the decree of the Council of Trent. This is true to the letter, whatever it may be in the spirit, for the date of the decree on these subjects in the Council of Trent is December 4, 1563, whilst the word *Romanensium* was placed in this Article in the previous January. The Tract then quotes some of the mythical stories of Purgatory which were rife in the middle ages, and intimates that these, with the abuses connected with them, constitute the '*Romish doctrine*' of purgatory condemned in this Article, and that the Tridentine doctrine is left untouched by it.

It is very important that the theological student should understand the ground taken by the active and conspicuous party in our Church, whose mode of dealing with our formularies has been for some years guided by the principles just described. Nothing but a court of law can decide whether special pleading of this sort might avail on a strictly legal interpretation of the words. But there can be no difficulty in ascertaining whether our Church has or has not wholly cast out, not this or that notion of Purgatory, but the very idea of Purgatory in every shape, from her formularies and her system.

In dealing further with the phrase 'Romish doctrine' in this Article, we shall now assume that we shall find it most fully represented in its binding form in the decrees of the Council of Trent, on these grounds. It is true that the particular decree on the matters contained in this Article was passed nearly a year after the word 'Romanensium' was inserted in it, and that, therefore, the *ipsissima verba* of that decree were not before the writers of our Article.

But it is notorious that if there ever was a Council under Roman influence, and reflecting, as far as was possible, in the then state of parties, Roman views, as distinguished from French, Spanish, or German, the Council of Trent is that one. It was recognised at the time—it has been recognised ever since—as distinctly and truly Romish.

Such writers as Field and others, in our Church, have always written of the Council of Trent as the great agent in severing the Papal Communion formally and specifically from that which was Catholic, and stamping it as Papal and Roman. It cannot be seriously argued that such a Council which had been sitting at intervals for seventeen years when our present Article was revised, and had already enacted the larger part of its decrees, was not in the mind of the revisers of such an Article when they altered the word '*Scholasticorum*' to '*Romanensium*.' Nor can it be reasonably doubted that when, a year later, the decree of the Council of Trent on the subjects now under consideration did appear, its statement was recognised as an enunciation of the doctrine already called '*Romish*' in this Article. Further, we must remember that the Thirty-nine Articles have subsequently obtained parliamentary sanction in 1571, and again in 1662, when there can be no question whether or no the word '*Romish*' would be fully understood as implying Tridentine. For these reasons we shall not hesitate in alleging the definitions of Trent as properly describing the '*Romish doctrines*' stigmatised in the Article now before us.

Our task, therefore, will be a simple one. We have merely to cite the portions of the Tridentine decrees bearing on the matters indicated in this Article. We shall then have before us what is unquestionable *Romish doctrine*, and what no one acquainted, even moderately, with the writings of our Reformers, can doubt was meant by them in this place.

1. *Purgatory.*

Our space will not allow us to sketch in any detail the history of this doctrine. It is traced from the fanciful interpretations of Origen in the third century, who thought that *at the day of judgment* there would be a purgatorial fire by which all should be tested. From his time this idea may be followed in numerous varieties of expression in the subsequent Christian writers. In the dark ages monkish visions and legends laid open the strange and ghastly arrangements of a land of purgatory, from which Dante afterwards derived the horrible pictures of his great poem. The schoolmen fashioned all this into a system, and defined the position, arrangements, and pains of purgatory.

The Council of Trent passed its decree on the subjects named in this Article in the hurry of its final session, which the anticipation of the pope's death brought to a hasty conclusion. The decree on Purgatory [1] is as follows: —' Since the Catholic Church, instructed by the Holy Spirit out of the sacred writings, and the ancient tradition of the Fathers, hath taught in Holy Councils, and lastly in this Œcumenical Synod that there is a Purgatory; and that the souls detained there are aided by the suffrages of the faithful, but most of all by the acceptable sacrifice of the altar; this Holy Synod enjoins all bishops diligently to endeavour that the wholesome doctrine of purgatory, handed down by Holy Fathers and Sacred Councils be believed by Christ's faithful, held, taught, and everywhere preached. But let the more difficult and subtle questions, and those which do not conduce to edification and from which often there is no increase of piety, be banished from popular discourses before the uneducated people. Moreover, they should not permit uncertain matters, or those which have the appearance of falsity, to be published or handled. But those which tend to curiosity or superstition, or savour of base gain, let them prohibit, as the scandals and offence of the faithful. Let bishops take care that the suffrages of the living faithful, viz., sacrifices of masses, prayers, alms, and other works of piety which have been customably performed by the faithful, for other faithful persons departed, be piously and religiously performed according to the institutions of the Church; and let them take care that the services which are due on behalf of the departed by the

[1] Session xxv.

foundations of testators, or in any other manner, be performed, not in a perfunctory way, but diligently and exactly by the priests and ministers of the Church, and others who are under obligation to perform this duty.'

It will be observed, that though this decree includes the whole belief, yet that it is cautiously worded, and avoids pronouncing on matters on which Romish divines were divided, and on which, when not writing for Protestant readers, they have often written very positively. But it follows from this that the prohibition of our Church is the more absolute against *the whole system* and not against some of its *details*. We may observe that even so acute a controversialist as Bellarmine follows the schoolmen in placing purgatory in the centre of the earth. He describes its four divisions, and appeals to visions and appearances in volcanic eruptions, in proof of his assertions.

2. *Pardons or Indulgences.*

The history of these may be traced in Ecclesiastical history from the relaxations of penitential discipline in the restoration of offenders to Church communion. These indulgences became more common as the Church was gradually more and more identified with the world after Constantine's days. And when the notion of purgatory became developed, and the limits of Church authority transcended the bounds of the visible, the indulgence found further place for its exercise in abridging purgatorial pains.

The satirist might not unfairly say that the realm of purgatory, which was so absolutely a mediæval creation, must surely be under the control of its creators. The pains of purgatory, together with Church censures, constitute the *temporal*, as distinguished from the eternal, punishment of sin. Over these temporal penalties the Roman Church claims full and absolute dispensing power. The results of the audacious sale of indulgences in Switzerland and Germany in the sixteenth century will be fresh in the reader's mind. Tetzel and Sampson had no small share in setting Luther and Zwingle free. Yet the Church of Rome was pledged to the system, and the

Council of Trent touched it with a light hand in the following decree :

'Since the power of conferring indulgences hath been granted by Christ to the Church ; and since even from the most ancient times the Church hath used a power of this kind, divinely delivered to her, the Holy Synod teaches and enjoins that the use of indulgences, most salutary to Christian people, and approved by the authority of sacred Councils, shall be retained in the Church ; and it anathematises those who either assert that they are useless, or deny that the Church hath the power of granting them ; yet in granting them the Council desires moderation to be used, in accordance with the old and approved custom in the Church, lest by too great facility ecclesiastical discipline should be weakened. But the Council desiring the abuses to be corrected, which have crept into them, and by occasion of which this illustrious name of indulgences is blasphemed by heretics, by this present decree orders in general terms, that all base profits for their purchase, whence very many causes of abuses have spread among Christian people, be altogether abolished. But with regard to the rest of the abuses proceeding from ignorance, superstition, irreverence, or any other cause whatever, since they cannot be severally prohibited on account of the multiplicity of corruptions of divers places and provinces, the Council commands each bishop diligently to collect abuses of this sort existing in his own Church, and refer them to the first provincial Synod, in order that, having been recognised by the opinion of other bishops also, they may forthwith be laid before the Supreme Roman Pontiff, by whose authority and prudence such regulations may be made, as shall be expedient for the universal Church, so that the gift of sacred indulgences may be dispensed to the faithful in a pious, holy, and incorrupt manner.'

When we remember that there was a very strong party in the Roman Church demanding considerable reforms, after the recent scandals of Tetzel and his brethren, and when we further bear in mind that the pope would not suffer any part of his prerogative to be even called in question by the Council, we shall the better understand this vague, ineffectual decree,

which defines nothing, and enacts indefinite reforms, of which
the pope was to be the final judge.

Practically, the question remains as it did in Luther's day.
The open market has been spoiled, but profuse grants of
indulgences for visits to certain shrines and localities, and in
return for other considerations, are still the opprobrium of the
Roman Church, and, in the highest degree, of the city of Rome
itself.

3. *The Veneration of Images and Relics.*

If there are germs of these practices traceable within the
first three centuries, they are of the most inoffensive character,
and connected with the natural affectionate celebrations of
martyrs' anniversaries. But in the fourth century the con-
cessions to heathenish customs, recommended by Constantine
at the Council of Nice, rapidly bore fruit. There were still
vigorous protests even to the end of the fourth century. Epiphanius, Augustine, and others, raised their voice against such
corruptions of the faith. But the heathen came in crowds
into the Church, and brought their heathenism, scarcely dis-
guised, with them. Monasticism, in its most fanatical form,
spread within less than a century over the Church. The history of Martin of Tours, written by a contemporary, presents
us with the full ideal of a mediæval saint, within the latter
half of the fourth century. Uncleanliness and squalor of person and of dress, strange visions and questionable miracles,
make the reader hesitate how fairly to apportion the share of
responsibility between fanaticism, imposture, and insanity.
But, indeed, in our day, what reasonable person, moderately
acquainted with human physiology, would expect results of
sanity from a brain physically unnourished by proper food,
worn out by unnatural vigils, and kept in constant excitement
by superstitious notions, and the visits of admiring devotees?

The history of Paulinus, a wealthy and learned Roman
Gaul in the same half-century illustrates the special subject
now before us. His own poems show him to be distinctly
a saint worshipper. He placed pictures in his church at Nola,
and attributed extraordinary power to the relics of Felix, his

patron saint. For further information on the struggle carried on in the Church during this century with regard to the veneration of relics and images, reference may be made to Neander.[1] 'Vigilantius and his Times,' by the late Dr. Gilly, is an interesting monograph on the same subject.

During the fifth and sixth centuries the practice in question became almost universal. In the seventh there was a reaction, and the iconoclastic controversy distracted the Eastern Empire. In 787 the second Council of Nice made a decree in favour of the use of images. This decree was received by Rome, but rejected by 300 bishops from France, Germany, and Italy, at the Council of Frankfort, under Charlemagne. From that time, however, the use of pictures and images prevailed more and more.

The Council of Trent dealt with this subject in somewhat general terms. It follows that the testimony of our Church against the *Romish doctrine* becomes more absolutely directed against the whole system, rather than against some supposed Romish excesses or details. The decree is as follows :

'Let them also diligently teach the faithful, that the holy bodies of the holy martyrs and of others living with Christ, which were living members of Christ, and the temple of the Holy Ghost, and are by Him to be raised to eternal life and glorified, are to be venerated by the faithful, for through them many benefits are bestowed upon men by God. So that they are to be altogether condemned, as the Church has long ago condemned, and now condemns them, who affirm that veneration and honour are not due to the relics of saints, or that these and other sacred monuments are unprofitably honoured by the faithful, or that the memorials of the saints are in vain frequented in order to obtain their aid.

'Moreover, let them teach that the images of Christ, of the God-bearing Virgin, and of other saints, are to be had and retained especially in Churches; and that due honour and veneration be paid to them ; not that any divinity or power is believed to be in them on account of which they are to be

---

[1] 'Ecc. Hist.' vol. iii. pp. 386-398 and 448-461.

worshipped; or that anything is to be sought from them, or
that confidence is to be reposed in the images, as formerly was
done by the Gentiles, who placed their hope in idols; but the
honour which is shown to them is referred to the persons
whom they represent, so that by the images which we kiss, and
before which we uncover our heads and prostrate ourselves, we
adore Christ, and venerate the saints whose similitude they
bear. This is that which has been sanctioned by the decrees of
Councils, and in particular by the second Synod of Nice against
those who oppugn images.' The decree then expatiates on
the use of pictures and images for purposes of instruction, for
keeping the miracles of the saints in mind, and to incite the
faithful to pious deeds. Finally it urges the bishops to guard
against abuses, *e.g.* to teach the unlearned, that when the
Deity is represented, they are not to suppose that a likeness of
God can be delineated. Base gain and indecent or unseemly
pictures of the saints are prohibited, as also licentious festivals
in their honour. New images and claims of new miracles are
to be approved by the bishop, or ultimately by the pope.

Such is the decree of those who would be wiser than God,
and attempt to use images for worship, and yet stop short of
idolatry. It is obvious to remark that all educated Pagans
would give precisely the same account of their use of images,
as merely highly honoured symbols of those who, under those
memorials, were worshipped. In accordance with the second
commandment, the Church of England in this Article pro-
hibits the above plausible *Romish doctrine*, and not merely the
popular excesses in the use of images, which are allowed to be
flagrant idolatry.

4. *The Invocation of Saints.*

This practice grew up *pari passu* with the use of images, and
we may at once quote the decree of the Council of Trent on
the subject. 'The saints who reign with Christ offer their
prayers to God for men : it is good and useful suppliantly to
invoke them, and to flee to their prayers, help and assistance,
because of the benefits to be obtained from God through his
Son, Jesus Christ, our Lord, who is our only Redeemer and

Saviour. Those are of impious opinions who deny that the saints enjoying eternal felicity in heaven are to be invoked—or who affirm that they do not pray for men; or that to invoke them to pray for us individually is idolatry; or that it is contrary to the word of God, and opposed to the honour of Jesus Christ, the One Mediator between God and man; or that it is folly to supplicate verbally or mentally those who reign in heaven.'

Here, again, the Church of England protests not merely against such frantic excesses as the votaries of the Virgin Mary commit, but against the whole system of invocation of saints. We may note here the distinction by which the scholastic divines evaded the consequence of idolatry in allowing image worship and invocation of saints. In the second Council of Nice, the Greeks asserted that λατρεία was due to none but God himself, whilst τιμητικὴ προσκύνησις was due to images. Peter Lombard, following this, ascribed Latria to God alone, and asserted that there are two species of Dulia, one of which may be paid to a creature, and the other to the human nature of Christ only. Thomas Aquinas called this latter hyperdulia, and ascribed it to the Virgin Mary also.[1] If anything further need be added, it is that the Church of England has interpreted her own meaning in this Article by the absolute exclusion from her services of every vestige of the practices stigmatised in it. Judicial decisions have further confirmed this, prohibiting so much as a cross upon the communion table, while permitting sculpture for the purpose of architectural ornament. The Homily *against peril of idolatry* ought to be read. It treats the whole subject copiously both from Scripture and history. The second part contains a very complete abstract of the history of the rise and growth of image worship in the Church. On the Invocation of Saints the second part of the brief Homily *concerning prayer* may be consulted, and on Purgatory and Prayer for the Dead the third part of the same Homily.

[1] Hagenbach, 'Hist. Doctrine,' § 188.

SUGGESTIONS AS TO THE SCRIPTURE PROOF OF ARTICLE XXII.

I. In the very first rank may be placed the *negative* argument from Scripture in dealing with these subjects. When we come to details of ecclesiastical arrangements, and of the administration of the Sacraments, the silence of Scripture proves little, simply because they do not come under review. But when such questions as those noted in the present Article are raised, the silence of Scripture is conclusive. It would be simply impossible for the writers of the Epistles to have omitted directions about prayers for the dead, notices of purgatory, and invocation of saints, if these had been any part of their system. No theory of ' economy ' or ' reserve ' can account for so extraordinary an omission. The Epistles often touch on the state of the departed, and are, above measure, copious on the subjects and nature of prayer ; yet these things are omitted precisely where no Romish divine could avoid giving them the foremost place. The inference is as strong as it is obvious. The student will see that the force of this argument lies not in the mere fact of omission (for many things are omitted in Scripture), but in the peculiar relation of what is omitted to what is mentioned and enjoined. In urging this negative argument, passages may be selected in which the nature of the subject brings out into strong relief the absence of the dogmas controverted here. This argument applies in a very high degree to the modern Roman worship of the Virgin Mary, the extravagances of which will be more or less familiar to the reader. The passages in the New Testament in which she is mentioned are so few, as to be easily collected and remembered ; and the conclusion to be drawn from them, and yet more from the absolute silence of the Epistles with regard even to her name, is of the most decisive character.

II. The second mode of dealing with these subjects will be to select passages in which the state of the departed, prayer, etc., are spoken of in terms absolutely inconsistent with the *Romish doctrines* in question.

III. With regard to image worship, absolute prohibitions of Scripture are not wanting.

IV. The true nature of justification, and the completeness of the satisfaction made by Christ for our sins, may be shown to exclude the notion of purgatory, indulgences, and whatever else belongs to that system.

V. The mediatorial relation of Christ to His Church, and the close communion which the believer enjoys with Him, will exclude secondary mediators.

VI. The passages chiefly alleged by Romanists as favouring their views may be found discussed in Bishop Browne on this Article.

ARTICLES XXIII. AND XXXVI.

ARTICLE XXIII.

Of Ministering in the Congregation.

It is not lawful for any man to take upon him the office of public preaching, or ministering the Sacraments in the Congregation, before he be lawfully called, and sent to execute the same. And those we ought to judge lawfully called and sent, which be chosen and called to this work by men who have public authority given unto them in the Congregation, to call and send Ministers into the Lord's vineyard.

De ministrando in Ecclesia.

Non licet cuiquam sumere sibi munus publice prædicandi, aut administrandi Sacramenta in Ecclesia, nisi prius fuerit ad hæc obeunda legitime vocatus et missus. Atque illos legitime vocatos et missos existimare debemus, qui per homines, quibus potestas vocandi ministros, atque mittendi in vineam Domini, publice concessa est in Ecclesia, cooptati fuerint, et adsciti in hoc opus.

ARTICLE XXXVI.

Of Consecration of Bishops and Ministers.

The Book of Consecration of Archbishops and Bishops, and ordering of Priests and Deacons, lately set forth in the time of *Edward* the Sixth, and confirmed at the same time by authority of Parliament, doth contain all things necessary to such Consecration and Ordering:

De Episcoporum et Ministrorum consecratione.

Libellus de consecratione Archiepiscoporum, et Episcoporum, et de ordinatione Presbyterorum et Diaconorum editus nuper temporibus Edwardi VI. et auctoritate Parliamenti illis ipsis temporibus confirmatus, omnia ad ejusmodi consecrationem et ordinationem necessaria continet, et

neither hath it anything that of itself is superstitious or ungodly. And therefore whosoever are consecrated or ordered according to the Rites of that Book, since the second year of the aforenamed King *Edward* unto this time, or hereafter shall be consecrated or ordered according to the same Rites; we decree all such to be rightly, orderly, and lawfully consecrated and ordered.

nihil habet, quod ex se sit, aut superstitiosum, aut impium; itaque quicunque juxta ritus illius libri consecrati aut ordinati sunt, ab anno secundo prædicti regis Edwardi, usque ad hoc tempus, aut in posterum juxta eosdem ritus consecrabuntur, aut ordinabuntur, rite atque ordine, atque legitime statuimus esse et fore consecratos et ordinatos.

Notes on the Text of Articles XXIII and XXXVI.

In Article XXIII. the following equivalents may be noted. ' In the congregation; ' Latin, *in ecclesiâ* (as in Article XIX.). 'Lawfully called;' Latin, *legitime vocatos.* 'Authority;' Latin, *potestas.*

In Article XXXVI. we may note the phrase 'rightly, orderly, and lawfully; ' Latin, *rite, atque ordine, atque legitime.*' The word ' rightly,' therefore, in this place signifies *correctly in respect of form and manner.*

Article XXIII. is identical with the twenty-fourth of 1552. It is partly taken from the Confession of Augsburgh, which declares,[1] ' No one ought to teach publicly in the congregation (ecclesia), or to administer the Sacraments, *nisi rite vocatus.*' Article XXXVI. was entirely recast in 1562. It takes the place of Art. XXXV. of 1552, which asserted that the second Prayer book of King Edward (*Liber nuperrime traditus,* &c.), together with the Ordinal, was in accordance with the Gospel, and to be received by the people.

Observations on Articles XXIII. and XXXVI.

Article XXIII. is so general in its terms that it might be admitted by any body of Christians who maintain the prin-

[1] Art. XIV.

ciple of an order of ministers set apart for the service of the Church.

The question, therefore, which arises, and which will need illustration from competent English sources, will be how far the twenty-third Article is interpreted or limited by the thirty-sixth, or by any other Church of England document.

Our enquiry in the first instance resolves itself into the question whether the thirty-sixth Article is meant to have simply an inclusive force, or also an exclusive force. That is, whether it means only to maintain the validity of the English mode of ordination as against objectors to the same, or also to pronounce against the validity of other modes. It seems clear that the thirty-sixth Article can have no such exclusive force for this reason. If it excludes *any*, it excludes *all* who are not consecrated or ordained according to our form, whether episcopally or not; which would prove too much. This Article therefore asserts the validity of our orders, and leaves the question of other modes of ordination untouched.

The preface to the Ordinal may at first sight be considered more exclusive. It declares that the three orders of bishops, priests, and deacons have continued from the time of the apostles; and it proceeds to order that none shall be accounted to be a lawful bishop, priest, or deacon of the Church of England who has not been ordained according to this ritual, or has not previously received episcopal ordination.

This prohibitory clause was added in 1662. It, therefore, stands as part of the more exclusive system adopted at the Restoration, and embodied in the Act of Uniformity of Charles II. Before that time, an Act of parliament, 1571, permitted men ordained otherwise than by the form of the English Church to hold benefices in England, on condition of their duly subscribing the Articles of Religion, and reading them during morning service in their own church.[1]

That this continued to be the practice is witnessed by the unexceptionable testimony of Bishop Cosin in a letter written in 1650, quoted in Dean Goode's ' Rule of Faith.' [2] 'Therefore, if at any time a minister so ordained in these French

---

[1] Strype's 'Annals,' B. I. c. 7.   [2] Vol. ii. p. 293, 2nd ed.

churches came to incorporate himself in ours, and to receive a public charge or cure of souls among us in the Church of England (as I have known some of them to have so done of late, and can instance in many other before my time), our bishops did not reordain him to his charge, as they must have done if his former ordination here in France had been void. Nor did our laws require more of him than to declare his public consent to the religion received amongst us, and to subscribe the Articles established.'

It appears, therefore, that previously to the Act of Uniformity of 1662, the Church of England admitted the validity of the ordinations in the foreign Protestant churches. That act for the first time required that episcopal ordination should be an absolute requisite for ministering in our Church, and at the same time the above clause was added in the preface to the Ordination Service denying the character of a minister of the Church of England to any one not episcopally ordained. The change thus introduced will be judged of in different ways according to the sympathies of different persons. But the conclusion is inevitable that our Church has passed no opinion in any of her formularies on the usages of foreign non-episcopal Churches ; but has simply ruled since 1662 that their ministers shall not be admissible, as such, into her service.

Our position, therefore, so far, is this. The Church of England has pronounced episcopacy to be of primitive and apostolical antiquity. She has also for the last two hundred years absolutely required episcopal ordination for all her own ministers. With regard to other differently constituted foreign churches, she is silent.

We may now endeavour to describe the position of different parties in relation to the subject before us. The Episcopalian (as such) usually asserts, with the preface to our Ordinal, the historico-ecclesiastical fact of the primitive antiquity of the three orders of the ministry. He also asserts either that he can trace them in the New Testament, or at least that nothing in the New Testament is inconsistent with their early existence. But he can scarcely fail to acknowledge that there

is no scheme of Church government definitely drawn out in the
New Testament; nor any command enforcing any particular
form of order or discipline on the Church at large. Many
would add to this, that such a precept would be inconsistent
with the genius of Christianity as a universal religion, flexible
and adaptable as regards its outer organisation.

Agreeing in the above general statement, Episcopalians vary
much in their deductions and resulting opinions.

I. The most extreme school sees in the historical fact, the
equivalent of an apostolical precept binding for ever on the
Church. It thus refuses to recognise the existence of a church
where regular episcopal organisation is not found.

II. The general tone of English divinity, as represented
from the first by men of different schools, has been more
moderate than this. It has accepted the historical fact, and
grounded upon it a satisfactory confidence in the apostolicity
and regularity of the constitution of the English Church. But
it has refused to admit anything into the category of the
essentials of a Christian church, which is not positively laid
down in the New Testament, or derived from it by direct
inference. For this moderation the student will have been
prepared already by the discussion of the *Notes of the Church*
under Article XIX. With these views most of our leading
divines have admitted the validity of foreign non-episcopal
ordination, some sparingly and grudgingly, others fully and
cheerfully.

The regular transmission of holy orders from generation to
generation, in episcopal lines from the apostles' time to our
own, is usually styled apostolical succession. We shall next,
in pursuance of the plan of this work, exhibit the opinions of
some representative English divines on the *necessity*, not the
fact, of this succession. We may first refer to Hooker, the
great defender of the Church of England. Book vii. 14, he
thus writes: 'Now whereas hereupon some do infer, that no
ordination can stand but only such as is made by bishops, which
have had their ordination likewise by other bishops before
them, till we come to the very apostles of Christ themselves....
To this we answer that there may be sometimes very just and

sufficient reason to allow ordination made without a bishop. The whole Church visible being the true original subject of all power, it hath not ordinarily allowed any other than bishops alone to ordain; howbeit, as the ordinary course is ordinarily in all things to be observed, so it may be in some cases not unnecessary that we decline from those ordinary ways. Men may be extraordinarily, yet allowably, two ways admitted unto spiritual functions in the Church. One is, when God himself doth of himself raise up any, whose labour he useth without requiring that men should authorise them. . . . Another extraordinary kind of vocation is, when the exigence of necessity doth constrain to leave the usual ways of the Church, which otherwise we would willingly keep: where the Church must needs have some ordained, and neither hath, nor can have possibly, a bishop to ordain: in case of such necessity the ordinary institution of God hath given oftentimes, and may give, place. And, therefore, we are not simply without exception, to urge a lineal descent of power from the apostles by continued succession of bishops in every effectual ordination.' The reader who examines this passage in the original will see that it appears to contemplate and defend the case of Beza, ordained by Calvin.

We have already referred (under Art. XIX.) to Field, 'Of the Church,' and his discussion of succession as one of Bellarmine's 'Notes of the Church.'[1] The subject is further treated[2] by him in the following important passage: 'There is no reason to be given, but that in case of necessity, wherein all bishops were extinguished by death, or, being fallen into heresy, should refuse to ordain any to serve God in his true worship, but that presbyters, as they may do all other acts, whatsoever special challenge bishops in ordinary course make upon them, may do this also (i.e. may ordain). Who, then, dare condemn all those worthy ministers of God that were ordained by presbyters, in sundry churches of the world, at such times as bishops, in those parts where they lived, opposed themselves against the truth of God, and persecuted such as professed it?' Again, 'If the bishops become enemies to God

---

[1] Book II. c. 6.   [2] Book III. c. 39.

and true religion, in case of such necessity, as the care and government of the Church is devolved to the presbyters remaining Catholic and being of a better spirit, so the duty of ordaining such as are to assist or succeed them in the work of the ministry pertains to them likewise.'

There can be no question that this was the tone of the leading English divines in the reigns of Elizabeth and James I. They did not meet their violent Puritan opponents, who claimed the divine right of Presbyterianism, with an absolute counter-claim of the indefeasible divine right of Episcopacy. They were content to prove it lawful in its use, and primitive in its origin. It is well known, however, that in the time of Charles I. the increasing bitterness of controversy induced the episcopal divines to make larger claims on behalf of their Church polity. Still they stopped short of rejecting the validity of other modes of ordination, and denying that the foreign Protestant communities were churches of Christ. Perhaps, among the Stuart divines of this class, no more typical names could be alleged than those of Archbishop Laud and Bishop Cosin. The Archbishop, in his 'Conference with Fisher the Jesuit,'[1] denies the necessity of 'continued visible succession,' or the existence of any promise that it should be uninterruptedly continued in any Church. He proceeds to say, 'for succession in the general I shall say this; it is a great happiness where it may be had visible and continued, and a great conquest over the mutability of this present world. But I do not find anyone of the ancient Fathers that makes local, personal, visible, and continued succession a necessary mark or sign of the true Church in any one place.'

Bishop Cosin, in a letter quoted by Dean Goode,[2] severely censures the Protestant churches of France and Geneva for their 'defect of episcopacy,' but says, 'I dare not take upon me to condemn or determine a nullity of their own ordinations against them.' He further acknowledges that in the face of certain passages in St. Jerome, some schoolmen, Jewel, Field,

[1] Section 39, vii.

[2] 'Divine Rule of Faith,' vol. ii. p. 293, 2nd ed.

Hooker, and others, he cannot say 'that the ministers of the reformed French Churches, for want of episcopal ordination, have no order at all.' He recommends his correspondent to communicate, if need be, with the French Protestants, rather than with the Roman Church. For a further copious treatment of this subject, reference may be made to Dean Goode.[1]

It has been the unhappy lot of our own days to see the ground taken by the great writers of our Church abandoned, and the definitions of our Articles and of our recognised divines forsaken for the 'Notes of the Church,' maintained by Bellarmine or other Roman controversialists.

III. Having so far attempted to give the student information on the views of *Succession* which have been held by various members of our Church, we may now add some notice of the varying opinions as to the precise status of the bishop as distinguished from the presbyter.

Omitting minor variations, there have been two principal classes of opinion. First, that of those who hold that the office of a bishop is in itself, and always has been, absolutely distinct from that of the presbyter, and can only be given by the laying on of hands by other bishops, themselves lawfully consecrated. It need scarcely be added that very various consequences are deduced from this opinion by men of different schools, some holding very strong notions of indefectible episcopal grace, and connecting absolutely with such a *succession* the grace of the sacraments and the transmission of the powers of the Christian ministry ; others being content to view this as the ordinary organisation of the Church, apostolical in its origin, but like all *positive* institutions, yielding either to necessity, or the higher claims of the *moral* obligation.

The class of opinions which we have placed second has been held by many divines, including (it is asserted) early Fathers and schoolmen, as well as Anglican bishops. This class of opinion regards the primitive bishop as little more than a kind of president among the presbyters, but not of a different order, strictly speaking. It will be seen under Article XXV.

---

[1] 'Divine Rule of Faith,' vol. ii. pp. 247–348, 2nd ed.

that among the seven orders reckoned by the Church of Rome as sacraments, the priesthood is the highest, and episcopacy is not named.   And it is natural that those who exalt the powers of the priesthood as the official instrument of accomplishing a corporal presence of our Lord in, with, or under, the elements in the Eucharist and, as the depositary of the sacramental power of remitting sin in absolution, may be slow to acknowledge an episcopal virtue and efficacy yet greater than this, saving for the general purposes of government.   It is equally natural, on the other hand, that this identification of the episcopal status with that of a presbyter, so far as regards the essential powers of the Christian ministry, should be used by persons desirous of establishing new Christian communities. Accordingly, Wesley, in his later years, maintained this view, and in accordance with it gave organisation to the Methodist Episcopal Church in the United States, and ordination to the Wesleyan ministers in England.

This theory of Church government must not be confused with Presbyterianism.   It holds that the Church is governed monarchically by a presbyter set apart for that purpose, and usually and properly (but not necessarily) consecrated by other bishops ; though the designation and appointment of an ordained presbyter to that office, by the Church, will suffice to constitute him bishop.   Presbyterianism, on the other hand, treats all presbyters on the same level, and governs the Church in a republican manner by representative bodies of presbyters and lay deputies.   For further information on this view of the rightful position of a bishop, together with a copious discussion of authorities, reference may be made to Dean Goode's ' Divine Rule of Faith,' [1] also to Field ' Of the Church.' [2]   A dissertation by Professor Lightfoot in his recent commentary on the Epistle to the Philippians discusses a branch of the same subject.

A final caution may be added.   The distinction is very important between what is irregular and what is invalid.   An act may be irregular, and yet may be valid if done.   Nay, in

[1] ' Divine Rule of Faith,' vol. ii. p. 259, 2nd ed.
[2] Book III. c. 39, and Book V. c. 27.

some cases of necessity, it may be an absolute duty to act irregularly. Lay baptism is undoubtedly irregular, and yet it is acknowledged to be valid if duly administered as to essentials.

THE THREE ORDERS OF THE MINISTRY TRACED IN THE NEW TESTAMENT.

ACTS I.-V.—The history of the Church is confined to Jerusalem, and the Apostles are the only order of ministers named.

ACTS VI.—' The Seven ' are ordained to a distinct office, bearing no name in Scripture, but subsequently identified with the Diaconate.

ACTS XIV. 23.—Presbyters are everywhere ordained by Paul and Barnabas.

ACTS XV. 6, 22.—Presbyters are spoken of as existing in the Church at Jerusalem, and meeting in council with the apostles.

ACTS XX. 17.—There were presbyters (plural) in the Church of Ephesus; the same men are called in v. 28 ἐπίσκοποι.

ACTS XXI. 18.—The presbyters of Jerusalem, with St. James, receive St. Paul.

There were therefore, in the Church at Jerusalem, apostles, presbyters, and deacons. And towards the close of the history of the Acts of the Apostles (i.e. about A.D. 58) there was a president, St. James (probably not an apostle, see dissertation in Professor Lightfoot on the Galatians), presbyters, and (we presume) still deacons.

PHILIPPIANS I. 1.—There were ἐπίσκοποι and deacons at Philippi. Some hold that Epaphroditus, then at Rome, (II. 25) and styled the ἀπόστολος of the Philippians, was (in modern language) their bishop.

1 TIM. III. 1.—The due qualifications of an ἐπίσκοπος.

1 TIM. III. 8.—The qualifications of a deacon.

1 TIM. V. 19.—Timothy may judge the presbyters.

1 TIM. V. 22.—Timothy has the power of ordination.

1 Tim. I. 3.—Timothy is to be watchful over the doctrine of the teachers.

Titus I. 5.—Titus is to ordain presbyters, who are called also ἐπίσκοποι in v. 7.

Titus III. 10.—Titus is to reject heretics after due admonition.

It is maintained that the two epistles last named contain the three orders, viz. that of Timothy and Titus corresponding to what has been since named a bishop, presbyters or ἐπίσκοποι, and deacons.

Rev. II. 1, &c.—St. John is directed to write to the 'Angels' of the Seven Churches of Asia. These have been very generally interpreted as the presiding ministers of the Churches, and that not only by Episcopal divines, but by many others, as Beza, Bullinger, Grotius, &c.

ARTICLE XXIV.

Of speaking in the Congregation in such a tongue as the people understandeth.

De loquendo in Ecclesia lingua quam populus intelligit.

It is a thing plainly repugnant to the word of God, and the custom of the Primitive Church, to have public Prayer in the Church, or to minister the Sacraments, in a tongue not understanded of the people.

Lingua populo non intellecta, publicas in Ecclesia preces peragere aut Sacramenta administrare, verbo Dei, et primitivæ Ecclesiæ consuetudini plane repugnat.

NOTES ON THE TEXT OF ARTICLE XXIV.

No special comment is needed on either the Latin or English text of the Article. The twenty-fifth Article of 1552 was to the same effect, but less strongly worded. ' It is most seemly, and most agreeable to the word of God, that in the congregation nothing be openly read or spoken in a tongue unknown to the people, the which thing St. Paul did forbid, except some were present that should declare the same.'

OBSERVATIONS ON ARTICLE XXIV.

The strangely irrational and unscriptural custom against which this Article protests belongs not only to the Roman Church. Several sections of the Christian Church persist in the use of service-books, or of translations of the Scriptures, in dialects long obsolete. But the use of Latin in the services of the Roman Church was the occasion of this Article. Little more can be needed than to show how this usage arose.

When the Western Roman Empire was broken up, Latin had superseded the native dialects throughout Italy, Gaul,

Spain, and probably Britain, excepting in the more remote and mountainous or less civilized provinces. The Church, therefore, through these regions was a Latin Church. In Italy, Gaul, and Spain the invading barbarians either pro-- fessed or adopted Christianity, and merged their own lan- guage in the provincial Latin. Thus, throughout those countries, the Church as well as the people continued to use Latin. It is not necessary to go into the question how far the provincial Latin was already a corrupt patois. Hallam [1] shows that Latin was still spoken in France in the sixth and seventh centuries; faulty in point of grammar, but still Latin, and intelligible to the people. In the eighth and ninth centuries we read of the 'rustic Roman,' and find that vulgar patois of broken Latin prevailed, out of which, in course of time, modern French arose. In Italy and Spain similar changes and developments of dialects were proceeding. But Hallam says that he does not find any express evidence of a vulgar Italian dialect different from the Latin earlier than the close of the tenth century.

From this sketch it will be manifest that the change of lan- guage was so very gradual that it was only by little and little that the Church services became unintelligible to the people. By the time that the new dialects had assumed a definite type, and had received some little literary culture, there was not sufficient enlightenment in the people to make them desire vernacular services.

This explanation will not apply to Germany, nor to England after the Saxon conquest. In both these countries Teutonic dialects prevailed. But they received Christianity so late, and chiefly through Latin sources, that the Latin service-books were everywhere introduced. The priesthood cherished Latin as the language of books, and of such learning and divinity as they possessed. It was also the instrument of intercourse with Rome and their foreign brethren. It was, therefore, prized as at once a pledge and means of learning, and a matter of ecclesiastical convenience. Subsequently it was found to be too valuable an instrument of ecclesiastical

[1] 'History of Middle Ages,' chap. ix. Pt. I.

domination to be abandoned by the Church of Rome, even in the face of the fourteenth chapter of the First Epistle to the Corinthians. Accordingly the Council of Trent [1] decreed that it was 'not expedient that the mass should be everywhere celebrated in the vernacular tongue.' The mode of defending this practice usually employed by Romanist writers appears to be of the following nature : 1. The canon of the mass is peculiarly sacred and perfect, and translations would naturally vary, and risk imperfections which might vitiate the whole. 2. Priests could only officiate in their own country if accustomed to the vernacular only. 3. The mass is a sacrifice, a thing done, which the worshipper is to contemplate and adore with all the powers of his heart. The words used do not, therefore, concern him. 4. In fact, the priest utters the canon of the mass in a low voice *to God*, and not to the people. Hence the language used is, to them, a matter of no consequence. It is, however, customary now in England, and probably in other countries of similar enlightenment, to place in the hands of the people vernacular books of devotion, explaining the nature of the services, and containing translations of some portions of them, and meditations and prayers in harmony with other parts.

It will be scarcely needful to point out that the Scriptural mode of dealing with the subject of this Article may be thus classified :—

I. Direct Scripture examples.

II. The nature of prayer, and its true requisites.

III. Direct Scripture precepts.

[1] Session XXII. chap. viii.

ARTICLE XXV.

Of the Sacraments.

Sacraments ordained of Christ be not only badges or tokens of Christian men's profession, but rather they be certain sure witnesses, and effectual signs of grace, and God's good will towards us, by the which he doth work invisibly in us, and doth not only quicken, but also strengthen and confirm our Faith in him.

There are two Sacraments ordained of Christ our Lord in the Gospel, that is to say, Baptism, and the Supper of the Lord.

Those five commonly called Sacraments, that is to say, Confirmation, Penance, Orders, Matrimony, and extreme Unction, are not to be counted for Sacraments of the Gospel, being such as have grown partly of the corrupt following of the apostles, partly are states of life allowed in the Scriptures ; but yet have not like nature of Sacraments with Baptism, and the Lord's Supper, for that they have not any visible sign or ceremony ordained of God.

The Sacraments were not

De Sacramentis.

Sacramenta, a Christo instituta, non tantum sunt notæ professionis Christianorum, sed certa quædam potius testimonia, et efficacia signa gratiæ atque bonæ in nos voluntatis Dei, per quæ invisibiliter ipse in nos operatur, nostramque fidem in se non solum excitat, verum etiam confirmat.

Duo a Christo Domino nostro in Evangelio instituta sunt Sacramenta : scilicet, Baptismus, et Cœna Domini.

Quinque illa vulgo nominata Sacramenta : scilicet, confirmatio, pœnitentia, ordo, matrimonium, et extrema unctio, pro Sacramentis Evangelicis habenda non sunt, ut quæ, partim a prava Apostolorum imitatione profluxerunt, partim vitæ status sunt in Scripturis quidem probati : sed sacramentorum eandem cum Baptismo et Cœna Domini rationem non habentes, ut quæ signum aliquod visibile, seu cæremoniam, a Deo institutam, non habeant.

Sacramenta non in hoc instituta sunt a Christo ut spectarentur, aut circumferrentur, sed ut rite illis utere-

ordained of Christ to be gazed upon, or to be carried about, but that we should duly use them. And in such only as worthily receive the same they have a wholesome effect or operation : But they that receive them unworthily purchase to themselves damnation, as St. *Paul* saith.

mur, et in his duntaxat qui digne percipiunt salutarem habent effectum : Qui vero indigne percipiunt, damnationem (ut inquit Paulus) sibi ipsis acquirunt.

NOTES ON THE TEXT OF ARTICLE XXV.

The following equivalents may be noted: ' Badges or tokens,' Latin, *notæ*; 'effectual signs,' Latin, *efficacia signa*; 'penance,' Latin, *pœnitentia*; 'nature,' Latin, *rationem*, as in Article IX. &c. ' Quicken,' Latin, *excitat*; not applied, therefore, to the *first* quickening or bringing to life. ' Duly,' Latin, *rite*, not *recte* :—that is in due *manner* and order, as opposed to gazing upon them, &c. ' In such only,' Latin, *in his duntaxat*.

The word *Sacrament* not being found in the Scripture, and being of Latin origin, owes its theological meaning to ecclesiastical writers. It is disputed whether this use arose from *sacramentum* in its sense of a military oath, or of a thing sacred. The word was very loosely used by early Christian writers, instances of which may be seen in Bingham.[1]

There is a very clear explanation of this absence of precision in the use of the word in the Homily on Common Prayer and the sacraments : ' In a general acceptation the name of a sacrament may be attributed to anything whereby a holy thing is signified. In which understanding of the word, the ancient writers have given this name, not only to the other five, commonly of late years taken and used for supplying the number of the seven sacraments; but also to divers and sundry other ceremonies, as to oil, washing of feet, and such like; not meaning thereby to repute them as sacraments, in the same signification that the two forenamed sacraments are.' The Homily proceeds to refer to passages in St. Augustine

[1] Antiq. xii. i. 4.

P

speaking expressly of the sacraments of the Gospel as only
two in number. The Homily moderately says of other things
that ' no man ought to take them for sacraments, in such signification and meaning as the sacraments of Baptism and the
Lord's Supper are.' The danger of confusing ideas in the
popular mind by using the same name for religious ceremonies
of different origin and degrees of obligation is obvious.

For this reason our Church has avoided giving the name of
sacrament to any ordinance excepting the two instituted by
Christ. The Homily has noticed the absence of precision in
the early use of the word. It is in the Catechism that our
Church gives the definition of the word sacrament.

' Q. How many sacraments has Christ ordained in His
Church?

' A. Two only as generally necessary to salvation, that is to
say, Baptism and the Supper of our Lord.

' Q. What meanest thou by this word sacrament?

' A. I mean an outward and visible sign of an inward and
spiritual grace, given unto us, ordained by Christ Himself,
as a means whereby we receive the same, and a pledge to
assure us thereof.'

According to these statements there are three essential con-
stituents of a sacrament, which are these :—

1. It has an outward sign.

2. It has an inward grace of which it is the pledge and
means.

3. It was ordained by Christ.

The Article gives no definition, but its statements are in
perfect harmony with that obtained from the Catechism, and
presuppose the above three essential parts of a sacrament.

The effect of the above definition is not only positive, but
also negative and exclusive; for by necessary consequence it
denies the name of *sacrament* to every rite excepting the two.
This is obviously the safer course, as tending to perspicuity,
and excluding the confusion of ideas which follows on the confusion of terms.

The corresponding Article of 1552 (the Twenty-sixth) differed considerably from the present form. It ran thus: 'Our

Lord Jesus Christ hath knit together a company of new people with sacraments, most few in number, most easy to be kept, most excellent in signification, as is Baptism and the Lord's Supper. The sacraments were not ordained of Christ to be gazed upon, or to be carried about, but that we should duly use them. And in such only as worthily receive the same, they have a wholesome effect and operation, and yet not that of the work wrought, as some men speak, which word, as it is strange, and unknown to Holy Scripture, so it engendereth no godly, but a very superstitious sense. But they that receive the sacraments unworthily, purchase to themselves damnation, as Saint Paul saith.' To this is appended what is now the first clause of the Article, and which is, therefore, not transcribed here.

There are sufficient verbal coincidences between this Article and the Thirteenth of the Augsburgh Confession, to prove that the latter formula was before the compilers of our Articles, but not sufficient to justify an assertion of the one being to any great extent taken from the other. For instance, we have the expressions *notæ professionis—signa et testimonia voluntatis Dei erga nos—proposita ad excitandum et confirmandum fidem*—which are common, with slight differences, to both documents.

The Five Rejected Romish Sacraments.

That the word *sacrament* was loosely used in the early ages has been seen. It is said that Peter Lombard in the twelfth century was the first who precisely enumerated the mystic number of seven sacraments. His Book of Sentences was a text-book in theology until the Reformation, and his enumeration became regarded as Catholic.[1]

It is a material point for consideration whether in our difference with the Church of Rome on this subject we are contending about words or facts and doctrines. The following passage will illustrate this.[2]

[1] See Hagenbach, 'History of Doctrines;' Clark's edit., § 189. Also Hey on this Article.

[2] 'Council of Trent,' Session vii. Canon i.

'If any one shall say that the sacraments of the New Law were not all instituted by Jesus Christ our Lord; or are more or fewer than seven, viz.: Baptism, Confirmation, the Eucharist, Penance, Extreme Unction, Orders, and Matrimony; or that any of these seven is not truly and properly a sacrament; let him be anathema.' Here it is plain that the third note of a sacrament in our own definition, Institution by Christ, is claimed for the five in question. The other two notes in our definition are contained in this extract from the Catechism of the Council of Trent.[1] 'A sacrament is a visible sign of an invisible grace, instituted for our justification.'

This makes it abundantly clear that we are not engaged in a strife of words, but that, meaning the same thing, the Church of Rome asserts that there are *seven* sacraments; the Church of England asserts that there are '*two only.*'

To one who admits the supremacy of Holy Scripture, and is even moderately acquainted with what is genuine in Christian antiquity, it will suffice, in justification of our Article, to state plainly what the Romish Teachers are able to allege in support of their theory of seven sacraments. For this purpose the Catechism of the Council of Trent is taken, in which clear, simple, and absolute statements of doctrine for the instruction of the people are everywhere to be found.

In order to understand what follows, the definition[2] must be first considered. There it is explained that the outer or '*sensible thing*' in the sacrament 'consists of two things, one of which has the nature of *matter*, and is called *the Element*: the other has the force of *form*, and is designated by a common appellation, *the word.*' It will be seen, therefore, that to bear out its own definitions, the Catechism is constrained to discover an Institution by Christ of *matter* and *form of words* for each sacrament. How boldly but hopelessly it labours at such a task, even with the aid of the forged decretals,[3] will be seen in the sequel.

The five Romish sacraments are taken in the order in which they occur in our Article.

[1] Pt. ii. chap. i. Q. 3.   [2] Ibid. Q. 10.   [3] See p. 177.

I. Confirmation.

Q. 6. 'Pastors must explain that not only was it instituted by Christ our Lord ; but that by Him were also ordained, as St. Fabian, pontiff of Rome, testifieth, the rite of Chrism, and the words which the Catholic Church uses in its administration.'

Q. 7. The '*matter*' of this sacrament is defined to be '*the Chrism*, or that ointment only which is compounded of oil and balsam, with the solemn consecration of the bishop.' It is further asserted that this is 'handed down to us by St. Dionysius, and by many other Fathers of the gravest authority, particularly by Pope Fabian, who testifies that the Apostles received the composition of chrism from our Lord, and transmitted it to us.'

Q. 11. The *form* in this sacrament is said to be as follows. 'I sign thee with the sign of the cross, and I confirm thee with the chrism of salvation, in the name of the Father and of the Son and of the Holy Ghost.' According to the exigencies of the Tridentine definition, it ought to be proved that Christ appointed these words. Unable to advance anything on this head beyond what was alleged under Question 6, the point is thus evaded. *Q.* 12. 'Were we even unable to prove by reason that this is the true and absolute form of this sacrament, the authority of the Catholic Church, under whose mastership we have always been thus taught, suffers us not to entertain the least doubt on the subject.'

II. Penance.[2]

Q. 10. 'Christ the Lord was pleased to give it a place among the sacraments.'.

Q. 13. 'Penance differs from the other sacraments principally in this, that the *matter* of the others is some production of nature or art, but the "*quasi materia*" of the sacrament of Penance consists, as has been defined by the Council of Trent, of the acts of the penitent, that is of contrition, confession, and satisfaction.'

---

[1] 'Catechism of Trent,' Pt. ii. chap. iii.   [2] Ibid. chap v.

Q. 14. ' The *form* is, *I absolve thee,* as not only may be
inferred from these words, *Whatsoever ye shall bind on earth
shall be bound also in heaven ;* but as we have also learned
from the same doctrine of Christ our Lord, handed down to
us by apostolic tradition.'

III. Orders.[1]

Q. 9. ' Comprising as the ministry does, many gradations
and various functions, and disposed as all these gradations
and functions are, with regularity, it is appropriately and
suitably called the sacrament of *Order.*'

Q. 10. ' The bishop, handing to him, who is being ordained priest, a cup containing wine and water, and a paten
with bread, says : *Receive the power of offering sacrifice &c. &c ;*
by which words the Church hath always taught that, whilst the
matter is presented, the power of consecrating the Eucharist
is conferred.' There is not, either in the Canons or Catechism of Trent, any more exact definition of the *institution,
matter,* or *form* of this rite.

Q. 12. ' According to the uniform tradition of the
Catholic Church, the number of these orders is seven ; and
they are called porter, reader, exorcist, acolyte, sub-deacon,
deacon, priest. . . . of these some are greater which are also
called holy, some lesser, called minor orders. The greater,
or holy, are sub-deaconship, deaconship, and priesthood ; the
lesser orders are porter, reader, exorcist, and acolyte.'

It will be observed that the episcopate is not reckoned as a
separate order. *Q.* 25. speaks of it as a priesthood having a
different degree of dignity and power.[2]

IV. Matrimony.[3]

Q. 15. Asserts that Matrimony received the dignity of a
sacrament from Christ.

Q. 16. Asserts that Matrimony is a sacrament because
the words (Eph. v. 32) *sacramentum hoc magnum est* are the
Latin rendering of the Greek τὸ μυστήριον τοῦτο μέγα ἐστί.

---

[1] ' Trent Catechism,' Pt. ii. chap. vii.   [2] See Article XXIII.
[3] ' Trent Catechism,' Pt. ii. chap. viii.

Neither the Catechism nor the Canons of Trent explain the *institution, form,* or *matter* of Matrimony considered as a sacrament. As it will be an instructive example to the student, we follow this somewhat further to illustrate the force of assumption and assertion with which Romish Theologians *break their way* through difficulties of this nature.

Few theological works have a more extensive use and authority in Romanist Colleges for the education of priests, than the *Theologia Moralis et Dogmatica* of Peter Dens. In the ' *Tractatus de Matrimonio,*' N. 26, we are told, ' so far as Matrimony is a sacrament, it was instituted by Christ our Lord, as the Council of Trent hath laid down, but when this was, does not appear certain.' Different opinions are then given. Some say this was done at the marriage in Cana; some, when Christ said ' What God hath joined together let no man put asunder; ' some, that it must have been done during the forty days after the resurrection ; some, that the time is uncertain, and that the time of the institution of Baptism is equally uncertain.

N. 28. The proof that Matrimony is a sacrament is thus arranged. 1. By the decrees of the Councils of Trent and Florence. 2. From tradition and prescription. 3. From Eph. v. 32.

N. 30. treats of the matter and form of the sacrament of Matrimony. This is said to depend on the question, Who is the minister of this sacrament? Some say that the contracting parties themselves are the actual ministers. Those who maintain this opinion are not agreed, but they most commonly hold the signs of consent, by which the parties mutually surrender to each other the right over their own body, to constitute the *matter,* and the words of such surrender to be the *form.*

The more approved opinion seems to make the *priest* the minister of this sacrament. According to this opinion the *matter* is the matrimonial contract of surrender of bodily rights to each other, and the *form* is the sentence of the priest, *I join you in matrimony in the name of the Father, &c.*

It is no exaggeration thus to sum up this treatment of the subject. Marriage is a sacrament, because it has been so defined by Councils and long received. Therefore Christ must have instituted it, though when He did so cannot be shown. Therefore, also, He must have instituted both *matter* and *form*, although both are so uncertain that the Council of Trent did not venture to define them.

V. Extreme Unction.[1]

Q. 2. ' Of all the other sacred unctions prescribed by our Lord and Saviour to His Church, this is the last to be administered.'

Q. 3. ' That extreme unction possesses the true nature of a sacrament can be clearly established from the words in which the Apostle St. James has promulgated the law of this sacrament.

Q. 5. ' The *matter* is oil consecrated by the bishop, that is to say, oil of olive berries, and not that expressed from any rich or fatty matter.'

Q. 6. ' The form of this sacrament is the word and that solemn prayer used by the priest at each anointing : *By this holy unction may God indulge thee, whatever sins thou hast committed by sight, smell, touch,' &c.*

Q. 8. ' It having been shown that extreme unction is truly and properly to be numbered among the sacraments, it also follows that it derives its institution from Christ our Lord, having been subsequently proposed and promulgated to the faithful by the Apostle St. James.'

It is important to add another mediæval theory of the effect of some sacraments, inasmuch as it has left some traces on our own usages. Three of the sacraments, Baptism, Confirmation, and Holy Orders, have been said to impress on the soul what is called ' *a character.*' The Catechism of the Council of Trent explains this to mean ' a certain distinctive mark impressed on the soul, which inhering perpetually can never be blotted out.' This is a necessary part of a system which holds that sacraments contain and give grace *ex opere operato*, when dealing with those which, from their nature,

---

[1] 'Trent Catechism,' Pt. ii. chap. vi.

cannot be repeated. The distinction between this and the
earlier statements on the subject is clearly given by Bingham.[1]

THE EFFICACY OF THE SACRAMENTS.

It will suffice here to note the two assertions made by this
Article on the efficacy of the two sacraments:

1. They are not bare 'tokens,' but are effectual signs (*efficacia signa*) of grace, through which God works.

2. This is not to be taken absolutely and invariably (*ex
opere operato*), but is conditional on the worthy receiving,
'In such only as worthily receive the same, they have a wholesome effect or operation.'

As these two statements will accompany us in the separate
treatment of the two sacraments, it is only necessary here to
call the student's attention to the preliminary fact that our
Church asserts the necessity of 'the worthy reception' to the
'wholesome effect' of both sacraments equally. This must,
therefore, be understood as underlying and qualifying the
subsequent statements about Baptism and the Lord's Supper.

The doctrine of our Church will be sufficiently illustrated
for our present purpose by contrasting the Tridentine statements with those of the illustrious Hooker.[2]

Canon 6. 'If any one shall say that the sacraments of the
New Law do not contain the grace which they signify, or do
not confer the grace itself on those not placing a bar (*non
ponentibus obicem*) &c., let him be anathema.'

Canon 8. 'If any one shall say that grace is not conferred
by these sacraments of the New Law, *ex opere operato*, but
that faith in the Divine promise alone suffices to obtain grace,
let him be anathema.'

It may be observed that the idea of sacraments *containing*
grace and *conveying* grace involves a philosophical or metaphysical theory. According to this, grace is a sort of spiritual
substantiality capable of this kind of residence in matter, and
of a transfer into the soul apart from the soul's own action or

---

[1] Antiq. b. xvii. chap. ii. 5.
[2] Council of Trent. Sess. vii. De Sacramento.

consciousness. Thus when the body is in contact with the sacramental matter the grace contained is conveyed into the soul. This is really a product of the scholastic subtleties of the middle ages.

The following passage from Hooker[1] will fully illustrate this Article, and is a true type of the English doctrine:

'Grace is a *consequent* of sacraments, a thing which accompanieth them as their end, a benefit which they have received from God Himself, the author of sacraments, and not from any other natural or supernatural quality in them. It may hereby both be understood that sacraments are necessary, and that the manner of their necessity is not in all respects as food unto natural life, because they contain in themselves no vital force or efficacy: they are not physical, but moral instruments of salvation, duties of service and worship; which unless we perform as the Author of grace requireth, they are unprofitable; for all receive not the grace of God, which receive the sacraments of His grace. Neither is it ordinarily His will to bestow the grace of sacraments on any but by the sacraments; which grace also, they that receive by sacraments or with sacraments, receive it from Him, and not from them. . . . . . Sacraments serve as the instrument of God to that end and purpose; moral instruments, the use whereof is in our hands, the effect in His: for the use we have His express commandment; for the effect His conditional promise: so that without our obedience to the one, there is of the other no apparent assurance; as contrariwise, where the signs and sacraments of His grace are not either through contempt unreceived, or received with contempt, we are not to doubt but that they really give what they promise, and are what they signify. For we take not baptism nor the Eucharist for bare resemblances or memorials of things absent, neither for naked signs and testimonies assuring us of grace received before, but (as they are indeed and in verity) for means effectual, whereby God, when we take the sacraments, delivereth into our hands that grace available unto eternal life, which grace the sacraments represent or signify.'

It may excite some surprise that a practice, obviously pos-

[1] Ecc. Pol. v. 57.

sible with regard to one of the sacraments only, should be referred to both. 'The sacraments' (not the elements of the Lord's Supper only) 'were not ordained of Christ to be gazed upon, or to be carried about'

There was undoubtedly a reason for this form of expression. Carelessness of diction finds no place in the Articles. That reason seems to be an intention more emphatically to deny the superstitious practices in question. The two sacraments are treated in this Article precisely on the same footing. They are spoken of, not in respect of their essential differences, but in respect of their essential similarities, by virtue of which they are properly sacraments, and by virtue of which grace is received 'by or with' both of them on precisely the same terms. Hence if the water in baptism is not to be carried about and elevated, neither are the bread and wine in the Lord's Supper. The only purpose of the elements in either sacrament is 'that we should duly use them.' Thus the use of the plural word 'sacraments' illustrates and enforces, more strongly than the singular number would, the denial of a practice which in fact has only been carried out with regard to the Eucharistic elements.

ARTICLE XXVI.

Of the Unworthiness of the Ministers, which hinder not the Effect of the Sacrament.

Although in the visible Church the evil be ever mingled with the good, and sometimes the evil have chief authority in the Ministration of the Word and Sacraments, yet forasmuch as they do not the same in their own name, but in Christ's, and do minister by his commission and authority, we may use their Ministry, both in hearing the Word of God, and in the receiving of the sacraments. Neither is the effect of Christ's ordinance taken away by their wickedness, nor the grace of God's gifts diminished from such as by faith and rightly do receive the Sacraments ministered unto them; which be effectual, because of Christ's institution and promise, although they be ministered by evil men.

Nevertheless, it appertaineth to the discipline of the Church, that inquiry be made of evil Ministers, and that they be accused by those that have knowledge of their offences; and finally being found guilty by just judgment, be deposed.

De vi institutionum divinarum, quod eam non tollat malitia Ministrorum.

Quamvis in Ecclesia visibili, bonis mali semper sunt admixti, atque interdum ministerio verbi et Sacramentorum administrationi præsint; tamen cum non suo, sed Christi nomine agant, ejusque mandato et auctoritate ministrent, illorum ministerio uti licet, cum in verbo Dei audiendo, tum in Sacramentis percipiendis. Neque per illorum malitiam effectus institutorum Christi tollitur, aut gratia donorum Dei minuitur, quoad eos qui fide et rite sibi oblata percipiunt, quæ propter institutionem Christi et promissionem efficacia sunt, licet per malos administrentur.

Ad Ecclesiæ tamen disciplinam pertinet, ut in malos ministros inquiratur, accusenturque ab his, qui eorum flagitia noverint, atque tandem justo convicti judicio deponantur.

Notes on the Text of Article XXVI.

The comparison of the Latin with the English suggests scarcely any illustrative matter. The student will, however, note that the Latin for 'rightly' is *rite*, which will refer to the essentials of *administration*, the manner of *reception* being qualified by the word *fide*, ' by *faith*.'

It will be also observed that the distinction between the Church visible and invisible is implied in the wording of this Article, as well as in the Nineteenth.

The Eighth Article of the Confession of Augsburgh was evidently before the compilers of the present Article. It remains, with only a verbal change, as it stood in the formulary of King Edward.

Observations on Article XXVI.

In the parallel Article of the Augsburgh Confession the Donatists *et similes* are condemned as having deemed the ministration of evil ministers ineffectual. But this Article no doubt chiefly regarded some of the Anabaptists of the day who held extreme views on this point. But in addition to this the reformed Church of England had special difficulties in this respect. The changes introduced into doctrine in the days of Edward and Elizabeth were ostensibly accepted by the mass of the existing clergy. The consequence was that the reformed ritual was performed in the first instance by men, the majority of whom were Romanists at heart, and too many of whom were grossly ignorant or even immoral.

This may be freely illustrated from any history of the English Reformation, and, indeed, is scarcely denied by any one. Protestants of earnest convictions, little open to consider and allow for the political or ecclesiastical exigencies from which such a state of the Church resulted, often gave vent to strong manifestations of their abhorrence of the ministrations of such persons.

This revulsion, perhaps, more than anything else, prepared the ground in which the seeds of the Puritan schism flourished so luxuriantly. To this was added in Elizabeth's

reign the unhappy objection raised by a section of the Eng
lish Reformers to the cap and surplice, and a few of the
minor ceremonies of the Prayer Book. In the conflict with
the royal supremacy, administered through the bishops, which
followed, not a few clergymen of piety, learning, and great
personal influence, were silenced for nonconformity in these
respects. The scandal was great in the eyes of many to find
the law depriving them of the ministers they trusted, and com-
manding them to attend the Parish Church, served perhaps by
a man who had conformed to every change of Henry, Edward,
Mary, and Elizabeth, and whose morals and learning they
equally held cheap. The Zurich Letters, published by the
Parker Society, or the lives of Archbishops Parker and Grindal, will fully illustrate the intensity of this feeling.[1] To
such feelings the present Article might offer an answer theo-
retically and theologically true; but it could not control those
instincts and sympathies which really govern the majority of
mankind in such matters.

All who are in earnest about religion know that the life of
the pastor setting forth the life of Christ which he preaches is
the most eloquent and persuasive illustration of the truth.
And comparatively few of such persons have been held in
allegiance to the Church, when the appointed minister has
stood in discreditable contrast to a less regularly appointed
rival, simply on account of a theological truth such as the one
before us.

Practically speaking, therefore, it would appear that while
on the one hand this Article maintains a doctrine of great importance, namely : that the efficacy of Christ's ordinances flows
directly from the Lord Himself through His Spirit—yet, on
the other hand, no Church can long maintain the loyalty and
affection of its members, excepting by the personal character
and influence of an enlightened and pious clergy.

On another matter of vast importance this Article is altogether silent. God may honour His own sacraments and
word in spite of man's guilt; but it is contrary to reason,

[1] See 'Examination of Certain Londoners.' Grindal's Remains.
Parker Soc.

to experience, to history, to Scripture, to suppose that an ungodly, still less a vicious, ministry can issue in anything but
an ungodly and corrupt state of the people. No conspicuous
work of grace has shown itself apart from a faithful, devoted,
prayerful administration of the word and ordinances of Christ.

One other subject is usually treated under this Article :
' the Roman doctrine of Intention.' The Council of Trent[1]
agrees with us that a minister living in sin may confer a valid
sacrament. But it requires (Canon II.) ' the intention,' on the
part of the administrator, ' to do that which the Church does.'
The student, desirous of further information on the meaning of
this, may find what the priests of the Roman Church are actually taught on the subject in ' Dens' Theology.'[2] It appears
from the elaborate classification there made of different kinds
of intention, that it implies of necessity an act of the will on
the part of the minister to do what the Church requires.
Minor acts of mental carelessness, forgetfulness, and wandering
during the service will not invalidate the sacrament; but a mere
habitual state of the will which could be, but is not, aroused to
intend the administration at the time will not suffice. It must
follow à fortiori that the administration by an infidel priest
who in his heart rejects the whole sacramental doctrine, must
be absolutely invalid. Those who know from history what
the state of the Roman clergy has been at some periods will
see what disastrous consequences must follow from such a
theory to those who rely for the perpetuation of the Church
on the valid administration of the sacraments.

All these extreme views on either hand disappear before the
true Scriptural ground maintained by the Church of England.
Christ is received, whether in His word, or through His sacraments, by faith [3]—the faith of the recipient. Christ, therefore, cannot be debarred from ' coming to him ' (John xiv. 23)
by the neglect, wickedness, or unbelief of any other, whether
official of the Church or not. Nothing can keep Christ from
the heart but our own impenitence and unbelief.

Finally, Hooker remarks that ' what every man's private

[1] Sess. vii. De Sac. Canon xii.   [2] ' De Sacramentis,' N. 39, 40, 41, 42.
[3] Arts. XXVI., XXVII.

mind is, we cannot know, and are not bound to examine;
therefore always in these cases the known intent of the Church
generally doth suffice ; and where the contrary is not manifest, we may presume that he which outwardly doth the work,
hath inwardly the purpose of the Church of God.'[1]

[1] Ecc. Pol. v. 58.

ARTICLE XXVII.

Of Baptism.	*De Baptismo.*
Baptism is not only a sign of profession and mark of difference whereby Christian men are discerned from other that be not christened : but is also a sign of regeneration or new birth, whereby, as by an instrument, they that receive Baptism rightly are grafted into the Church : the promises of the forgiveness of sin, and of our adoption to be the sons of God by the Holy Ghost, are visibly signed and sealed : faith is confirmed : and grace increased by virtue of prayer unto God. The Baptism of young children is in any wise to be retained in the Church, as most agreeable with the institution of Christ.	Baptismus non est tantum professionis signum, ac discriminis nota, qua Christiani a non Christianis discernantur, sed etiam est signum regenerationis, per quod, tanquam per instrumentum, recte baptismum suscipientes, Ecclesiæ inseruntur, promissiones de remissione peccatorum, atque adoptione nostra in filios Dei per Spiritum Sanctum visibiliter obsignantur, fides confirmatur, et vi divinæ invocationis gratia augetur.
	Baptismus parvulorum omnino in Ecclesia retinendus est, ut qui cum Christi institutione optime congruat.

Notes on the Text of Article XXVII.

In comparing the Latin with the English we may observe these equivalents :—(1) As by an instrument : Latin, *tanquam per instrumentum.* Some have given the legal meaning of *title-deed* to the word *instrument,* but the metaphor used requires that of a *grafting-tool.* (2) 'They that receive baptism rightly ' : Latin *recte,* not 'rite,' for *ritual* defect (if not touching the essence of the Sacrament) does not invalidate it. Lay and other irregular baptisms are admitted to be valid.

Omitting one or two verbal changes, the present Article is distinguished from the 28th of 1552 by containing a stronger statement on the subject of Infant Baptism. For in King Edward's Article it was simply asserted that ' the custom of the Church to christen young children is to be commended, and in any wise to be retained in the Church.'

In the wording of this Article our Reformers seem to have borrowed little or nothing from other sources.[1]

The Roman Doctrine of Baptism.

The Roman doctrine as to the spiritual result of the Sacrament of Baptism has already received some elucidation under Article IX. on Original Sin. For the most distinct, and perhaps the most authoritative, doctrinal statements we may further refer to the ' Catechism of the Council of Trent.'[2]   The ordinary administration of this Sacrament has been loaded by the Roman Church with many ceremonies ; but it holds the simplest possible form to be *valid,* and encourages ' all from among the laity, whether men or women,' and ' even Jews, infidels, and heretics,' in case of necessity, to baptize.[3]   This laxity seems to arise of necessity from the extreme view held as to the importance of this Sacrament. The faithful are to be taught[4] that ' unless they be regenerated unto God through the grace of Baptism, whether their parents be Christian or infidel, they are born to eternal misery and perdition.' Further,[5] ' No other means of salvation remains for infant children except Baptism.' This will explain the otherwise unintelligible anxiety of zealous Roman missionaries to baptize (even surreptitiously) the infant children of heathen parents, where there is no prospect of an opportunity of imparting subsequent Christian instruction.[6]

[1] Hardwick, ' History of Arts,' p. 393.   [2] Part II. chap. ii.
[3] Question xxiii.   [4] Question xxx.   [5] Question xxxiii.
[6] To this must also be referred a most revolting chapter of Dens, ' Theologia Moralis et Dogmatica,' a work much used, and of high authority in training the Roman priesthood ; ' Tractatus de Baptismo,' 23, 24, 25 ; ' An infantes baptizentur in utero materno ; ' ' De sectione Cæsarea ; ' ' De fœtu abortivo.'

The degree of suffering to be endured by infants dying unbaptized is much disputed, but ' parents may be consoled by the assurance that it is not certain that they endure the penalty of fire, but that it is certain that their penalty will be the lightest of all.' [1]

The chief effects of Baptism are defined [2] thus : ' Sin is remitted and pardoned, whether originally contracted from our first parents or actually committed by ourselves, however great its enormity '—' The remaining concupiscence or innate predisposition to sin does not really possess the nature of sin '— ' Why a state of uncorrupt nature is not straightway restored by Baptism ' is said to be ' because we are not to be more honoured than Christ, our Head, who did not lay aside the fragility of human nature,' and because what we have to struggle with gives us ' the germs and materials of virtue, from which we may afterwards obtain more abundant fruit of glory and more ample rewards.' For the further results of Baptism it is asserted that ' the soul is replenished with divine grace. But grace is (as the Council of Trent has decreed under pain of anathema) not only that whereby sin is remitted, but is, also, a divine quality inherent in the soul, and, as it were, a certain splendour and light, that efface all the stains of our souls, and render the souls themselves brighter and more beautiful. To this is added a most noble train of all virtues, which are divinely infused into the soul with grace.' The question why the baptized, nevertheless, are so slow to practise piety is answered from the consideration of ' the severe conflict of the flesh against the spirit.' But it is finally ' confessed that all do not participate in an equal degree of its heavenly graces and fruits.'

THE DOCTRINE OF THE ENGLISH CHURCH ON ARTICLE XXVII.

It is a difficult task to attempt to lay before the student a succinct and clear, and at the same sufficiently accurate and satisfactory, account of English theology on the subject of

---

[1] Dens, ' Theol. Tract. de quatuor novissimis,' **19.**

[2] Catech. Trent, Part II. chap. ii. Q. 41–57.

Baptism. And this must be so, if Dean Goode's account of the matter be (as it undoubtedly is) correct. He thus writes in his learned work on ' The Doctrine of the Church of England as to the effects of Baptism in the case of infants : [1] ' The matter is often spoken of as if the Church of England must of necessity have laid down, and had in fact laid down, a certain definite, precise view upon this subject, and peremptorily enjoined it upon all her ministers for their acceptance and belief. . . . It appears to me, after long and anxious consideration, that all which our Church has done upon this question is to lay down certain *limits* on both sides, within which the views of her ministers are to be confined.' Those limits he thus traces. In the early days of the Reformation on the Continent, crude and imperfect views on the Sacraments arose in some quarters out of the revulsion from the gross materialism of the Romish dogma. Such views have been generally identified (perhaps not altogether justly) with the name of Zwingle, and are conveniently, at least, and commonly known as *Zwinglian.* According to them the Sacraments were regarded as *mere* signs without any special promise of grace. But the leading divines of the various sections of the Reformed Churches unanimously rejected this imperfect teaching, and came to a practical agreement, thus far at least, that the Sacraments are not empty figures or mere signs, but that God through them efficaciously works that which they represent. [See this copiously illustrated from the foreign Reformed Confessions, and the works of Luther, Bullinger, Calvin, &c., by Dean Goode on Infant Baptism, chap. iii.] This leads us to the limit imposed by the Church of England on the one hand, that the Sacraments in general, and (as in this article) Baptism in particular, are ' not only badges and tokens,' but rather 'effectual signs of grace by which God doth work invisibly in us.' ' Baptism is not only a sign of profession and mark of difference.' As this limitation fronts and excludes what may be briefly called Zwinglian opinions, so the other faces in the opposite direction, and excludes the Roman doctrine of grace given *ex opere operato,* and *contained* as if it were (so to speak) a certain

[1] Chap. i.

matter deposited in the matter of the Sacrament and conveyed along with it. We have already seen (p. 217) how this Roman view of the Sacrament stands contrasted with English theology. These, then, are the limits which our Church has laid down in the Articles as those within which the opinions of her ministers are to be confined. How far the formularies admit of all the variations of doctrine which lie between those limits is another and very difficult question.

But having thus stated the extremes within which, according to our Articles, variation is not forbidden, it will be needful to attempt to lay before the student some classification which may, with sufficient accuracy, group together the leading shades of doctrine which have. prevailed within the borders of the English Church.

The differences in question have been based mainly on expressions in the Catechism and the Baptismal service. The following may be taken as the most marked of those expressions:—

'Baptism, wherein I was made a member of Christ, a child of God, and an inheritor of the kingdom of Heaven.'

'A death unto sin, and a new birth unto righteousness; for being by nature born in sin, and the children of wrath, we are hereby made the children of grace.'

'Seeing now that this child is regenerate and grafted into the body of Christ's Church, let us give thanks unto Almighty God for these benefits.'

'We yield Thee hearty thanks, most merciful Father, that it hath pleased Thee to regenerate this infant with Thy Holy Spirit, to receive him for Thine own child by adoption, and to incorporate him into Thy holy Church.'

The opinions resulting from a consideration of these passages, together with the Articles and Scriptural and other sources of theological system, may be first broadly classified into these two:—

A. Those which understand the above expressions as literally and absolutely fulfilled in every case of Baptism. Obviously these will differ according to the scope and comprehensiveness of meaning given to the words *Regeneration*, *Adoption*, *Child of God*, &c.

B. Those which understand the expressions in question to be used not absolutely but conditionally : as conveying not a known certainty, resulting from known and ascertained spiritual conditions, but hypothetically in the language of faith, which assumes the implied conditions to be present, and thereupon pronounces the fulfilment of the Gospel covenant of grace to the person baptized. In this view, however, that fulfilment (at least in its complete and absolute sense) still remains a contingency depending on spiritual conditions, the presence or absence of which will hereafter become manifest in the life.

The class A may be broken into these three principal sections :—

A 1. Those who more or less closely approximate to the Tridentine view of the Sacrament containing grace and giving it *ex opere operato*, the soul being absolutely and invariably restored to primeval purity in Baptism.[1] Opinions of this class seem to have altogether exceeded the limits of comprehensiveness allowed by the Church of England and described above.

A 2. Those who hold the class of doctrine to be included in our second section usually belong to those who are generally and popularly known as moderate High Churchmen. These generally hold that, in the case of an infant, its inability to oppose any barrier of unbelief and impenitence to the entrance of grace assures us that the covenanted grace has been certainly conferred in Baptism. For they allege that unbelief and impenitence alone can bar the flow of covenant grace. Accordingly an impenitent adult is able to resist (the technical mediæval phrase is *ponere obicem*) the reception of grace ; but an unconscious infant cannot do so, and in such an one Baptism fulfils its entire purpose.

Divines of a purely English school must, by virtue of their national character, have a respect for *facts*, which they are not permitted to override altogether by any theory. Hence in

[1] See Art. IX. p. 79.

claiming the *spiritual regeneration* of all infants in Baptism in a sense which shall reach the moral nature within, this class of divines conceives that ' a seed ' of goodness is invariably implanted at Baptism which may or may not afterwards become developed and bear fruit. Or the doctrine may be otherwise stated as the bringing of the soul into direct and covenanted connexion with the Holy Spirit, whose help is thenceforth positively assured. The grace of the Spirit will plead with the soul as the reason opens, and will ultimately sanctify it, if ' that grace be not stifled, disregarded, or abused.'

A 3. Another school of divines reconciles the observed facts as to the moral condition of the mass of the baptized with the literal interpretation of our formularies by excluding the moral element from the definition of the word *regeneration*, which is explained solely in an ecclesiastical sense. In Baptism, say they, the child is admitted to all the privileges of the Church, and is brought into a covenant relation to God. It is claimed that such a change of condition is so great and signal as to deserve the name of *regeneration*, and even of *spiritual regeneration*, inasmuch as it is the admission to great spiritual privileges. Some would take this as one of many senses in which regeneration may be used. Others would limit the theological use of the word to this sense, and apply the words *conversion, renovation*, and the like, to the moral and spiritual transformation of the soul.

It will be readily understood that different writers on this subject have used varied language, and have not always sharply defined their opinions. Still it is believed that the above forms a fairly approximate classification of English opinion. It need scarcely be added that A 2 and A 3, with their legitimate variations, are universally held to be fairly within the limits allowed by the English Church.

B. We come next to the classes of interpreters who understand the disputed expressions in the Catechism and baptismal services, not as the assertion of an ascertained and universal fact, but as the language of faith and charity, which *presumes* the presence of the grace signified by the Sacrament until the contrary shall have been manifested by the life of the person

baptized. These understand the word *regeneration* in its full
spiritual signification, reaching the moral nature within.
Their view at least has the merit of reconciling fully the
observed facts in the conduct of the baptized with the doctrinal theory of the effect of Baptism.

It is urged by the supporters of this view of the subject
that both in the Articles and in the Catechism the Sacraments
are dealt with in their ideal completeness. All that is
requisite to their efficacy is presumed to be present, both as
respects the administration and the spiritual qualities of the
recipient.[1] The two Sacraments are treated alike in this
respect. The Catechism definitely requires repentance and
faith for the complete result of either Sacrament. It assumes
with respect to infants that these graces will in due time be
manifested. In this event, and not till then, the Sacrament will
be spiritually complete. Strictly speaking, our Church has
not defined the result of Infant Baptism, but has been content
with statements which assume the right reception as well as
the·right administration, and with a general declaration that
infants ought to be baptized. Thus in the eye of the Church
the Sacrament is assumed to be complete in all its parts. But
the divine part therein can only be spoken of hypothetically
and conditionally. Whether the spiritual regeneration assumed has really taken place or not can be known to man
only from the after fruits. It is further urged that this is
the model on which all our services are composed. Each
grace contemplated in the several acts of worship—repentance,
faith, love, humility—is assumed to be present in the language
put into the mouths of the worshippers. The language of
doubt and hesitation is nowhere admitted, not even into a
service of such almost miscellaneous use as that for the burial
of the dead. All bears the same glow of faith and hope.
But, it is urged, this language of faith ought not to be
paraphrased in the case of Baptism, any more than in the other
services, into theological assertions of the invariable presence
of the graces thus assumed.

[1] See Art. XXV.

It will now be necessary to elucidate by examples these schools of doctrine. It is not deemed necessary or advisable to notice further the class A 1. Tridentine and scholastic theology is broadly contrasted with that of the English Church, and has been sufficiently set forth in the words of Trent. We turn to class A 2. It is often very difficult to find a passage containing language sufficiently definite to identify the class of doctrine of any given divine to our absolute satisfaction. But it appears that Hammond and Thorndike belong to this present class, and (though not without hesitation) Bishop Bethell's work on Regeneration, which has had much authority within the last fifty years, must be assigned to it also. He speaks of Waterland with approval, but seems, in the author's opinion, to go beyond him. Certainly he lacks the admirable power of making himself distinctly understood which characterized that great divine. Bishop Bethell, with Waterland and others, distinguishes between Regeneration and Renovation, when he defines regeneration as conveying the 'spirit of grace, which is designed to be a principle of spiritual life,' but 'is merely a potential principle.' And when he speaks of 'the infused virtue of the Holy Ghost,' though 'dormant and inactive,' he seems to fall within the class now under consideration.

Proceeding to class A 3, we shall have the great advantage of the lucid statement of Dr. Waterland in his *Regeneration Stated and Explained*, of which we proceed to give some account :—

'Regeneration is but another word for the new birth of a Christian. . . . This is a spiritual change wrought upon any person, by the Holy Spirit, in the use of Baptism, whereby he is translated from his natural state in Adam to a spiritual state in Christ. This change, translation, or adoption, carries in it many Christian blessings and privileges, but all reducible to two, viz., remission of sins (absolute or conditional), and a covenant claim for the time being to eternal happiness. . . . Regeneration complete stands in two things which are, as it were, its two integral parts—the grant made over to the person, and the reception of that grant. The grant, once made, continues always the same, but the reception may vary, because it depends upon the condition of the recipient.

'Renovation, I understand, is a renewal of heart and mind. Indeed, regeneration is itself a kind of renewal ; but then it is of *the spiritual state*, considered at large; whereas renovation seems to mean a more particular kind of renewal; namely, of the inward frame or disposition of the man . . . Renovation may be, and should be, with respect to adults, before, and in, and after Baptism.'

'The distinction which I have hitherto insisted upon between regeneration and renovation has been carefully kept up by the Lutheran divines generally. And it is what our Church appears to have gone upon in her offices of Baptism, as likewise in the Catechism.'

Waterland afterwards takes the cases of adults and infants. With regard to the former there can be no *salutary* regeneration without renovation accompanying it, or until in after years renovation is wrought in the soul. With regard to infants, he says that, being in a state of innocence and incapacity, they need no repentance and cannot have faith ; ' that ' they are consecrated in solemn form to God : pardon, mercy, and other covenant privileges, are made over to them ; and the Holy Spirit translates them out of their state of nature (to which a curse belongs) to a state of grace, favour, and blessing ; this is their regeneration.'

According to these very clear statements and definitions it is manifest that this able divine did not consider that any real moral and spiritual change was wrought *in the soul*, of necessity, in Baptism. All that change he separates from regeneration under the name renovation. Accordingly he proceeds to say that ' the renewing also of the *heart* may come gradually on with their first dawnings of reason in such measures as they shall yet be capable of. . . . . In this case, it is to be noted that regeneration precedes, and renovation can only follow after : though infants may perhaps be found capable of receiving some seeds of internal grace sooner than is commonly imagined.' This last definite expression of doctrine as to the case of

infants leaves no hesitation as to the correctness of the classification here made.

The class B will be sufficiently illustrated by the sketch
of the celebrated Gorham case which will follow. The work
of Dean Goode on 'Infant Baptism' is a powerful and learned
treatise advocating this mode of interpretation.

It is probable that the great majority of those usually
known as the Evangelical party in the Church of England hold
opinions falling under this head. But not a few of them, including men of considerable learning, belong to the class A 3.
It will, however, be admitted that individual writers, while
holding these general principles of interpretation, arrange the
details with some considerable variety. For a general view of
the whole question there is no more masterly summary than
the 'Review of the Baptismal Controversy,' by Dr. Mozley, the
Regius Professor of Divinity, Oxford.

From a consideration of the several statements so far made,
it will be manifest that one who desires to estimate accurately
the opinions of others on this subject, or to state distinctly his
own, must carefully define two things—first, in what sense
the word regeneration is used and asserted in respect of Baptism; secondly, whether such regeneration is held to be absolutely and invariably attached to Baptism or not. Failing
this, it is apparent that such a gross absurdity might result, and
in fact has resulted, in ignorant or careless minds, as the confusing of an extreme Tridentine divine with a moderate English
Churchman of the class A 3; for each of them teaches
invariable baptismal regeneration, but each means a widely
different thing.

With regard to the word *Regeneration* Dr. Mozley (chap. iv.)
writes thus: 'Two definitions of regeneration may be said to
divide theological opinion; according to one of which it is a
state of pardon and of *actual goodness*, according to the other
a state of pardon, and a new *capacity* only for goodness, or an
assisting grace.' The extreme phase of the former of these is
the scholastic and Tridentine view of an infusion of all virtues
into the soul of the baptized.[1] This would be absolutely re-

[1] See page 227.

pudiated by those divines who may be called moderate Anglicans. Waterland, for example, speaking of the regeneration of infants, says that he does not believe that a *moral* change takes place in them, and ' for this plain reason, because I am persuaded that the thing is impossible, morality and immorality being alike incompatible with their state of being.' Bishop Bethell also (chap. viii.) says that ' in the case of infants the spirit of grace, which is designed to be a principle of spiritual life, is merely a potential principle. . . . . The infused virtue of the Holy Ghost is, to speak in the mildest terms, dormant and inactive when religious instruction and moral discipline are neglected.' And he proceeds in strong language to reject, in the name of our Church, the 'scholastic speculations' on the implantation of all virtues.

It will appear, therefore, upon the whole, setting aside the influence of Roman theology, that those in our Church who distinguish the word *regenerate* from its kindred expressions—*renewed, converted, born of God,* &c.—which involve an actual change of moral and spiritual character and affections, maintain an universal baptismal regeneration. Those who take the word *regenerate* as a comprehensive word, involving the change just noticed, maintain that it can only be asserted in baptism hypothetically and in the language of faith and hope.

The internal controversies of the Church of England of late years have turned so much on the baptismal question that a few notes on this subject may be added. Dr. Mozley writes : ' The baptismal controversy was the controversy of the first half of this century. It produced treatises from a succession of writers—Archbishop Lawrence, Bishop Mant, Mr. Biddulph, Mr. Faber, Bishop Bethell, Dr. Pusey, Dr. Goode, Archdeacon Wilberforce, and others. It came to a head in the Gorham trial, and has since dropped.' If this be so, a slight sketch of the points in debate, and the bearing of the decision in the Gorham case, will be useful to illustrate what may be legally held in the Church of England on this subject. In 1847, whilst that controversy was at its height, the Rev. G. C. Gorham was presented to the living of Brampford Speke, in Devonshire. Dr. Philpotts, then Bishop of Exeter, after a prolonged personal examination, refused to institute Mr. Gorham to the living, on the ground of unsound doctrine on the subject of Baptism. An action was brought against the Bishop, in the Court of Arches, to rebut this charge and procure institution to the living. Sir Herbert Jenner Fust, then judge of that court, pronounced against Mr. Gorham in an elaborate judgment, declaring the doctrine of the Church of England to be that infants are undoubtedly, and without any exception, regenerated in Baptism.

The agitation produced by this decision was intense. Neither of the two contending parties probably represented the general body of the English clergy. Bishop Philpotts declared in one of his charges that on the subject of Baptism we are agreed with Rome. How far this is from being the case anyone comparing the Tridentine statements with the language of such an acknowledged English divine as Waterland would see in a moment. On the other hand, Mr. Gorham made statements with regard to Baptism with which many, who might agree with him generally, would refuse to symbolize. But it was felt that the issue was raised between an absolute unconditional interpretation of the baptismal service and that hypothetical charitable construction of its language which had been held ever since the Reformation by many great divines. The judgment had rejected the latter altogether, and cast it out from any place in the Church of England.

From the sentence of the Court of Arches an appeal was made to the Judicial Committee of the Privy Council, consisting of five eminent judges, the two Archbishops, and the Bishop of London. The two Archbishops and four judges concurred in reversing the decision of the inferior court. The Bishop of London and one judge refused to concur.

In the judgment delivered by Lord Langdale, in the name of the Judicial Committee, the following five propositions were selected from the statements of Mr. Gorham, as containing the doctrines which had been condemned :—

1. That Baptism is a sacrament generally necessary to salvation ; but that the grace of regeneration does not so neces-

sarily accompany the act of Baptism that regeneration *invariably* takes place in Baptism.

2. That the grace may be granted before, in, or after Baptism.

3. That Baptism is an effectual sign of grace by which God works invisibly in us, but only in such as *worthily* receive it; in them alone it has a wholesome effect; and that without reference to the qualification of the recipient it is not in itself an effectual sign of grace.

4. That infants baptized, and dying before actual sin, are certainly saved.

5. But that *in no case* is regeneration in Baptism unconditional.

The judgment passed in review the baptismal and other offices of our Church, together with the Articles. It came to the conclusion that 'the services abound with expressions which must be construed in a charitable and qualified sense, and cannot with any appearance of reason be taken as proofs of doctrine.' It further declared that 'there are other points of doctrine respecting the Sacrament of Baptism which are capable of being honestly understood in different senses.' It proceeded to fortify this position by showing that opinions, in the main not distinguishable from Mr. Gorham's, had been held from the first by eminent prelates and divines, without censure or reproach. Among these, Bishop Jewel, Hooker, Archbishop Usher, Bishop Jeremy Taylor, Bishop Carlton, and Bishop Prideaux, were cited.

On these grounds Mr. Gorham was acquitted of the charge of holding false doctrine, and he was ultimately instituted to the disputed benefice.

It will be seen, therefore, that, as the law stands, the hypothetical interpretation of the expressions in the baptismal service is equally legal with the more absolute and invariable interpretation. It must not, however, be inferred that there are no limits to the license allowed by our Church on this matter. It was intended by our Reformers to exclude equally Roman excess on the one hand and Zwinglian defect on the other. Neither ought the student of divinity to allow himself to suppose it a matter of indifference which opinion he should espouse within the legal limits of the Church of England. But rather he should seek with all prayer and diligence to know what opinion most nearly harmonises with the whole body of revealed truth.

The foregoing observations will make it almost superfluous to say that it is difficult to allege passages from divines of established reputation which may be accepted as typical representations of the doctrine of the Church of England on the effects of Infant Baptism. It is conceived that there is no such difficulty with regard to the main doctrines of the faith, or with regard to the other Sacrament. One chief reason for this difficulty will be found in the age of the ordinary recipient of Baptism. An infant seems to be outside of our usual means for estimating spiritual results. Were the subject Adult Baptism there would be less scope for difference. There would be a variety of opinion about the exact nature of the grace conveyed in this rite, and as to how far it was conveyed in and with the Sacrament, or how far the Sacrament was a sign and seal of grace already received; but all would agree that without faith and repentance in the adult recipient the spiritual grace was not given. Any general discussion of English theology, much more of patristic theology, on the doctrine of Baptism, is far too large for this work. The student must be referred to treatises expressly dealing with the subject, some of which have been mentioned above. One name, however, is so prominent as that of a recognised English divine, and has been so frequently and generally used in this work, that we cannot omit consideration of his statements. Hooker has devoted eight chapters (58–65) of the fifth book of his Ecclesiastical Polity to the discussion of the nature, effects, and ritual of Baptism. What are usually considered the most important passages, as bearing upon this Article, are the following :—

1. 'If outward Baptism were a cause in itself possessed of that power, either natural or supernatural, without the present operation whereof no such effect could possibly grow; it must then follow that, seeing effects do never prevent [i.e., *precede*]

the necessary causes out of which they spring, no man could ever receive grace before Baptism; which being apparently both known and also confessed to be otherwise in many particulars, although in the rest we make not Baptism a cause of grace; yet the grace which is given them with their Baptism doth so far forth depend on the very outward Sacrament, that God will have it embraced, not only as a sign or token of what we receive, but also as an instrument or mean whereby we receive grace. Because Baptism is a Sacrament which God hath instituted in His Church, to the end that they which receive the same might thereby be incorporated into Christ; and so through His most precious merit obtain, as well that saving grace of imputation which taketh away all former guiltiness, as also that infused divine virtue of the Holy Ghost which giveth to the powers of the soul their first disposition towards future newness of life.' [1]

2. 'Predestination bringeth not to life without the grace of external vocation, wherein our Baptism is implied. For as we are not naturally men without birth, so neither are we Christian men in the eye of the Church of God but by new birth; nor, according to the manifest ordinary course of divine dispensation new-born, but by that Baptism which both declareth and maketh us Christians. In which respect, we justly hold it to be the door of our actual entrance into God's house, the first apparent beginning of life, a seal, perhaps, to the grace of election before received; but to our sanctification here a step that hath not any before it.'[2]

3. 'The law of Christ, which in these considerations maketh Baptism necessary, must be construed and understood according to rules of natural equity . . . . . . And (because equity so teacheth) it is on all parts gladly confessed that there may be in divers cases life by virtue of inward Baptism, even where outward is not found . . . . . . Touching infants which die unbaptized, since they neither have this Sacrament itself, nor any sense or conceit thereof, the judgment of many hath gone hard against them. But yet, seeing grace is not absolutely tied unto Sacraments: and besides, such is the lenity of God that

[1] B. V. c. lx.   [2] Ibid.

unto things altogether impossible He bindeth no man; but where we cannot do what is enjoined us, accepteth our will to do instead of the deed itself; again, forasmuch as there is in their Christian parents, and in the Church of God, a presumed desire that the Sacrament of Baptism might be given them, yea, a purpose also that it shall be given: remorse of equity hath moved divers of the school divines in these considerations ingenuously to grant that God, all-merciful to such as are not able in themselves to desire Baptism, imputeth the secret desire that others have in their behalf, and accepteth the same as theirs, rather than casteth away their souls for that which no man is able to help.'[1]

4. 'How should we practise iteration of Baptism, and yet teach that we are by Baptism born anew; that by Baptism we are admitted unto the heavenly society of saints; that those things be really and effectually done by Baptism which are no more possibly to be often done than a man can naturally be often born? . . . . As Christ hath therefore died and risen from the dead but once, so that Sacrament which both extinguisheth in Him our former sin and beginneth in us a new condition of life is by one only actual administration for ever available; according to that in the Nicene Creed, 'I believe one Baptism for remission of sins.'[2]

5. 'The fruit of Baptism dependeth only upon the covenant which God hath made; that God by covenant requireth in the elder sort faith and Baptism; in children the Sacrament of Baptism alone, whereunto He hath also given them right by special privilege of birth within the bosom of the Holy Church; that infants, therefore, which have received Baptism complete, as touching the mystical perfection thereof, are by virtue of his own covenant and promise cleansed from all sin; forasmuch as all other laws, concerning that which in Baptism is either moral or ecclesiastical, do bind the Church which giveth Baptism, and not the infant which receiveth it of the Church.'[3]

6. 'The whole Church is a multitude of believers, all honoured with that title; even hypocrites for their profession's

[1] B. V. c. 60.   [2] B. V. c. 62.   [3] *Ibid.*

sake, as well as saints because of their inward sincere persua-
sion, and " infants as being in the first degree of their ghostly
motion towards the actual habit of faith." The first sort are
faithful in the eye of the world ; the second faithful in the sight
of God ; the last in the ready direct way to become both, if all
things after be suitable to these their present beginnings.'[1]

7. ' Were St. Augustine now living, there are which would
tell him, for his better instruction, that to say of a child it is
elect, and to say it doth believe, are all one ; for which cause,
since no man is able precisely to affirm the one of any infant
in particular, it followeth that, precisely and absolutely,
we ought not to say the other. Which precise and absolute terms are needless in this case. We speak of infants as
the rule of charity alloweth both to speak and think. They
that can take to themselves, in ordinary talk, a charitable kind
of liberty to name men of their own sort God's dear children
(notwithstanding the large reign of hypocrisy), should not,
methinks, be so strict and rigorous against the Church for
presuming as it doth of a Christian innocent. For when we
know how Christ in general hath said that " of such is the kingdom of heaven ; " which kingdom is the inheritance of God's
elect ; and do withal behold how His providence hath called
them to the first beginnings of eternal life, and presented them
at the well-spring of new birth, wherein original sin is purged;
besides which sin, there is no hindrance of their salvation
known to us, as themselves will grant; hard it were that,
having so many fair inducements whereupon to ground, we
should not be thought to utter (at the least) a truth as probable
and allowable, in terming any such particular infant an elect
babe, as in presuming the like of others whose safety nevertheless we are not absolutely able to warrant.'[2]

8. ' Baptism implieth a covenant or league between God
and man : wherein as God doth bestow presently remission of
sins and the Holy Ghost, binding Himself also to add (in process of time) what grace soever shall be further necessary for
the attainment of everlasting life; so every baptized soul,

¹ B. V. c. 64.   ² *Ibid.*

receiving the same grace at the hands of God, tieth likewise itself for ever to the observation of His law.'[1]

These appear to be all the principal passages in this work distinctly setting forth Hooker's doctrine of Baptism. It is of great importance, and it requires great care and theological accuracy to assign to these statements the place which Hooker intended. The closing words of quotation 1 and the greater part of 2 have often been torn from their place in Hooker's theological system, and exhibited as a proof that this great divine held the doctrine of universal spiritual regeneration in Baptism with an almost Tridentine interpretation of infused habits of virtue. Those who know what Hooker's doctrines really were must conclude that either there was some great inconsistency not to be attributed to so deep a thinker and so cautious and systematic a divine, or else that the bearing of his teaching on Baptism has been in many quarters misapprehended. We refer especially to his Discourses on Justification, and on the Perpetuity of Faith in the Elect. The student may notice particularly the twenty-sixth section of the former, from which the following brief extract may serve as a specimen :—

9. 'If, therefore, he which once hath the Son may cease to have the Son, though it be but for a moment, he ceaseth for that moment to have life. But the life of them which have the Son of God is everlasting in the world to come. But because as Christ being raised from the dead died no more, death hath no more power over Him, so justified man, being allied to God in Jesus Christ our Lord, doth as necessarily from that time forward always live, as Christ, by whom he hath life, liveth always.'

Many striking passages to the same effect may be alleged. See particularly[2] one which sets forth the communion between Christ and the Church, founding the doctrine on the eternal purpose of God for the salvation of his true mystical Church. In short Hooker, together with the Elizabethan divines (with scarcely an exception), held what would *now be called* Calvinistic opinions, and was favoured by Archbishop Whit-

[1] B. V. c. 64.   [2] Ecc. Pol. B. V. c. 56.

gift, the chief author of the Lambeth Articles. It is not
meant that he advocated the more harsh and severe parts of
Calvinism, or that he approved of the unqualified reprobation
asserted in the Lambeth Articles. We must, therefore, read
Hooker's account of the effects of Baptism together with such
statements as the following :—[1]

10. 'We participate Christ, partly by imputation, as when
those things which He did and suffered for us are imputed
unto us for righteousness; partly by habitual and real infusion,
as when grace is inwardly bestowed while we are on earth
and afterwards more fully both our souls and bodies made
like unto His in glory. The first thing of His so infused into
our hearts in this life is the Spirit of Christ; whereupon,
because the rest, of what kind soever, do all both necessarily
depend and infallibly also ensue; therefore the Apostles term
it some time the seed of God, some time the pledge of our
heavenly inheritance, some time the handsel or earnest of that
which is to come.'

11. 'So that all His foreknown elect are predestinated,
called, justified, and advanced unto glory, according to that
determination and purpose which He hath of them : neither
is it possible that any other should be glorified, or can be
justified, and called, or were predestinated, beside them,
which in that manner are foreknown. . . It followeth :—1.
that God hath predestinated certain men, not all men. 2.
That the cause moving Him hereunto was not the foresight of
any virtue in us at all. 3. That to Him the number of His
elect is definitely known. 4. That it cannot be but their sins
must condemn them to whom the purpose of His saving mercy
doth not extend. 5. That to God's foreknown elect final
continuance of grace is given. 6. That inward grace whereby
to be saved is deservedly not given unto all men. 7. That no
man cometh unto Christ whom God by the inward grace of
His Spirit draweth not. 8. And that it is not in any man's
own mere ability, freedom, or power, to be saved; no man's
salvation being possible without grace. Howbeit God is no
favourer of sloth, and therefore there can be no such absolute

[1] Ecc. Pol. B. V. c. 56.

decree touching man's salvation as on our part includeth no necessity of care and travail, but shall certainly take effect whether we ourselves do wake or sleep.'[1]

On a review of the above statements we gather that Hooker maintained the following doctrines:—

1. The election to life of a predestined number.[2]

2. That these, and these only, are called and justified.[3]

3. That the justified man doth thenceforward always live as necessarily as Christ liveth.[4]

4. That when the soul participates Christ, the first thing of His infused into the heart is the Spirit of Christ, whereupon the rest, of *what kind soever*, necessarily depend and *infallibly ensue*.[5]

5. Those who are thus justified, and have participated Christ, and have His spirit infused into their heart, 'do not sin in anything any such sin as doth quite extinguish grace, clean cut them off from Christ Jesus; because the seed of God abideth in them, and doth shield them from receiving any irremediable wound.'[6]

To these statements we must now add with regard to Baptism:—

6. That through Baptism the soul is 'incorporated into Christ,' and so receives the 'saving grace of imputation' and the infused virtue of the Holy Ghost.[7]

7. That Baptism is 'the door of our actual entrance into God's house, the first apparent beginning of life, a seal perhaps to the grace of election, but to our sanctification here a step that hath not any before it.'[8]

8. That the case of unbaptized infants may nevertheless be excepted on principles of equity.[9]

9. That Baptism extinguishes our former sins in Christ, and begins in us a new condition of life.[10]

---

[1] 'Fragments of an Answer to a Letter of certain English Protestants.' Keble's Hooker, App. to B. V. No. 1, p. 751.

[2] Quotation 11.

[3] Quotation 11.

[4] Quotation 9.

[5] Quotation 10.

[6] Sermon on Perpetuity of Faith, vi.

[7] Quotation 1.

[8] Quotation 2.

[9] Quotation 3.

[10] Quotation 4.

10. That infants in Baptism are cleansed from all sins.[1]

11. That infants are in the first degree of their ghostly motion towards the actual habit of faith.[2]

12. That no one is able precisely to affirm of any infant that it is elect. But that we speak of infants as the rule of charity allows. It is as probable and allowable to term a particular infant an elect babe as to presume the like of adults, as some have done.[3]

This last paragraph contains in truth the key to the whole difficulty, and we may now arrange the foregoing conclusions in a consistent order, thus :—

It is known to God alone who are indeed His elect. He has not permitted us to judge. Hence we may, by the rule of charity, *presume* that any particular infant is one of the elect, and speak of it accordingly. *If it be one* of the elect (and not otherwise), it is in Baptism made a participant of Christ and receives the first fruits of the Spirit, from which all needful graces, and ultimately the glorified state, will in due time ' infallibly ensue ; ' and it will be preserved from final apostasy as long as it lives by the eternal life of Christ, its Head.

Such, it is believed, was the real system of Hooker. He distinguishes carefully[4] between the Church visible and the mystical Church, teaching us that ' the everlasting promises of love, mercy, and blessedness belong to the mystical Church,' but the duties belong to the visible Church.

In his language about the Sacraments it will be found, on a careful consideration, that this distinction is always tacitly assumed : the Church visible owes the duty of careful administration, the members of the Church mystical (and these alone) receive, and ' infallibly ' receive, all the grace which Sacraments are meant to convey. But he does not, while treating of the Sacraments perpetually throw in this chilling distinction. On the other hand, with a glow of charity he contemplates the partakers as indeed members of Christ, he views the Sacraments in their spiritual and re-

---

[1] Quotation 5. [3] Quotation 7.
[2] Quotation 6. [4] Ecc. Pol. B. III. 1.

ciprocal completeness, and he claims the full grace which they were meant to betoken and to convey.

Hence we conclude that Hooker really belongs to the class of those who interpret the expressions in the baptismal services as the language of charitable presumption.

If this seem strange to any, it can only be from lack of acquaintance with the language of Hooker's contemporaries, or from approaching his writings with preconceived ideas derived from other schools of theology.

The historical fact is very material to notice that, among all the controversies raised by the earlier Puritans about the baptismal service, none was ever raised about the doctrine of Regeneration as taught in it. It will be observed that Hooker contests with his opponents the answers of the sponsors, the use of the cross, the validity of lay baptism &c., but that he is not called upon to defend the expressions around which modern controversy has been waged. It was not until other ideas on the Sacraments had become prominent in the Church of England in the time of Charles, that Baptismal Regeneration was generally taught apart from election. Then the language of the service was soon called in question, and the controversy, so commenced, has continued to our day.

Indeed, Calvin himself used language with respect to Baptism quite as strong as that of Hooker.[1]

' Q. Do you attribute nothing more to the water than that it is a figure of ablution ?

' A. I understand it to be a figure, but still so that the reality is annexed to it : for God does not disappoint us when He promises us His gifts. Accordingly it is certain that both pardon of sins and newness of life are offered to us in Baptism and received by us.

' Q. Is this grace bestowed on all indiscriminately ?

' A. Many, precluding its entrance by their depravity, make it void to themselves. Hence the benefit extends to believers only, and yet the Sacrament loses nothing of its nature.

' Q. If repentance and faith are requisite to the legitimate use of Baptism, how comes it that we baptize infants ?

---

[1] Catechism of the Church of Geneva.

'*A*. It is not necessary that faith and repentance should always precede Baptism. They are only required from those whose age makes them capable of both. It will be sufficient then if, after infants have grown up, they exhibit the power of their Baptism.'

It is thought that these references and observations may suffice to introduce the student to the theological treatment of the effects of the Sacrament of Baptism. The accumulation of literature on this subject bearing upon its Patristic, Scholastic, Lutheran, Reformed, and Anglican treatment is enormous. It is important that all who are teachers of religion should understand clearly the general bearings of the different aspects of the questions raised. But it may be doubted whether much more than this may not frequently prove rather prejudicial than helpful to him who is called upon to minister and to teach among ordinary congregations. For theological subtleties of doctrine and precise theological definition are either distasteful or unintelligible, and are at least seldom edifying or instructive, to most of our people.

Infant Baptism.

The chief controversial work on this subject is Dr. Wall's learned *History of Infant Baptism*, published at the beginning of the last century. He received the thanks of the Lower House of Convocation. Later editions contain replies to various opponents, some of whom praise him for his candour and fairness. It contains a careful examination of the Patristic statements on the subject, and a discussion of the Scriptural argument. He also wrote a more popular and compendious abridgment, under the title of a *Conference between two men that had doubts about Infant Baptism*. This has been repeatedly reprinted by the Christian Knowledge Society. On the subject of Infant Baptism the language of our Church is studiously moderate. It is customary to discuss the scanty statements of the earliest fathers bearing upon it. But our Article seems to pass this by, simply saying that it is most agreeable with the institution of Christ. There is, doubtless, a reference here to the well-known passage alleged in the Gospel in the baptismal service, '*Of such is the kingdom of heaven.*' If the kingdom of heaven be taken in our Lord's usual meaning, as His visible Church or kingdom among men, and if baptism be the acknowledged rite of ordinary covenant admission into that Church or kingdom, it would seem at once to follow that the baptism of young children is most agreeable with the institution of Christ. It may also be shown to be 'most agreeable' with the words of institution which include '*every creature.*'

Dr. Hey, writing on this Article, gives this summary of precedents deducible from the Scriptures on this question:— 'On the one hand, they mention no instance of Infant Baptism; on the other hand, they afford no instance of Baptism being delayed. Some families are spoken of collectively as being baptized; but the children are not mentioned particularly.'

To this must be added the support afforded by the analogies of circumcision. It is unlikely that Christianity should have introduced a *restrictive* change in respect of admitting children without a special announcement of it. And this the more because the Church for some years was chiefly composed of converted Jews.

ARTICLE XXVIII.

Of the Lord's Supper.

The Supper of the Lord is not only a sign of the love that Christians ought to have among themselves one to another : but rather it is a Sacrament of our Redemption by Christ's death. Insomuch that to such as rightly, worthily, and with faith, receive the same, the Bread which we break is a partaking of the Body of Christ; and likewise the cup of blessing is a partaking of the Blood of Christ.

Transubstantiation (or the change of the substance of Bread and Wine) in the Supper of the Lord cannot be proved by Holy Writ; but is repugnant to the plain words of Scripture, overthroweth the nature of a Sacrament, and hath given occasion to many superstitions.

The Body of Christ is given, taken, and eaten, in the Supper, only after an heavenly and spiritual manner. And the mean whereby the Body of Christ is received and eaten in the Supper is Faith.

De Cœna Domini.

Cœna Domini non est tantum signum mutuæ benevolentiæ Christianorum inter sese, verum potius est Sacramentum nostræ per mortem Christi redemptionis.

Atque adeo, rite, digne, et cum fide sumentibus, panis quem frangimus est communicatio corporis Christi : similiter poculum benedictionis est communicatio sanguinis Christi.

Panis et vini transubstantiatio in Eucharistia ex sacris literis probari non potest. Sed apertis Scripturæ verbis adversatur, Sacramenti naturam evertit, et multarum superstitionum dedit occasionem.

Corpus Christi datur, accipitur, et manducatur in Cœna, tantum cœlesti et spirituali ratione. Medium autem, quo corpus Christi accipitur et manducatur in Cœna, fides est.

The Sacrament of the Lord's Supper was not by Christ's ordinance reserved, carried about, lifted up, or worshipped.	Sacramentum Eucharistiæ ex institutione Christi non servabatur, circumferebatur, elevabatur, nec adorabatur.

NOTES ON THE TEXT OF ARTICLE XXVIII.

'Rightly, worthily, and with faith,' corresponds to the Latin *rite, digne, et cum fide.* *Rite* refers to all that is essential in the administration. *Digne* (used also in Article XXV.) refers to the mode and spirit of reception, which is yet further qualified by the requirement *cum fide.*

The Latin word used here for ' partaking ' is *communicatio.*

It may be observed that our Church uses the Latin word *Eucharistia,* but prefers in the English version the simple expression, ' the Lord's Supper.'

If we compare the present Article with the corresponding one (XXIX.) of 1552, it will be noticed that there are a few verbal differences in the first part, and in the last clause, but that the intermediate portion, viz., ' The body of Christ is given . . . . is Faith,' has taken the place of the longer clause in the Article of 1552, which is here subjoined:—' Forasmuch as the truth of man's nature requireth that the body of one and the self-same man cannot be at one time in many and divers places, but must needs be in some one certain place : therefore the body of Christ cannot be present at one time in many and divers places. And because (as Holy Scripture doth teach) Christ was taken up into heaven, and there shall continue unto the end of the world, a faithful man ought not either to believe or openly to confess the real and bodily presence (as they term it) of Christ's flesh and blood in the Sacrament of the Lord's Supper.'

The same influence which struck out of Elizabeth's Prayer Book the advertisement at the end of the Communion Service (restored in 1662) appears to have operated against the above clause, so similar to it, in the line of reasoning adopted against the ubiquity of the Lord's body.

Archdeacon Hardwick [1] suggests no sources for the text of this Article.

THE PRESENCE OF CHRIST IN THE EUCHARIST.

The opinions which have prevailed on this subject may be arranged under three principal divisions, which will be considered in this order:—

I. The corporal presence.
II. The denial of any peculiar presence.
III. The spiritual presence.

I. *The Corporal Presence.*

This will fall under two separate heads, *transubstantiation* and *consubstantiation.* The former of these, after a struggle prolonged for some centuries (for which the reader is referred to ecclesiastical history), may be considered as finally decreed by the Church of Rome, A.D. 1216, at the Lateran Council, under Innocent III. This was confirmed by the following decree of the Council of Trent,[2] which also sufficiently defines the term transubstantiation :—' That, by consecration of the bread and wine, a conversion is made of the whole substance of the bread into the substance of the body of Christ our Lord, and of the whole substance of the wine into the substance of His blood : which conversion is conveniently and properly called transubstantiation by the Holy Catholic Church.'

The Council proceeds to decree (c. 5) that this ' most holy Sacrament shall be reverenced with the worship of latria which is due to the true God.'

Among the canons of the Council on this Sacrament are some to the following effect :—

1. That the body and blood of Christ, together with His soul and divinity, and therefore the whole Christ, are truly, really, and substantially *contained* in the Eucharist.

2. That the substance of the bread and wine do not remain

---

[1] History of Arts, p. 395.   [2] Sess. xiii. c. 4.

together with the body and blood of Christ; but there is a conversion of the whole substance of the bread into the body, and of the whole substance of the wine into the blood. The ' species ' of bread and wine only remaining.

3. That in each species, and under each individual part of each species when separated, the whole Christ is contained.

4. That this presence of the body and blood exists not only while being taken, but before and after ; and also in the consecrated hosts or particles which remain after communion.

[*Note.*—Under the last clause the Roman casuists have raised those offensive questions about a mouse taking the reserved host, and similar suppositions, which have been erroneously attributed to Protestant irreverence !]

The second mode of holding the corporal presence of Christ in the elements is called *consubstantiation.* It is the belief of the Lutherans. Rejecting the notion of the change of the earthly elements of bread and wine, it holds that in some way the real body and blood of Christ are locally present with them. The original documents of the Lutheran Church do not explain this.

The confession of Augsburgh (X.) briefly says that ' the body and blood of Christ are truly present, and are distributed to those eating in the Supper of the Lord.'

The Saxon Confession, A.D. 1551, asserts that ' in this com munion Christ is truly and substantially present, and the body and blood of Christ are truly exhibited to those receiving.'

The mode of this presence Luther himself usually shrank from defining. See the account in D'Aubigné's History of the Reformation of the Marburg Conference between him and Zwingle, together with other divines of both parties.

But D'Aubigné [1] gives this illustration from Luther's writings : ' Just as iron and fire, which are nevertheless two distinct substances, are confounded together in a heated mass of iron, so that in each of its parts there is at once iron and fire ; in like manner, and with much greater reason, the glorified body of Christ is found in all the parts of the bread.'

[1] B. XI. c. xi.

Luther's illustration fails before modern science, which tells us that cold and heat are only relative terms implying the presence of different degrees of heat.

This dogma involved another, when the possibility of such a bodily presence was discussed philosophically, viz., *ubiquitarianism*; or the doctrine that the glorified body of Christ is everywhere, *ubique*. This led to serious divisions in the Lutheran Church; some in their zeal for it maintaining opinions scarcely distinguishable from Monophysitism.

The Ultra-Lutherans maintained this dogma with great acrimony, arguing it after the old scholastic method. ' The Form of Concord ' A.D. 1576, a formula which caused much division in the Lutheran Church,[1] asserts ' that Christ truly fills all things and rules everywhere, present, not only as God, but also as man, from sea to sea and to the bounds of the earth.'

Further, that ' the right hand of God is not any certain and circumscribed place in heaven, but is nothing else than the omnipotent virtue of God, which fills heaven and earth.' Again, that ' the divine and human nature in the person of Christ are united, so as not only to have names in common, but really and in fact communicate between themselves, without confusion and equality of essences—according to the doctrine of *communicatio idiomatum*.'

Luther's own views may be seen from the following extract :[2] ' We are not so foolish as to believe that the body of Christ exists in the bread in the same visible manner in which bread is in the basket or wine in the goblet. . . . We believe that Christ's body is present; otherwise we are quite willing that any one should say : Christ is *in* the bread, or is *the* very bread, or is *there* where the bread is, or as he likes. We will not quarrel about words, but merely insist upon keeping to the literal meaning, viz., that it is not simply bread of which we partake in the Lord's Supper, but the body of Christ.' Luther himself, in his controversy with the Swiss party, maintained the ubiquity of Christ's body.

---

[1] Hagenbach's ' History of Doctrines,' vol. ii. p. 329.　　[2] *Ibid.* p. 299.

On this controversy our Church has made a positive declaration in the note appended to the Communion Service.

II. *The Denial of any Peculiar Presence.*

The name of Zwingle has been identified with that view of the Lord's Supper which makes it merely a commemorative sign, and not a special or effectual means of grace. This view is negatived by the first clause of Article XXV. Passages from the writings of Zwingle have been quoted to show that he did express himself to that effect. At the same time, that he knew a higher significance of the Sacrament appears from his confession of faith : [1] 'I believe that in the Holy Eucharist the true body of Christ is present to faith by contemplation.'

The Zwinglian doctrine on the Lord's Supper may probably be held and taught by many individuals in churches and sects, but it is not the avowed doctrine in the confession of any organized body of Christians who are orthodox on the Holy Trinity. Its consideration need not, therefore, delay us.

III. *The Spiritual Presence.*

Very early in the Reformation on the Continent arose, chiefly in Rhenish Germany, a party who stood midway between Luther and Zwingle, and attempted to moderate between them.

Bucer, who had so much influence in England in the reign of Edward VI., Oswald Myconius, and other eminent men, enunciated the doctrine of the Spiritual Presence of Christ to believers in the Lord's Supper, as opposed to his corporal presence in or with the elements, and to the notion of the Sacrament being a mere commemorative sign. [2]

This doctrine speedily prevailed against the crude and imperfect views of Zwingle through all those sections of Reformed Christendom which were not avowedly Lutheran. Thenceforward German writers acknowledged two main divisions in Protestant Christianity, *the Lutheran* and *the Reformed.* A reference to so familiar a work as Mosheim's 'History of the Church' will illustrate this. From the sixteenth century he

---

[1] Hagenbach, p. 297.   [2] See Hagenbach, § 258, note 10.

groups together under the latter name the Swiss, Belgic, French, English, and Scotch Churches, the dividing line being manifestly their adherence to the spiritual as against the corporal presence.

The reception of this doctrine in the English Church was due in the first place to Ridley, who satisfied himself by independent historical and scriptural enquiry as to its antiquity and truth.[1] By his influence Cranmer was led to study, and ultimately to adopt, the same opinion. The learned foreigners, Bucer, Peter Martyr, &c., introduced by Cranmer, belonged to the *Reformed* rather than to the *Lutheran* section of the Church.

The Spiritual Presence thus became the doctrine of the English Liturgy and Articles.

In other countries the enormous influence which Calvin's systematic treatises exercised tended in the same direction.

The following lucid and moderate passage may illustrate his views:[2]—'The presence of Christ in the Supper we must hold to be such as neither affixes Him to the element of bread, nor encloses Him in bread, nor circumscribes Him in any way (this would obviously detract from His eternal glory); and it must, moreover, be such as neither divests Him of His just dimensions, nor dissevers Him by distance of place, nor assigns to Him a body of boundless dimensions, diffused through heaven and earth. All these things are clearly repugnant to His true human nature. Let us never allow ourselves to lose sight of the two restrictions—

' First, let there be nothing derogatory to the heavenly glory of Christ. This happens whenever He is brought under the corruptible elements of this world or is affixed to any earthly creatures. Secondly, let no property be assigned to His body inconsistent with His human nature. This is done when it is either said to be infinite, or made to occupy a variety of places at the same time.

' But when these absurdities are discarded, I willingly admit anything which helps to express the true and substantial communication of the body and blood of our Lord as exhibited

[1] Soames' Hist. of English Reform, vol. iii. c. 2.

[2] Institutes, iv. xvii. 19.

to believers under the sacred symbols of the Supper, under-standing that they are received not by the imagination or intellect merely, but are enjoyed in reality as the food of eternal life.'

With these views the confessions of the principal ' *Reformed*' Churches—the Swiss, Dutch, Scotch Presbyterian, and the Church of England—will be found to be in substantial accordance.

For example, the Confession of Faith of the Established Church of Scotland [1] thus sets forth the doctrine of the presence :—

' Worthy receivers, outwardly partaking of the visible elements in this sacrament, do then also inwardly by faith, really and indeed, yet not carnally and corporally, but spiritually, receive and feed upon Christ crucified and all benefits of his death: the body and blood of Christ being then not corporally and carnally in, with, or under the bread and wine; yet as really, but spiritually, present to the faith of believers in that ordinance as the elements themselves are to their outward senses.'

It is well that the student in theology should thus learn how utterly inaccurate are statements continually put forth for popular circulation, attributing Zwinglianism to Calvin and the Calvinistic Churches.

In illustration of the doctrine of the Church of England on the nature of the presence in the Lord's Supper, we shall again allege the words of Hooker :—

' Christ is termed our life because through Him we obtain life; so the parts of this sacrament are his body and blood, for that they are so to us, who receiving them, receive that by them which they are termed. The bread and cup are his body and blood because they are causes instrumental upon the receipt whereof the participation of his body and blood ensueth. For that which produceth any certain effect is not vainly nor improperly said to be that very effect whereunto it tendeth. Every cause is in the effect which groweth from it.' [2]

' The real presence of Christ's most blessed body and blood is not to be sought in the sacrament, but in the worthy

---

[1] Chap. xxix. 7.   [2] 'Ecc. Pol.' v. 67.

S

receiver of the sacrament. . . . . I see not which way it should be gathered by the words of Christ when and where the bread is his body or the cup his blood; but only in the very heart and soul of him who receiveth them. As for the sacraments, they really exhibit, but for aught we can gather out of that which is written of them, they are not really, nor do really contain in themselves, that grace which, with them or by them, it pleaseth God to bestow.' [1]

The answer in the Church Catechism, ' The Body and Blood of Christ which are verily and indeed taken and received by the faithful in the Lord's Supper,' must be interpreted in conformity with these views of the presence. ' *The faithful* ' must mean those who have faith (not all persons baptized and calling themselves Christians). For ' the mean whereby Christ is received is faith.' Therefore without faith He is not received. ' *The Body and Blood are verily and indeed taken,*' but ' *only after a heavenly and spiritual manner.*' ' *The natural Body and Blood of our Saviour Christ are in heaven and not here.*' Nor is there ' *any corporal presence of Christ's natural Flesh and Blood.*' [2]

The phrase '*Real Presence*' has been, and is, used by many of our divines to express the genuine doctrine in opposition to Zwinglianism. It should, however, be observed that our Church has avoided it in her Liturgy and Articles; and it may be a needful caution to all who will exercise the office of public teachers, that they should be most wary (to say the least) about permitting this expression in their *popular teaching*. It is generally and popularly identified with the *corporal presence*. In spite of explanations to the contrary, the majority of hearers usually attribute to a word or phrase what *they* are accustomed to understand by it. It is the part of wisdom, therefore, to *avoid* as far as possible ambiguous expressions which tend to nurture distrust or misunderstanding.

This caution is added with the more confidence because it is adopted by Waterland.[3]

It is beyond the scope of this work to multiply quotations

---

[1] ' Ecc. Pol.' v. 67.   [2] Note appended to the Communion Service.
[3] ' Doctrine of the Eucharist,' chap. vii.

and authorities. But the work just referred to deserves special
notice on this ground. In the first half of the last century
some of the non-jurors propounded doctrines on the Lord's
Supper akin to Romanising views lately advocated so prominently in our own days. Dr. Waterland, then Archdeacon of
Middlesex, met these opinions in his ' Review of the Doctrine
of the Eucharist,' and in four Charges to the clergy of
Middlesex. These have been recently republished by the
present Bishop of London, ' at the request of the Archbishops
of Canterbury and York.' Under these circumstances this
work deserves special attention. In reference to the present
Article, the seventh chapter will be found to deal most
perspicuously with the mode of Christ's presence in the Lord's
Supper. It is illustrated from analogy, from the Old Testament,
from the Fathers, and from recognised divines of the Foreign
Reformed Churches, and of the English Church. The following
passage, cited with approval from Dr. Aldrich, will serve to
illustrate Waterland's doctrine :—

' It is evident that since the body broken and blood shed
neither do nor can now really exist, they neither can be really
present, nor literally eaten or drunk ; nor can we really
receive them, but only the benefits purchased by them. But
the body which now exists, whereof we partake, and to which
we are united, is the glorified body ; which is, therefore,
verily and indeed received. . . . . and by consequence said
to be really present, notwithstanding its local absence ; because a real participation and union must needs imply a real
presence, though they do not necessarily imply a local one.
For it is easy to conceive how a thing that is locally absent
may yet be really received. . . . . as when we commonly say
a man receives an estate or inheritance, when he receives the
deeds or conveyances of it. . . . . The reception is confessedly
real, though the thing itself is not locally or circumscriptively
present, or literally grasped in the arms of the receiver. . . .
The Protestants all agree that we spiritually eat Christ's
body and drink his blood ; that we neither eat nor drink nor
receive the dead body nor the blood shed, but only the
benefits purchased by them ; that those benefits are derived

to us by virtue of our union and communion with the glorified
body, and that our partaking of it and union with it is effected
by the mysterious and ineffable operation of the Holy Spirit.'

The last clause of this Article, referring to certain well-
known Mediæval and Roman uses of the consecrated elements
will, perhaps, need no illustration. These practices stand or
fall together with the doctrines to which they essentially
belong. One of these, however, stands partially on another
footing. In early times portions of the elements were sometimes reserved in order to be sent to the absent, the sick, and
the prisoners for Christ's sake.[1] Messengers who conveyed
the portion so reserved might be laymen. Our Church has
wisely declined to revive a practice which has given occasion
to manifold superstitions; she has ordered all that remains
of the consecrated elements after communion to be ' reverently '
eaten and drunk immediately after the blessing.[2] This was
also one of the early usages.[3]

[1] See Bingham, ' Antiq.' B. xv. c. viii. 1–5.
[2] Rubric after Communion Service.   [3] See Bingham, as above.

ARTICLE XXIX.

Of the wicked which do not eat the Body of Christ in the use of the Lord's Supper.

The wicked, and such as be void of a lively faith, although they do carnally and visibly press with their teeth (as Saint *Augustine* saith) the Sacrament of the Body and Blood of Christ : yet in nowise are they partakers of Christ, but rather to their condemnation do eat and drink the sign or Sacrament of so great a thing.

De manducatione corporis Christi, et impios illud non manducare.

Impii, et fide viva destituti, licet carnaliter et visibiliter (ut Augustinus loquitur) corporis et sanguinis Christi Sacramentum dentibus premant, nullo tamen modo Christi participes efficiuntur. Sed potius tantæ rei Sacramentum, seu symbolum, ad judicium sibi manducant et bibunt.

NOTES ON THE TEXT OF ARTICLE XXIX.

The Latin text appears to require no special comparison with the English.

This Article was introduced by Archbishop Parker in 1563, but was not finally adopted until 1571.[1]

The following is the passage of Augustine to which reference is made.[2] ' Qui non manet in Christo, et in quo non manet Christus, procul dubio nec manducat *spiritualiter* carnem ejus, nec bibit ejus sanguinem, *licet carnaliter et visibiliter premat dentibus sacramentum corporis et sanguinis Christi ;* sed magis tantæ rei sacramentum ad judicium sibi manducat et bibit.'

The Article obviously has been closely founded on this

---

[1] Hardwick, p. 396. [2] Super Joann. Tract. 26.

passage. The portions in italics (the very part most relied upon in our Article) are placed by the Benedictine editors in brackets, and there has been considerable controversy on the point. It was controverted in the days of Archbishop Parker himself.[1] But the Archbishop maintained his point, and alleged other passages in proof. It is the very opposite to probability that such words should be added as a gloss in the Middle Ages; while it is probable that a zealous transcriber might omit them. Moreover they are certainly as old as the days of Bede and Alcuin. This question, however, does not affect the authority of the Article. Whether the words be the genuine expression of Augustine or not, our Church has adopted them and propounded them as containing the true doctrine.

OBSERVATIONS ON ARTICLE XXIX.

This Article is a simple corollary to the last. If *faith* is the *mean* whereby the body of Christ is received and eaten, those who have not faith cannot receive and eat it. But, further, this Article categorically denies the possibility of the reception *in any wise*. Those without lively faith are ' in no wise ' (*nullo modo*) partakers of Christ. This seems intended to exclude every possible subterfuge which might bring them in as partakers in a subordinate sense.

This Article is therefore a great difficulty with those who maintain a real objective presence in or with the consecrated elements. If the body of Christ is in anywise brought into union with the matter of the elements themselves by the act of consecration, then in some sense *all* who partake of them must be partakers of Christ. So not only the Catechism of the Council of Trent,[2] but most of those who maintain a corporal presence, assert. The difficulties inherent in such an assertion, especially in connection with St. John vi. 54 (' Whoso eateth my flesh and drinketh my blood, hath eternal life; and I will raise him up at the last day ') are felt to be so great, that many able Romanist divines[3] do not interpret

[1] Strype's Parker, B. iv. c. 6.   [2] II. iv. 48.   [3] E.g. Cajetan.

the expressions in that chapter to mean feeding on Christ in the Eucharist. But the direct application of the chapter to the Lord's Supper is the usual Roman interpretation.[1]

On this subject the sixth chapter of Waterland on the Eucharist will be found very clear and satisfactory. It contains a brief review of the ancient and modern interpretations of the sixth chapter of St. John. It may be well to add some of the conclusions.

'There have been two extremes in the accounts given of the Fathers, and both of them owing, as I conceive, to a want of proper distinctions. They who judge that the Fathers, in general, or almost universally, do interpret John vi. of the Eucharist, appear not to distinguish between interpreting and applying. It was right to apply the general doctrine of John vi. to the particular case of the Eucharist considered as worthily received, because the spiritual feeding there mentioned is the thing signified in the Eucharist, yea and performed likewise. After we have sufficiently proved from other Scriptures that in and by the Eucharist, ordinarily, such spiritual food is conveyed, it is then right to apply all that our Lord, by St. John, says in the general, to that particular case; and this indeed the Fathers commonly did. But such application does not amount to interpreting that chapter of the Eucharist.'

Waterland then proceeds to discuss the language of Ignatius, Irenæus, Clemens Alexandrinus, Tertullian, Origen, Cyprian, &c. &c., and sums up his comments thus: 'From this summary view of the ancients it may be observed that they varied sometimes in their constructions of John vi. or of some parts of it; but what prevailed most, and was the general sentiment wherein they united, was, that Christ himself is properly and primarily our bread of life, considered as the Word made flesh, as God incarnate, and dying for us; and that whatever else might, in a secondary sense, be called heavenly bread (whether sacraments or doctrines, or any holy service), it was considered but as an antepast to the other, or as the same thing in the main, under a different form of expression.'

---

[1] E.g. Catechism of Trent, II. iv. 52.

The distinction thus drawn between ' *interpreting* ' and ' *applying*' a passage is most valuable. It will be the key by which the reader may open the perplexity of some strange apparent contradictions in quotations from the Fathers on other subjects beside this.

ARTICLE XXX.

Of both Kinds.	*De utraque specie.*
The Cup of the Lord is not to be denied to the lay-people. For both the parts of the Lord's Sacrament, by Christ's ordinance and commandment, ought to be ministered to all Christian men alike.	Calix Domini laicis non est denegandus, utraque enim pars Dominici Sacramenti, ex Christi institutione et præcepto, omnibus Christianis ex æquo administrari debet.

NOTES ON THE TEXT OF ARTICLE XXX.

The Latin and English versions of this Article are equally perspicuous, and require no special comment. The Article was added in Elizabeth's time; it appears to have been written by Archbishop Parker.

OBSERVATIONS ON ARTICLE XXX.

Romish advocates after the Reformation used to attempt to show that the administration in both kinds was not *universal* in primitive times. But the more candid amongst them are compelled to own that in public administration it was so. Cardinal Bona, quoted by Bingham,[1] says that 'the faithful always, and in all places, from the very first foundation of the Church to the 12th century, were used to communicate under the species of bread and wine. And in the beginning of that century the use of the cup began by little and little to be laid aside, whilst many of the bishops interdicted the people the use of the cup for fear of irreverence and effusion. And what they did at first for their own churches was afterwards

[1] XV. v. 1.

confirmed by a canonical sanction in the Council of Constance.[']
This may be admitted as a sufficient historical account of the
matter from the pen of an adversary. It is not much to the
purpose whether or not in ancient times *private* communion
was sometimes given in one kind only, as Bona maintains.
Supposing such cases made out, still it remains that the public
communion of the Church was uniformly, as Bona admits,
under both kinds. It will be observed that the denial of the
cup arose about the same time as the legal establishment of
the doctrine of transubstantiation, to which indeed it is a
corollary. Wickliffe, Huss, and other early reformers, brought
this abuse prominently forward.

The Bohemians, who rose against the decrees of the Council
of Constance, demanded the cup, and were hence called Calix-
tines.[1]

The denial of the cup is defended by the Council of Trent [2]
thus :

Cap. I. That Christ instituted the Supper under both kinds,
but did not make both binding on all the faithful. Also that
in St. John vi. Christ varied the expression, sometimes saying
eating and drinking, sometimes *eating* only.

Cap. II. That this is a matter which the Church has power
to regulate, according to the text, 'Let a man so account of
us as stewards of the mysteries of God.'

Cap. III. That under either species, the whole and entire
Christ is received, and that, therefore, the communicant under
one kind only is not defrauded.

The reasons for the denial of the cup are thus stated [3] :—

1. To avoid spilling the blood.
2. Because wine reserved might turn acid.
3. Because some cannot bear the smell or taste of wine.
4. Because in some countries wine is very scarce.
5. In order more plainly to oppose the heresy of those who
   deny that the *whole* Christ is contained under *either* species.

It is unnecessary to add anything in refutation of this un-
Scriptural and confessedly non-primitive practice.

---

[1] Mosheim, c. xv. p. ii. 5.   [2] Sess. xxi.
[3] Catechism of Trent, II. iv. 63.

ARTICLE XXXI.

Of the one Oblation of Christ finished upon the Cross.

The offering of Christ once made is the perfect redemption, propitiation, and satisfaction, for all the sins of the whole world, both original and actual, and there is none other satisfaction for sin but that alone. Wherefore the sacrifices of Masses, in the which it was commonly said, that the Priests did offer Christ for the quick and the dead, to have remission of pain or guilt, were blasphemous fables, and dangerous deceits.

De unica Christi oblatione in cruce perfecta.

Oblatio Christi semel facta, perfecta est redemptio, propitiatio, et satisfactio pro omnibus peccatis totius mundi, tam originalibus quam actualibus. Neque præter illam unicam est ulla alia pro peccatis expiatio. Unde missarum sacrificia, quibus vulgo dicebatur, sacerdotem offerre Christum in remissionem pœnæ, aut culpæ, pro vivis et defunctis, blasphema figmenta sunt, et perniciosæ imposturæ.

Notes on the Text of Article XXXI.

In this important doctrinal Article, the verbal criticism must not be overlooked. The following Latin equivalents may be noticed. ' Once made '—Latin, *semel facta, semel=* ἅπαξ, ' once only, and not again.' ' One oblation '—Latin, *unica*, not *una* : ' one only of its kind,' *unique*. ' Pain or guilt '—Latin, *pœnæ aut culpæ*. ' Fables '—Latin, *figmenta*. 'Dangerous deceits '—Latin, *perniciosæ imposturæ*.

This Article is one of the original series of 1552, and only received verbal change in Elizabeth's time. One such change is noticeable, namely, the substitution of the word *propitiation* in the English version for the original expression, *'the pacifying of God's displeasure.'*

This Article is said by Hardwick to be based on the Augsburgh Confession, Part II. 3, but the resemblance appears very slight, and only extends to some obvious expressions.

Observations on Article XXXI.

As first written, this Article was no doubt intended to meet the Roman doctrine of the *repetition* of the sacrifice of Christ in the Mass. In our day it has a further value. It will be found not only to meet the Romish error of excess, but also the modern rationalising errors of defect in the great doctrine of the Atonement.

It will be necessary first to state the Roman doctrine, which is as plainly opposed to the English as words can make it. We refer, as before, to the Council of Trent.[1]

Cap. II. ' Since the same Christ who once offered himself by his blood on the altar of the cross, is contained in this divine sacrifice which is celebrated in the Mass, and offered without blood, the holy Council teaches that this sacrifice is really propitiatory, and made by Christ himself. . . . . For assuredly God is appeased by this oblation, bestows grace and the gift of repentance, and forgives all crimes and sins, how great soever ; for the sacrifice which is now offered by the ministry of the priests is one and the same as that which Christ then offered on the cross, only the mode of offering is different. And the fruits of that bloody oblation are plentifully enjoyed by means of this unbloody one ; so untrue is it that the latter derogates from the glory of the former. Wherefore it is properly offered, according to apostolic tradition, not only for the sins, punishments, satisfactions, and other necessities of living believers, but also for the dead in Christ, who are not yet thoroughly purified.'

Canon 1. ' If any one shall affirm that a true and proper sacrifice is not offered to God in the Mass, or that nothing else is offered save that Christ is given to us to eat, let him be anathema.'

[1] Sess. xxii.

Canon 3. 'If any one shall affirm that the sacrifice of the Mass is only one of praise and thanksgiving, or a bare commemoration of the sacrifice accomplished on the cross, but not propitiatory; or that it only profits the receiver, and ought not to be offered for the living and the dead, for sins, punishments, satisfactions, and other necessities, let him be anathema.'

Canon 4. 'If any one shall affirm that the most holy sacrifice of Christ finished on the cross is blasphemed by the sacrifice of the Mass, or that the latter derogates from it, let him be anathema.'

The scriptural treatment of this subject is twofold. First, negative, from considerations of the silence of the Epistles upon this subject. The application of the sacrifice of the death of ·Christ for sin is the most vital point of Christianity; but not a word is breathed throughout the Epistles as to this mode of applying it to the sinner's needs. Second, positive, from the numerous passages which speak of the death of Christ, and the sinner's justification by faith in Him. But especially from a careful study of the Epistle to the Hebrews, which deals at large with the priestly functions of Christ.

Turning to the Article itself, it will be observed that four words are accumulated to express the effect of Christ's death, '*Redemptio, propitiatio, satisfactio, expiatio.*' These words are also used in the Communion Service (see especially the consecration prayer). Each of them expresses a particular bearing of the death of Christ on the salvation of a sinner. *Redemption* regards the price paid. *Propitiation* imports the restored favour of God. *Expiation* implies atonement made and accepted. But of all these words *Satisfaction* is in some respects the most important, as bringing the element of entire sufficiency into all these modes of expression. It is a word with a perfectly defined theological meaning, which may be illustrated by the following passage from Hooker.[1] 'Satisfaction is a work which justice requireth to be done for contentment of persons injured; neither is it in the eye of justice a sufficient satisfaction, unless it fully equal the injury for which we

[1] 'Ecc. Pol.' vi. 5.

satisfy. Seeing, then, that sin against God eternal and infinite must needs be an infinite wrong, justice in regard thereof doth necessarily exact an infinite recompense, or else inflicts upon the offender infinite punishment. Now, because God was thus to be satisfied, and man not able to make satisfaction in such sort, his unspeakable love and inclination to save mankind from eternal death ordained in our behalf a Mediator to do that which had been for any other impossible. Wherefore all sin is remitted in the only faith of Christ's passion, and no man without belief thereof justified. Faith alone maketh Christ's satisfaction ours, howbeit that faith alone, which, after sin, maketh us by conversion His.'

It is through these four words, but especially through the word *satisfaction*, that this Article meets certain prevalent errors which obscure, if they do not deny, the propitiatory and satisfactory work of Christ in His sacrifice.

With regard to the historical treatment of the general subject of the Article it may be observed that in very early times the words ' sacrifice ' and 'altar' were used in connexion with the Lord's Supper. When it is remembered that praise, almsgiving, self-devotion, &c., are called *sacrifices* in the New Testament, the student will not be unduly influenced by the above fact, but will enquire carefully further as to the sense in which such words were used. The words, however, having been once introduced, and having come into ordinary usage, suffered the usual fate of ambiguities. With the progress of doctrinal corruption the idea of expiatory sacrifice offered by the priest on an altar came in, and as with the doctrine of transubstantiation so with this; after centuries of oscillating and contradictory language, the doctrine of the propitiatory sacrifice of the Mass became firmly established. The student must therefore be prepared to meet with very contradictory statements confidently alleged from writers of the first ten centuries on this subject. For the further consideration of the subject of the Christian sacrifice, especially in its bearing on the Lord's Supper, a careful study is recommended of a very valuable chapter (the twelfth) of Waterland on the Eucharist.

Amongst its statements we may select the following. From Augustine it is shown that a ' true sacrifice is any work done with a view to our bond of holy union with God, having ,a reference to Him as our highest good.' Thus works of mercy are ' true sacrifices,' according to Augustine, ' if done with a view to God,' otherwise they are no sacrifice at all. This throws light on the meaning of the ancients when they call the Eucharist a ' true sacrifice.' They looked upon the spiritual sacrifices as true and proper sacrifices ; even more so than the legal offerings. And to make the Eucharist a material sacrifice would, in their estimation, have degraded it to the level of the legal ceremonies.

The ' true and evangelical sacrifices ' are thus enumerated.

1. The sacrifice of alms to the poor and oblations to the Church, with a religious intent, and offered through Christ. Phil. iv. 18. The offering goes to the poor, but *the service* is God's.

2. The sacrifice of prayer, from a pure heart, is evangelical incense. Rev. v. 8.

3. The sacrifice of praise and thanksgiving to the Father, through the Son. Heb. xiii. 15.

4. The sacrifice of a penitent and contrite heart. Ps. li. 17.

5. The sacrifice of ourselves, our souls, and our bodies. Rom. xii. 1.

6. The offering up of the mystical body of Christ, that is the Church, which is the same as the last taken collectively.

7. The offering up of true converts by their pastors, who have laboured successfully in this blessed work. Rom. xv. 16.

8. The sacrifice of faith and hope and self-humiliation in commemorating the grand sacrifice and resting finally upon it is another Gospel sacrifice, and eminently proper to the Eucharist.

' These, I think, are all so many true sacrifices, and may all meet together in the one great complicated sacrifice of the Eucharist. Into some one or more of these may be resolved (as I conceive) all that the ancients have ever taught of Christian sacrifices, or of the Eucharist under the name or notion of a true or proper sacrifice.'

After this follows an examination of the language of Fathers of the first four centuries when treating of Christian sacrifices. Waterland's conclusion is this: ' The Fathers well understood that to make Christ's natural body the real sacrifice of the Eucharist would not only be absurd in reason, but highly presumptuous and profane; and that to make the outward symbols a proper sacrifice, a material sacrifice, would be entirely contrary to Christian principles, degrading the Christian sacrifice into a Jewish one, yea, and making it much lower and meaner than the Jewish, both in value and dignity. The right way, therefore, was to make the sacrifice spiritual; and it could be no other on Gospel principles.'

The student may at least take this argument as a warning of the utter insecurity of relying upon isolated quotations from the Fathers, apart from an acquaintance with their phraseology, their habits of thought, and their mode of reasoning.

ARTICLE XXXII.

Of the Marriage of Priests.

Bishops, Priests, and Deacons, are not commanded by God's Law either to vow the estate of single life or abstain from marriage. Therefore it is lawful also for them, as for all other Christian men, to marry at their own discretion, as they shall judge the same to serve better to godliness.

De conjugio Sacerdotum.

Episcopis, presbyteris, et diaconis nullo mandato divino præceptum est, ut aut cœlibatum voveant, aut a matrimonio abstineant. Licet igitur etiam illis, ut cæteris omnibus Christianis, ubi hoc ad pietatem magis facere judicaverint, pro suo arbitratu matrimonium contrahere.

NOTES ON THE TEXT OF ARTICLE XXXII.

The comparison of the Latin with the English text appears to throw no additional light on the subject of this Article. The corresponding Article of 1552 consisted of the first clause only of the present form, and that with some verbal variation. The change thus introduced is somewhat material. In the earlier form of the Article it was simply asserted that the marriage of the clergy was not forbidden. It is now added that they are under no different obligation from other Christian men in this respect, and that it is lawful for them to marry.

The wording of the Article does not appear to be traced to any special source. In the negotiations between Henry VIII. and the Lutherans in 1538 for agreement on a confession of faith, it was on the point of clerical celibacy, together with transubstantiation and private masses, that they failed to agree.[1]

[1] Hardwick, c. iv.

T

Observations on Article XXXII.

The Scripture authority on this question is so clear, that little remains beyond the history of the growth of the restriction on the marriage of the clergy.

From very early times there was an undue regard paid to celibacy, as having in itself some peculiar virtue, instead of being a state of life profitable for the usefulness of some, according to the decision of St. Paul on this subject.[1] 'Every man hath his proper gift of God, one after this manner and another after that.'

The origin of these opinions may with high probability be traced up to those notions of evil connected with matter which had for centuries been a part of Eastern philosophy, and which led to ascetic practices long before the commencement of Christianity. Gnostic and Manichean doctrines were vanquished by the Church, but, as often happens, the conquerors became tinged with some of the views of the conquered.

At the Council of Nice a decree to enforce celibacy on the clergy was proposed, but it was rejected. But shortly before this, A.D. 305, the Council of Illiberis, a provincial council in Spain, had prohibited the clergy from marriage.[2] After this there was a struggle for centuries. The popular feeling undoubtedly attributed superior efficacy and sanctity to an unmarried priest. Gregory VII., A.D. 1074, is commonly spoken of as first effectually imposing celibacy on the clergy. In England Archbishop Anselm, A.D. 1108, finally enforced the same.

The doctrine of the Romish Church is stated thus by the Council of Trent[3]:

Canon 6. Marriage is disannulled if one of the parties enters into a religious order.

Canon 9 anathematises all who affirm that persons in holy orders, or regulars, who have made a solemn profession of chastity, may contract marriage.

The Greek Church requires marriage as a qualification for the priesthood, but does not permit a priest who is a widower to re-marry—so interpreting 1 Tim. iii. 2, 12.

[1] 1 Cor. vii. 7.   [2] Neander. iii. p. 197.   [3] Sess. xxiv.

The question of the celibacy of the clergy has been, and is, much discussed in the Roman Church. It seems to be maintained from a feeling of its importance to the *Papal* system. It isolates the clergy from the ordinary interests and associations of their fellow-countrymen, and fits them better to be the willing ministers of a foreign power. It is probable also that the laity may upon the whole prefer an unmarried clergy to receive the secrets of the confessional.

ARTICLE XXXIII.

Of excommunicate Persons, how they are to be avoided.

De excommunicatis vitandis.

That person which by open denunciation of the Church is rightly cut off from the unity of the Church, and excommunicated, ought to be taken of the whole multitude of the faithful, as an Heathen and Publican, until he be openly reconciled by penance, and received into the Church by a Judge that hath authority thereunto.

Qui per publicam Ecclesiæ denunciationem rite ab unitate Ecclesiæ præcisus est, et excommunicatus, is ab universa fidelium multitudine (donec per pœnitentiam publice reconciliatus fuerit arbitrio judicis competentis) habendus est tanquam ethnicus et publicanus.

Notes on the Text of Article XXXIII.

The Latin equivalent for ' rightly cut off,' is ' *rite* præcisus,' for it does not suffice that the excommunication be *right* in point of the offender's deserts, but it must be *in due order* as respects the *manner* of the action of the Church.   And one of the essentials in this is defined by the Article to be *publicity*, ' *open* denunciation,' or ' *publicam* denunciationem.' Penance—Latin, *pœnitentiam*.   Heathen—Latin, *ethnicus*, or Gentile : ' a stranger to the commonwealth of Israel.'

This was one of King Edward's Articles, and no special source is indicated for its style and language.

Observations on Article XXXIII.

It is manifestly a power inherent in any community, civil or religious, to exclude from their body, or to deprive wholly or partially of privileges, offenders against the rules or interests of the community.

The Jewish rabbis of old accordingly exercised this power in several degrees.[1] And, from the beginning, the Christian Church inflicted excommunication of various degrees on offenders. This was recognised by our Lord,[2] and in many passages of the Epistles.[3]

When, after the conversion of Constantine, the authority of the bishops was recognised by the State, a sentence of excommunication became a serious matter in a civil point of view. In course of time it drew with it civil disabilities, while the relaxation of discipline which pervaded the administration of the Church blunted its effect as a check upon immorality.

Further, when the power of the Popes assumed strength, their excommunication became a formidable weapon in dealing even with princes. But it lost its efficacy by excessive abuse; and the excommunications of Luther, of Henry VIII. and of Elizabeth, were effectual only in the recoil of the weapon.

The Roman law of excommunication may be seen in any treatise on the Canon Law, and will be found to legalise and require the religious tyranny and persecution of the Middle Ages. The Council of Trent speaks in guarded language on this point in its closing decree, but sufficiently indicates its demand for the exercise of the power of the State to persecute.

By the Canons of the Church of England (A.D. 1603) impugners of the king's supremacy, or of the doctrine and ceremonial of the Church, and all schismatics, are declared to be excommunicate. The same sentence is pronounced upon various offenders against sundry regulations, and also upon those guilty of grave immorality.

By the common law of England the civil courts formerly enforced penalties on the excommunicated. The progress of legal reform since the Reformation gradually diminished this exercise of the civil power; and it has been entirely removed

---

[1] See any Biblical Dictionary, under the word Anathema.
[2] Matt. xviii. 15–18.   [3] As 1 Cor. v. 3–5, &c.

by modern legislation, excepting so far as it may be in vindication of the proper discipline and jurisdiction of ecclesiastical courts over ecclesiastics.

Excommunication can only be pronounced by a lawful ecclesiastical judge, sitting in open court, and after a due hearing of the cause. The expression '*ipso facto excommunicated*,' in several of the Canons, implies no more than that *if* the person in question be ultimately sentenced, the excommunication will be retrospective and date back from the commission of the offence. But it does not empower anyone to deal with the supposed offender as an excommunicated person on his own private judgment. Nothing but a formal and legal sentence of excommunication can justify such a treatment. This is important, as bearing on the Rubrics in the Burial and Communion Services.

In the present state of the law it is doubtful how far an ecclesiastical court can pronounce sentence on a lay person in any case whatever.

ARTICLE XXXIV.

This article has been commented upon in combination with Article XX. See page 168.

PART V.

REGULATIONS AFFECTING THE CHURCH OF ENGLAND IN PARTICULAR.

ARTICLE XXXV.

Of Homilies.

The second Book of Homilies, the several titles whereof we have joined under this Article, doth contain a godly and wholesome Doctrine, and necessary for these times, as doth the former Book of Homilies, which were set forth in the time of *Edward* the Sixth; and therefore we judge them to be read in Churches by the Ministers, diligently and distinctly, that they may be understanded of the people.

De Homiliis.

Tomus secundus Homiliarum, quarum singulos titulos huic Articulo subjunximus, continet piam et salutarem doctrinam, et his temporibus necessariam, non minus quam prior Tomus Homiliarum, quæ editæ sunt tempore Edwardi sexti : Itaque eas in Ecclesiis per ministros diligenter, et clare, ut a populo intelligi possint, recitandas esse judicavimus.

Of the Names of the Homilies.

1. *Of the right use of the Church.*
2. *Against peril of Idolatry.*
3. *Of repairing and keeping clean of Churches.*
4. *Of good Works; first, of Fasting.*
5. *Against Gluttony and Drunkenness.*
6. *Against Excess of Apparel.*
7. *Of Prayer.*
8. *Of the Place and Time of Prayer.*
9. *That common Prayers and Sacraments ought to be ministered in a known Tongue.*
10. *Of the reverent estimation of God's Word.*
11. *Of Alms-doing.*
12. *Of the Nativity of Christ.*

De nominibus Homiliarum.

Of the right Use of the Church.
Against peril of Idolatry.
Of repairing and keeping clean of Churches.
Of good Works; first, of Fasting.

Against Gluttony and Drunkenness.
Against Excess of Apparel.
Of Prayer.
Of the Place and Time of Prayer.

That common Prayers and Sacraments ought to be ministered in a known Tongue.
Of the reverent estimation of God's Word.
Of Alms-doing.
Of the Nativity of Christ.

13. *Of the Passion of Christ.*	*Of the Passion of Christ.*
14. *Of the Resurrection of Christ.*	*Of the Resurrection of Christ.*
15. *Of the worthy receiving of the Sacrament of the Body and Blood of Christ.*	*Of the worthy receiving of the Sacrament of the Body and Blood of Christ.*
16. *Of the Gifts of the Holy Ghost.*	*Of the Gifts of the Holy Ghost.*
17. *For the Rogation-days.*	*For the Rogation-days.*
18. *Of the state of Matrimony.*	*Of the state of Matrimony.*
19. *Of Repentance.*	*Of Repentance.*
20. *Against Idleness.*	*Against Idleness.*
21. *Against Rebellion.*	*Against Rebellion.*

NOTES ON THE TEXT OF ARTICLE XXXV.

This Article was substituted in Elizabeth's time for the previous one of Edward, which was very similar in its terms, but, as a matter of course, recognised the First Book of Homilies only.

The name is of Greek origin, ὁμιλία, so called as being rather a familiar and instructive discourse than an oration. So also the Latin word *sermo*, which nearly corresponds.

OBSERVATIONS ON ARTICLE XXXV.

The only question can be as to the degree of assent hereby given to the Homilies. A quibbler might satisfy himself by finding in them the least modicum of doctrine with which he could agree, and say that they contained therefore ' a godly and wholesome doctrine.' But it would have been childish to insert such an Article, if it were not intended to affirm a general assent to the Homilies. They are popular discourses, and were not meant to be subjected to that verbal criticism and nicety of arrangement and expression required in a formulary of faith. But if the Article has any use or force at all, it must imply a general approval of the doctrines, as distinguished from any particular arguments used by the writers, or special illustrations or ideas adapted to those times. It will be remembered that the eleventh Article gives a yet higher authority to the Homily on Justification.

The great necessity for such volumes as the two collections of Homilies will at once be manifest when it is remembered that on the restoration of the Reformation under Elizabeth only eighty parish priests declined to conform. The great mass of the clergy, therefore, both in Edward's reign and in the early part of Elizabeth's, were those who had conformed to every change of Henry VIII., of Edward, of Mary, and of Elizabeth, and were incompetent and unfit in every point of view to preach.

The authorship of the Homilies is obscure. Cranmer is credited with the greater part of the First Book, and Jewel with the Second. Some, however, were certainly by other hands. Two were written by Taverner.

The two Books of Homilies are now usually published in one volume. It may be well to give here the list of the Homilies in the First Book.

1. A Fruitful Exhortation to the reading of Holy Scripture.
2. Of the misery of all mankind.
3. Of the salvation of all mankind.
4. Of the true and lively Faith.
5. Of good Works.
6. Of Christian Love and Charity.
7. Against Swearing and Perjury.
8. Of the declining from God.
9. An Exhortation against the Fear of Death.
10. An Exhortation to Obedience.
11. Against Whoredom and Adultery.
12. Against Strife and Contention.

ARTICLE XXXVI.

See Article XXIII., in conjunction with which this Article has been treated. See page 194.

ARTICLE XXXVII.

Of the Civil Magistrates.

The Queen's Majesty hath the chief power in this Realm of *England,* and other her dominions, unto whom the chief government of all estates of this Realm, whether they be Ecclesiastical or Civil, in all causes doth appertain, and is not, nor ought to be, subject to any foreign jurisdiction.

Where we attribute to the Queen's Majesty the chief government, by which titles we understand the minds of some slanderous folks to be offended ; we give not to our princes the ministering either of God's Word, or of Sacraments, the which thing the Injunctions also lately set forth by *Elizabeth* our Queen doth most plainly testify : But that only prerogative, which we see to have been given always to all godly princes in holy Scriptures by God himself ; that is, that they should rule all estates and degrees committed to their charge by God, whether

De civilibus Magistratibus.

Regia Majestas in hoc Angliæ regno, ac cæteris ejus dominiis, summam habet potestatem, ad quam omnium statuum hujus regni, sive illi ecclesiastici sint, sive civiles, in omnibus causis, suprema gubernatio pertinet, et nulli externæ jurisdictioni est subjecta, nec esse debet.

Cum Regiæ Majestati summam gubernationem tribuimus, quibus titulis intelligimus animos quorundam calumniatorum offendi, non damus Regibus nostris, aut verbi Dei, aut Sacramentorum administrationem, quod etiam Injunctiones ab Elizabetha Regina nostra, nuper editæ, apertissime testantur : sed eam tantum prærogativam, quam in sacris Scripturis a Deo ipso, omnibus piis Principibus, videmus semper fuisse attributam : hoc est, ut omnes status atque ordines fidei suæ a Deo commissos, sive illi ecclesiastici sint, sive civiles, in officio contineant, et con-

they be Ecclesiastical or Temporal, and restrain with the civil sword the stubborn and evildoers.

tumaces ac delinquentes gladio civili coerceant.

The Bishop of *Rome* hath no jurisdiction in this Realm of *England*.

Romanus pontifex nullam habet jurisdictionem in hoc regno Angliæ.

The laws of the Realm may punish Christian men with death, for heinous and grievous offences.

Leges regni possunt Christianos propter capitalia, et gravia crimina, morte punire.

It is lawful for Christian men, at the commandment of the Magistrate, to wear weapons, and serve in the wars.

Christianis licet, ex mandato magistratus, arma portare, et justa bella administrare.

Notes on the Text of Article XXXVII.

The Latin text calls for no special comment.

The corresponding Article (the 36th) of Edward differs from the present chiefly in the portion dealing with the royal supremacy, which was simply asserted as follows : ' The King of England is Supreme Head in earth, next under Christ, of the Church of England and Ireland.'

The Royal Supremacy.

For a full comment on this part of the Article we must refer to those portions of civil and ecclesiastical history which treat of the prolonged resistance of the English Crown to the papal claims ; the repudiation of those claims by Henry VIII. ; the intermediate struggles ; and the final establishment of the supremacy under Elizabeth ; to which we must add the extent to which this prerogative was strained by the Tudor and Stuart princes, and the stedfast opposition carried out through so many years by the Puritans.

In the original statute of 1534, which first declared the royal supremacy, the words used were these : The king ' shall be taken, accepted, and reputed the only and supreme head in earth of the Church of England.' The title *Head* was open to obvious objections as being applied in the New Testament to Christ. Papist and Puritan alike did not lose the opportunity thus opened for acrimonious attacks.

When the royal supremacy was restored by Parliament after Mary's death, the objectionable word was avoided, and *Governor* substituted for it. Furthermore this title was explained in the *Injunctions* to which reference is made in this Article. They were *set forth* by royal authority in 1559, the first year of Elizabeth, and deal at some length with ecclesiastical arrangements and discipline. The explanation of the oath of supremacy to which the Article refers is as follows : ' Her Majesty forbiddeth all manner her subjects to give ear or credit to such perverse and malicious persons which . . . labour to notify to her loving subjects, how by words of the said oath it may be collected, that the kings or queens of this realm, possessors of the crown, may challenge authority and power of ministry of divine service in the Church, wherein her said subjects be much abused by such evil disposed persons. For certainly her Majesty neither doth, nor ever will, challenge any authority, than that was challenged and lately used by the said noble kings of famous memory, King Henry VIII. and King Edward VI.; which is and was of ancient time due to the Imperial Crown of this realm ; that is, under God, to have the sovereignty and rule over all manner of persons born within these her realms, dominions, and countries, of what estate, either ecclesiastical or temporal soever they be, so as no other shall or ought to have any superiority over them.'

The supremacy thus given to the Tudor sovereigns was used by them in an arbitrary manner, under the authority of Acts of Parliament, which gave them very large powers over the Church. The truth seems to be that the boundaries of the ecclesiastical, as well as the civil power of the Crown, were very ill defined. They only became ascertained and limited after the severe struggles which culminated in the civil wars and were terminated by the Revolution.

In the present day the royal supremacy signifies little more than the supremacy of the civil law and courts over ecclesiastical legislation and jurisdiction. Still this general principle is in several respects brought to bear more closely on the Church of England than on other religious bodies within the realm. The latter are free to make any regulations they please for their own internal government, provided they do not contravene the law. The civil power will only interfere with them for purposes of the common peace and order; or when invoked by a member of any such body who alleges that he has suffered wrong by the violation in his case of the laws and regulations of that body. The civil court will then interpose, and compel such a religious body to give to the aggrieved member all the privileges and rights which he enjoys according to the rules under which that body has constituted itself. Striking instances of this have recently occurred in the history of the Free Church of Scotland, and of the Saurin convent case in the Church of Rome. These two ecclesiastical bodies have advanced claims of independence from the State beyond all others. But the civil courts allowed them no exemption from their jurisdiction.

The position of the Church of England, as established, gives to the civil power yet more control in her case. The Church of England has no power to change any portion of the Liturgy or Articles, or to modify any existing canon, or to enact a new one. The Liturgy is sanctioned by Act of Parliament, and can be altered by no other authority. The Convocation has no power to deliberate on a new canon without license from the Crown, nor has such canon, when agreed upon, any force without the royal assent. The patronage of bishoprics and benefices, generally, has perhaps not much to do with this subject, inasmuch as there might be patronage in a Church not established, as for instance in the case of Colonial Sees, or trustees of dissenting chapels. But the use of the royal supremacy which has attracted most attention, and created most discontent in some quarters, is that the final appeal in ecclesiastical causes has been reserved to the Crown ever since the Reformation. During the papal usurpation the right of appeal lay to the Pope from the bishop's or archbishop's court. Since the declaration of the royal supremacy that appeal has lain not to any ecclesiastical court, but to the

Crown. Subsequently to the accession of Elizabeth the Court of High Commission, usually consisting of bishops and ecclesiastical lawyers, exercised this jurisdiction. The Court of High Commission was abolished just before the civil war, and was not restored with Charles II. Its functions as a court of appeal were transferred to the Court of Delegates appointed by the Sovereign. This was abolished in 1833, and a committee of the Privy Council was specially organised to exercise jurisdiction in all cases in which the appeal lies to the Crown. The chief judges of the several courts are members of this board, and in ecclesiastical cases it is necessary that at least one bishop shall be present.

It will be observed that whether in the ecclesiastical court, or in the Privy Council, eminent lawyers are the judges. The difference is chiefly one of form. In the Bishop's Court, or that of Arches, the judge sits under the commission of the bishop or archbishop. In the Privy Council all is transacted in the name of the Sovereign; and the final sentence goes forth as the act of the Crown, and not in any ecclesiastical name. It must further be borne in mind that these courts are not legislative. Their province is to interpret the existing law, and that should be deemed the best tribunal which is most competent to investigate and declare the meaning and obligation of the laws.

THE PAPAL SUPREMACY.

On this point the Article is content simply to deny any jurisdiction of the Pope in this realm of England. But this opens the whole question of his claims. Among the most interesting of modern publications on this subject must be named ' The Pope and the Council, by Janus.' It shows with great historical grasp that the claims of the Popedom were unknown to antiquity; and it traces out step by step the story of usurpation and forgery which recounts the growth of the papal power. But it will be more satisfactory if, in accordance with the principles of this work, we take as our guide in dealing with this subject one of the masterpieces of English theology. For an exhaustive and unanswerable argument we

select Barrow's ' Treatise of the Pope's Supremacy.' Archbishop Tillotson says of it that ' many others have handled
the subject before, but he hath exhausted it. . . . He hath
said enough to silence the controversy for ever, and to deter
all wise men, of both sides, from meddling any further with
it. . . . There is neither from Scripture, nor reason, nor
antiquity, any evidence of the Pope's supremacy ; the past
and the present state of Christendom, the histories and records
of all ages, are a perpetual demonstration against it, and there
is no other ground in the whole world for it, but that now of
a long time it hath been by the Pope's janizaries boldly asserted
and stiffly contended for, without reason.'

The following analysis of the principal portions of Barrow's
great treatise may serve to put the student in possession of the
main points of the argument. In the Introduction the author
takes this preliminary view of the question.

' The disagreement of the Roman doctors about the nature
and extent of papal authority is a shrewd prejudice against
it. If a man should sue for a piece of land, and his
advocates (the notablest that could be had, and well paid)
could not find where it lieth, how it is butted and bounded,
from whom it was conveyed to him, one would be very
apt to suspect his title. If God had instituted such an
office, it is highly probable we might satisfactorily know what
the nature and use of it were: the patents and charters for it
would declare it. Yet for resolution in this great case we are
left to seek ; they not having the will, or the courage, or the
power to determine it. . . . Hence even the anathematizing
definers of Trent (the boldest undertakers to decide controversies that ever were) did waive this point : the legates of
the Pope being enjoined to advertise, that they should not for
any cause whatever come to dispute of the Pope's authority.'

Barrow then proceeds to examine, with numerous quotations
from leading Romish divines and papal bulls, what is the most
received doctrine on the supremacy. He admits that there
have been and are lower opinions of it in the Roman Church,
e.g. that the Pope is subject more or less to a General Council.
or to the established canons of the Church. It is notorious

U

that this was maintained in the Councils of Pisa, Constance and Basil. But although these decisions received papal confirmation, it is certain that they have been repeatedly repudiated. Barrow brings a strong array of papal and other quotations to prove that the papal supremacy has been most generally held to involve universal dominion. In the words of the bull of Pius V. against Elizabeth, 'this one [the Pope] he hath constituted prince over all nations and all kingdoms, that he might pluck up, destroy, dissipate, ruinate, plant, build.'

The degree in which temporal power over Christendom is really claimed, is (as is well known) much disputed. Bellarmine vouches for the common opinion of Catholics that 'by reason of the spiritual power, the Pope, at least indirectly, hath a supreme power even in temporal matters.' This, in the opinion of Barrow, really amounts to the same thing. We may now add to this the famous encyclical of the present Pope (1864), distinctly re-asserting the subjection of the civil power, and its obligation to punish heresy at the call of the Church. And the decree of the recent Vatican Council has made binding on all Romanists what were previously the private opinions of the Ultramontanes among them. But although the civil supremacy thus claimed makes the assumption the more glaring to those who know history, yet the ecclesiastical supremacy alone, together with its essential consequences, is necessary to Barrow's argument.

To clear thinking, clearness of arrangement is indispensable. Each grows out of, and leads to, the other by an inevitable law. In proceeding to discuss the question of the papal supremacy, Barrow distributes the Roman claim to a perpetual primacy and authority, derived from St. Peter and transmissible to all future ages, into the following seven suppositions:—

I. That Peter had a primacy over the apostles.

II. That Peter's primacy, with its rights and prerogatives, was not personal, but derivable to his successors.

III. That Peter was Bishop of Rome.

IV. That Peter did continue Bishop of Rome, after his translation, and was so at his decease.

V. That the Bishops of Rome (according to God's ordinance
and by original right derived thence) should have a
universal supremacy and jurisdiction over the Christian
Church.

VI. That in point of fact the Roman bishops continually, from
Peter's time, have enjoyed and exercised this sovereign
power.

VII. That this power is indefectible and unalterable.

To fix these seven suppositions carefully in the mind, and to
consider them in the light of the scriptural and historical
knowledge already (as it is hoped) possessed by the student,
must at once, in his mind, be fatal to the papal claims. The
strength of a chain consists in the tenacity and hold of *each*
link. If one link fail the chain is broken. If any one of these
seven suppositions be false, the argument for the papacy has
failed.

The examination of these seven suppositions forms so many
sections, into which the work is divided. It is proposed now
to give the outline of the consideration of each supposition.

SUPPOSITION I.

That St. Peter had a Primacy over the Apostles.

There are four kinds of Primacy :—

I. Of Personal Excellence.
II. Of Reputation.
III. Of Order or Precedence.
IV. Of Power or Jurisdiction.

I. The first of these Barrow grants to St. Peter on the consideration of several passages of Scripture.

II. The second he is also ready to grant, referring to
Gal. ii. 2, 6, 9, &c.

III. On examining several passages Barrow thinks that
St. Peter was the first called to be an apostle—the first who
avowed our Lord's divinity—perhaps the oldest—first in the
list of the apostles, &c. He would, therefore, grant a sort
of precedence of order, but not of degree or rank.

IV. Barrow denies a primacy of jurisdiction, on the following grounds :—

1. That there would have been a clear divine commission to such a primacy.

2. That there is no account of the time, manner, &c., of St. Peter being vested with such authority, nor of the nature and rules of such an office.

3. When was such an office instituted ? Barrow examines St. Peter's position at different times; and observes that the Lord did enjoin humility towards each other, but never submission to him as superior.

4. Peter's office would have been distinct in character and title from that of the other apostles.

5. No higher title than apostle was known. (Eph. iv. 11.)

6. Our Lord positively declared against such a primacy. (Luke xxii. 24–30.)

7. Particular passages having been examined, it is concluded that no administration was given to St. Peter which was not elsewhere granted to the other apostles.

8. Peter in his two Epistles makes no intimation of such a power.

9. In the Acts of the Apostles, where Christ's words are reduced to action, no trace whatever of such power is to be found, but rather the contrary.

10. In all controversies in Scripture no appeal is ever made to St. Peter's judgment—nothing said of obeying or disobeying him.

11. St. Peter nowhere appears as a judge. Also 1 Cor. i. 12 (I am of Cephas, &c.) is inconsistent with a popedom in St. Peter.

12. The apostles acted independently of each other in Church organisation. This was especially true of St. Paul.

13. The apostolic ministry was exercised through such remote regions that St. Peter could not exercise such a power.

14. The apostles had the only superintendence they needed, the promised Paraclete.

15. St. Paul's conduct towards St. Peter showed that he acknowledged no subjection to him.

16. On the supposition of this primacy, St. Peter ought to have outlived the other apostles. Otherwise, during the last thirty years of the first century, was St. John subordinate to the Bishop of Rome?

17. The other apostles might claim superiority on the same grounds as St. Peter.

18. The Fathers down to Jerome and Chrysostom assert the equality of power and authority among the apostles.

19. The most eminent Fathers, speaking at length of St. Peter, mention no such prerogative.

20. Romish arguments for the superiority of St. Peter are refuted—especially these six particulars are closely examined:

(1) Peter the Rock. Matt. xvi. 18.

(2) The keys. Matt. xvi. 19.

(3) Feed my sheep. John xxi. 16.

(4) Sundry other passages in which Peter is prominent in action.

(5) The order of the names in the lists of the apostles.

(6) Patristic testimony.

Supposition II.

That St. Peter's Primacy, with its rights and prerogatives, was not personal, but derivable to his successors.

Whatever may have been the nature of St. Peter's authority, Barrow lays down the following conclusions relating to it:—

I. It was grounded on personal acts and qualities.

II. That all the passages relied upon by Romanists (*see* above) are accomplished and exhausted in St. Peter's own person.

III. That a foundation is laid once for all; successors must be only superstructure.

IV. That the apostleship was in its nature extraordinary and personal, and, therefore, not derivable.

V. That the other apostles (as such) had no successors.

Hence there could be no remaining primacy among the apostles, if there was no such body.

VI. If some privileges of St. Peter are derivable, why not all ?

VII. If it be said that the bishops are successors of the apostles, it may be granted in certain respects, they having originally received jurisdiction and authority from the apostles. But inasmuch as they existed *with* the apostles, they cannot, as Bellarmine argues, be properly their successors.

VIII. In the permissible sense of the word, all bishops are equally successors of the apostles.

IX. That this last is the sense in which Cyprian and others hold this transmission.

X. That St. Peter and other apostles transmitted this derivable power equally to the bishop of every church they founded.

XI. That thus Irenæus and others claim this succession even for bishops of churches not planted by the apostles.

XII. That the distinction claimed by Romanists for something peculiarly transmissible in Peter has no ground.

XIII. That so momentous a claim could not have been avoided by Scripture and by the first Fathers, all of whom are silent upon it.

XIV. If such a succession had been designed and known, it is impossible that Origen, Chrysostom, Cyril, Jerome, &c., expounding the very passages relied on by Romanists, should not in some way have touched upon it.

Supposition III.

That St. Peter was Bishop of Rome.

The following considerations make against such a supposition :—

I. This would confound the two offices of bishop and apostle distinct by God's appointment ;—

II. Distinct also by the nature of their duties.

III. For St. Peter to become Bishop of Rome would be as if the King should become Lord Mayor of London.

IV. Having the superior charge, St. Peter would not need the inferior and particular authority.

V. St. Peter's apostleship of the circumcision gave him special charge of the Jews throughout the world.

VI. In fact, as far as we can gather, St. Peter travelled much, and could seldom reside in Rome. Various circumstances related of Peter are here examined to show this.

VII. Repeats III. and IV.

VIII. He would have given a bad example of non-residence, censured by all primitive canons.

IX. For St. Peter to be Bishop of Rome would offend against the earliest church rules—especially against

X. One forbidding the translation of a bishop to another see—for the Romanists make Peter to have been first Bishop of Antioch, then of Rome—

XI. And against another forbidding two bishops to preside in the same city.

Supposition IV.

That St. Peter did continue Bishop of Rome after his translation (from Antioch), and was so at his decease.

The following opposing considerations are alleged :—

I. Early writers give different accounts of this, saying that Peter, or Peter and Paul, appointed other persons to be bishop, Linus, or Clemens, or Anacletus. Hence he was either never bishop or did not continue so, for—

II. This would have been a great irregularity according to early canons, which forbade a bishop even at the point of death to appoint a successor.

III. Yet if he were bishop, he divested himself of the office by appointing Linus or Clemens.

IV. In short, either St. Peter retained the episcopacy, in which case there were more Bishops of Rome than one at the same time ; or else he resigned it, and did not die Bishop of Rome.

V. Hence the ancient expressions about St. Peter's bishopric must be understood of his exercising the apostleship in that city, as Ruffinus says, while there was a bishop there in the proper sense.

VI. The most ancient writers never expressly style St. Peter Bishop of Rome.

VII. The lists of Roman bishops sometimes count in the apostles, sometimes not, as in other churches also.

VIII. Other churches besides Rome were called apostolical sees, as Ephesus, &c.

IX. The apostolical constitutions, recounting the first bishops, never reckon any of the apostles.

X. All apostles had full episcopal power, wherever they were, as the greater includes the less.

XI. It is argued that James, an apostle, was Bishop of Jerusalem. Answer, The weight of testimony is against James the son of Alphæus, who was an apostle, being identical with James, the Lord's brother, who was Bishop of Jerusalem. [See Lightfoot's Dissertation, in his ' Commentary on the Epistle to Galatians.'] But if he were an apostle, there were special reasons why one of the apostles should have a fixed residence in the city which was the fountain and centre of Christianity.

SUPPOSITION V.

That the Bishops of Rome (according to God's institution and by original right derived from thence) should have an universal supremacy and jurisdiction over the Christian Church.

This supposition is treated under the following heads :—

I. The previous four suppositions failing, this of necessity falls to the ground.

II. But admitting those suppositions, this fifth does not of necessity follow. For the jurisdiction of St. Peter might have existed, and might have been transmitted, and yet not to the Bishop of Rome, but, for example, to the whole college of bishops.

III. This kind of transmission of the apostolical authority, in fact, was the doctrine of the early Fathers, especially of Cyprian, the Apostolical Constitutions, &c.

IV. Other bishops of churches of apostolical foundation claimed to be successors of the apostles in the same sense as they admitted the Bishop of Rome to be successor of Peter. Yet they did not claim jurisdiction out of their own diocese.

V. St. James, Bishop of Jerusalem (called an apostle in the Roman liturgy) was more certainly Bishop of Jerusalem than St. Peter was of Rome. And Jerusalem, not Rome, was called mother of all the churches by the Second General Council. Yet the Bishops of Jerusalem, successors of St. James, claimed no general jurisdiction.

VI. As St. Peter founded other churches, and is called by some writers Bishop of Antioch, why should not such succession, if existing, appertain to the Bishop of Antioch ?

VII. They say the succession came to Rome by St. Peter's will. It is asked where such will is to be found.

VIII. Bellarmine asserts positively God's command to St. Peter to fix his see at Rome. But afterward overturns this by saying *Non est improbabile* that God commanded, &c.

IX. Antioch at least has a plea for a share in Peter's prerogatives. Query, what share ?

X. St. John, perhaps, might have, at least, equal claim with St. Peter, as the surviving apostle.

XI. The Bishop of Jerusalem might put in his claim as successor of Christ Himself, even although St. Peter might have had jurisdiction for his life.

XII. A successor of St. Peter would more fairly be appointed by the suffrages of the whole Church, than by the votes of a few persons at Rome for a bishop there.

XIII. If God had purposed such a succession of universal sovereignty, He would not have left the mode of election so uncertain as that to the see of Rome has been.

XIV. Other sovereignties, though assured at first, have passed into uncertain channels. ' Who is heir-at-law of Adam ? ' So there might be a monarchy in Peter and in some successors, and yet by defect of title it might now be lost.

XV. It cannot be proved that God intended the Church to have any one unvarying mode of government.

XVI. In fact there have been long intervals when there was no Bishop of Rome at all. Of which vacancies Barrow gives ten classes.

Direct Arguments against the Papal Supremacy.

This portion of the Treatise must be very briefly epitomised.

I. The papal supremacy has neither divine nor human testimony, as shown in the following particulars.

1. On such a point God would have plainly declared His will.

2. The New Testament does contain precepts on the order and ministers of the Church, &c. How could a mention of the spiritual monarch have been avoided, if he existed?

3. Obedience to higher powers is inculcated. How could obedience to the universal pastor be omitted?

4. The apostles remember the temporal sovereign; how could they forget the Pope?

5. St. Peter (1. Ep. ii. 13–17) urges obedience to kings. Why did he forget his successor? The false decretals everywhere urge obedience to the Pope.

6. St. Paul, writing to the Romans, and also from Rome, omits altogether any privileges of that see.

7. No early Father, though noticing many traditions, has any relating to papal authority.

8. Eusebius gives a full list of Roman bishops, but has nothing about their supremacy.

9–11. It is unnoticed by any ancient summary of doctrine, catechetical discourses, or synods.

12, 13. Early popes did not assert it, and persons denying popes' decrees were not called heretics.

14. A universal empire would have been most offensive to pagans, but not one names such a thing.

16. Constantine and other emperors would not have embraced a religion with such claims.

16, 17, 18. The apostolical canons and the Pseudo-Dionysius Areopagita and Ignatius define ecclesiastical orders, but do not name the supremacy.

19, 20, 21. Early popes do not use any sovereign style, and other bishops address them as equals.

22–26. This dogma is never alleged against heretics by the Fathers, nor by early Popes, all of whom do, however, appeal to Church tradition against heretics.

27. The voluminous works of ancient Fathers from Origen to Augustine, contain no such dogma, not even when treating on *Tu es Petrus*.

II. This pretence is contrary to Scripture.

1. It invades the prerogative of Christ.

2. It makes the Church a temporal dominion.

3. It destroys the brotherly equality of bishops.

4. It denies the Scriptural rights of individual churches.

5. It takes away the liberties of Christian people.

6. It deprives princes of their rights over part of their subjects.

III. As Romanists little regard Scripture proofs, further, it crosses tradition and the Fathers.

1. Usage shows right—there was no such usage.

2. The state of the early Church did not admit it.

3. The Fathers knew nothing above a bishop.

IV. Arguments against the papal supremacy from abstract considerations.

1. The inconvenience of such a dependence of distant Churches ; and the impossibility of one man governing an overgrown dominion.

2. By its very nature such a power would be encroaching and exorbitant.

3. It would naturally make religion and doctrine subserve its own interests.

4. Errors so introduced would be unchangeable.

5–7. The officers of such a power would inevitably become corrupt, and such corruption would be perpetual, and re-act unfavourably on the pontiff.

8, 9. It must clash from time to time with civil power, and hence indispose princes to Christianity itself.

10. It is more safe and natural that national Churches should exist independently of each other.

11. Such a power is needless and useless.

V. and VI. The ancients considered all the bishops independent in their own diocese, and equal amongst each other.

VII. The ancient bishops, when occasion arose, asserted their equality with the Roman bishops.

VIII. The primitive bishops addressed the Roman bishops as ' brother or colleague,' and *vice versâ*.

IX. The original ground of eminence given to the see of Rome is shown to be its dignity and importance as the capital of the empire.

X. All prerogatives of particular sees were of human ordinance, for purposes of order or of local or other convenience. This is proved by a careful examination of the patriarchal and other jurisdictions in the early Church.

Finally, the growth of papal power is historically traced to a concurrence of causes, arranged under thirty-six heads.

Supposition VI.

That in fact the Roman Bishops continually, from St. Peter's time, have enjoyed and exercised this sovereign power.

This is a question of fact, to decide which the principal branches of sovereignty are individually examined.

I. Such a sovereign would have power to convene supreme councils, &c., and would have used it.

It is proved, on the contrary, that this never was done but by the emperors, and that sometimes on the Pope's application.

II. Such a sovereign would preside over, and moderate in, all general synods. But it is shown that the Emperor or his commissaries presided.

III. Legislative power would belong to such a sovereign of the Church, or at least a power of veto. It is, however, proved that acts of the general councils were ratified by the Emperors, not by the Popes.

IV. Such absolute sovereignty would enact or dispense with laws. The legislative usages of the early Church negatives such a power in the Pope.

V. Such a sovereign as the Pope claims to be would exercise

universal jurisdiction. It is shown that such an authority was unknown.

VI. Thé appointment or confirmation of inferior offices would appertain to such a sovereign. The early modes of electing bishops, popes, and other ministers of the Church being examined, it is shown that the popes had no such power.

VII.–X. Powers of censure and deprivation, of absolving and restoring bishops, would appertain to such a sovereign, but it is shown that these belonged to synods. Power also of receiving appeals, and commissioning other bishops, would belong to him. But it is shown that this only became so by gradual encroachment.

XI. Such a sovereign could be neither censured nor deposed. But popes have suffered both of these.

XII.–XIX. Other branches of sovereignty are similarly examined.

All these are claimed by the popes, and are all unknown to the early Church.

Supposition VII.

That the Papal Supremacy is indefectible and unalterable.

Supposing that the Pope had a universal sovereignty, nevertheless change of circumstances might have brought it to an end. But especially departure from the true doctrine of Holy Scripture would terminate it, as Ambrose says, ' They have not the inheritance of Peter who have not the faith of Peter.' This leads the author to a detailed statement of the doctrinal errors of the Roman Church, with which the Treatise closes.

The remaining two clauses of the thirty-seventh Article will be examined in connexion with the thirty-eighth and thirty-ninth, belonging, as they do, to questions raised by the same classes of schismatics.

Part VI.

CIVIL RIGHTS AND DUTIES.

ARTICLES XXXVIII. AND XXXIX.

ARTICLE XXXVIII.

Of Christian men's Goods, which are not common.

The riches and goods of Christians are not common as touching the right, title, and possession of the same, as certain Anabaptists do falsely boast. Notwithstanding, every man ought, of such things as he possesseth, liberally to give alms to the poor, according to his ability.

De illicita bonorum communicatione.

Facultates et bona Christianorum non sunt communia, quoad jus et possessionem (ut quidam Anabaptistæ falso jactant); debet tamen quisque de his quæ possidet, pro facultatum ratione, pauperibus eleemosynas benigne distribuere.

ARTICLE XXXIX.

Of a Christian man's Oath.

As we confess that vain and rash Swearing is forbidden Christian men by our Lord Jesus Christ, and *James* his Apostle: So we judge, that Christian Religion doth not prohibit, but that a man may swear when the Magistrate requireth, in a cause of faith and charity, so it be done according to the Prophet's teaching, in justice, judgment, and truth.

De jurejurando.

Quemadmodum juramentum vanum et temerarium a Domino nostro Jesu Christo, et Apostolo ejus Jacobo, Christianis hominibus interdictum esse fatemur; ita Christianorum Religionem minime prohibere censemus, quin jubente magistratu in causa fidei et charitatis jurare liceat, modo id fiat juxta Prophetæ doctrinam, in justitia, in judicio, et veritate.

x

NOTES ON THE TEXT OF ARTICLES XXXVIII. AND XXXIX.

The Latin version of these Articles throws no new light upon the English. They are found in their present form in the formulary of Edward as well as that of Elizabeth.

No direct source is suggested for these Articles. But the Augsburgh Confession,[1] the Helvetic[2] and other foreign Reformed Confessions contain similar articles. The calumnies of their Roman opponents made the Reformed Churches very anxious to destroy any possible identification of themselves with the fanatical sects.[3]

OBSERVATIONS ON ARTICLES XXXVIII. AND XXXIX.

For general consideration we take, together with these Articles, the two last clauses of the thirty-seventh. We have thus before us four allied subjects.

1. The lawfulness of capital punishment.
2. The lawfulness of military service.
3. That community of goods is not the Christian law.
4. That judicial oaths are lawful.

The negative to these propositions was maintained by some of those fanatical sects who are grouped together under the name of Anabaptists. We may again refer the reader to Article VII., p. 62, for some account of these disturbing sects. And for further illustration we may quote Luther. ' They teach that the Christian must possess nothing, must take no oath, must hold no magistracy, must give effect to no judgment, must slay none, must not defend himself, must desert his wife and children, with other portentous precepts.' The same errors are copiously illustrated in the Parker Society's series.[4]

The notions combated in these Articles have been maintained at different periods of history by various obscure sects. The most prominent of those who, in modern times, have

---

[1] xvi. de Rebus Civilibus.   [2] xxx. de Magistratu.
[3] See Jewel's ' Apology,' P. iii. C. ii. Div. 1.
[4] See article Anabaptist in the General Index.

denied the first, second, and fourth of these, has been that of
the Quakers. They were not, however, within the view of
the framers of the Article, since they arose subsequently, in
the time of the Commonwealth. Nevertheless, in the opinion
of Mosheim,[1] George Fox, the founder of Quakerism, derived
his doctrines indirectly from some of the Dutch mystics ; and
these were certainly connected with some sections of those
known as Anabaptists. And it is also true that the mystic
and fanatical notions, which had been rife in Germany for
some centuries, found expression during the ferment of the
Reformation among the Anabaptists. The fanaticism of
George Fox was reduced into a philosophical and theological
system, with much learning and ability, by Robert Barclay
in 1675. Since that time Quakerism has been a consistent
and coherent creed, and has dropped all its earlier extravagances. This part of its code of morality will be found
considered in the Fifteenth Proposition of Barclay's Apology.

The Scriptural Treatment of these Subjects.

Old Testament examples will scarcely suffice under any of
these heads, inasmuch as our opponents contend that in this
respect the law of the New Testament is in advance of the
Old Testament.

It is needful to draw a preliminary distinction between
what is lawful to man in his private capacity as an individual,
and what is lawful to him as an official person, being, as St.
Paul says, a ' minister of God.' The student will recall the
argument, pressed so often in Butler's Analogy, that the organisation of human society is distinctly from God, inasmuch
as it is a necessary consequence of man's nature, as a social
being formed to live as a member of society. Hence, in a
certain sense, all rulers of men have responsible duties and
powers, distinct from their duties as individuals, and are, as
St. Paul calls them, 'God's ministers.' Care must be taken
to allow no confusion of moral principle in drawing this dis-

[1] Cent. xvii. II. ii. 6.

tinction. The law of love and of care for human life, feelings, and happiness, binds alike ruler and subject. The *application* of that law in a particular case may require the individual to forgive, and the ruler to punish. Without this distinction between the *principle* and the *mode of applying* the principle, many precepts of Scripture (even the simplest) must often be a mass of confusion.

Thus Matt. v. 16 commands us to let our good works be seen; Matt. vi. 4 bids us carefully to conceal our alms; Matt. vii. 1 absolutely forbids us to judge; Matt. vii. 16 gives us the rule by which we may judge. Probably few persons are, even for a moment, perplexed by these apparent opposites in dealing with the outcomings of certain principles in different cases. But we must style it a perverse treatment of similar unqualified announcements of the Christian duty of individuals, which has led to the tenets condemned in the Articles now under consideration.

1. *The Lawfulness of Capital Punishments.*

In the New Testament the leading persons are continually brought into collision with the authorities. It will be uniformly found on examining the instances that the *authority* is recognised, however wrongfully a particular officer may act.

We have further the direct recognition of this exercise of the power. (Acts xxv. 11; Rom. xiii. 1–4; 1 Pet. iv. 15.)

To this must be added that the original command (Gen. ix. 6) was primæval, universal, and distinct from the Jewish law.

2. *The Lawfulness of Military Service.*

The distinction between public and private duties must here be strongly insisted upon. In the execution of justice, which God has in a certain degree committed to man; in the defence of the weak, and of the welfare and happiness of those who are entrusted to the care of the community; some amount of force and violence is, to say the least, necessary. If there is to be a ruler (under whatever name) that ruler must be empowered to exercise force. No property, no right, no happiness can be preserved without it. In a word, without it society could not exist, and the non-employment of force in a sinful world would lead to the reign of wicked force. If, therefore, the law of love, of charity, of the protection of the affections and interests of human life, requires force, it follows that the forceful agent of the ruling power exercises a lawful calling, and is empowered to use what amount of violence (even to death) may be requisite to carry out his duty. If this be so, it is impossible to draw the line of right between the employment of the policeman against violence and wrong emanating from a domestic foe to society, and of the soldier against the multitudinous violence and wrong offered by a foreign enemy. This is quite apart from the right or wrong of any particular war. It is probable that these will usually be more or less intermixed in the present confused state of human affairs; and it will follow that in ordinary cases it will not be the soldier's duty to act on his own private judgment as to the merits of the war in which he may be engaged.

These principles being premised, we are prepared to find that the New Testament recognises the military profession as an incident of the present state of man, and nowhere hints that it is unlawful.

See the cases of instructions to soldiers, Luke iii. 14, and of the centurion received, as such, into the Church (Acts x). Many metaphors are drawn from military service in a manner which could scarcely have been done were it unlawful.

Moreover, Rom. xiii. 4, recognises the use of the *sword*.

3. *That Community of Goods is not the Christian Law.*

This subject is easily dealt with. The *principles* involved will be these :—

1. The ideas of property arising out of the fruits of industry, which are involved in the notion of *society* as it exists by virtue of the *natural* law of God.

2. The necessity for liberality and bounty, which have no place if the Christian has nothing individually his own to give.

3. The exact treatment will be the consideration of the cases

in Acts iv. 32, 34, 35, and v. 1–10. It will be needful first to examine how far the transactions there described were *required* as a law of the Church (Acts v. 4), and then further to enquire whether in point of fact the community of goods was afterwards imposed as a law in the Churches founded by the apostles, and recognised in the Epistles as existing or needful. There can be no question as to the result of such an examination.

4. *That Judicial Oaths are Lawful.*

It may well appear that, apart from the general question of oaths, the English formula may be thoroughly defended. For it simply consists of a solemn (at least such it ought to be) petition to the Almighty that the person so attesting may speak the truth, or perform the truth in the premises. The simple ceremony added to this of kissing the book of the Holy Gospels, appears (to say the least) an innocent and significant testimony that the person so attested has that faith which is the basis of such an appeal.

But the general lawfulness of judicial oaths is usually defended, apart from the Old Testament, by our Lord submitting to be put on his oath before Caiaphas (Matt. xxvi. 63, 64). By the language of St. Paul in many passages (e.g. Rom. ix. 1; Gal. i. 20, &c.). And by the apparent recognition of such oaths (Heb. vi. 16–18).

In this case the declarations in Matt. v. 34–37, and James v. 12, must be classed with many positive assertions alluded to in p. 308, which must be understood not by our arbitrary decision, but as they stand qualified by other passages. Nor can there be any difficulty in this to one who has closely studied the manner and the phraseology of Holy Scripture.

INDEX.